Marriage and Violence

Marriage and Violence

The Early Modern Legacy

FRANCES E. DOLAN

PENN

University of Pennsylvania Press

Philadelphia

Published by
University of Pennsylvania Press
Philadelphia, Pennsylvania 19104-4112

Printed in the United States of America on acid-free paper

10   9   8   7   6   5   4   3   2   1

A Cataloging-in-Publication record is available from the Library of Congress
ISBN-13: 978-0-8122-4075-7
ISBN-10: 0-8122-4075-8

Contents

Introduction

Today, marriage is celebrated as the bedrock on which the rest of society builds. For instance, in his 2004 State of the Union Address, President George W. Bush described marriage as "one of the most fundamental, enduring institutions of our civilization."[1] As James Dobson puts it in *Marriage Under Fire*, "the institution of marriage represents the very foundation of human social order." Yet this claim that marriage is a foundation almost always, as in these two examples, precedes the claim that it needs to be shored up. Marriage requires "defense" and "protection" in the form of educational programs and financial incentives that would promote "healthy marriage" and bans on same-sex marriage. For someone like Dobson, even the Defense of Marriage Act of 1996, the first to define marriage at a federal level, is not enough.[2] Dobson proposes a federal marriage amendment to the Constitution in order "to define this historic institution exclusively as being between one man and one woman." Dobson urges his readers to "find the wisdom and strength to defend the legacy of marriage," through political action and personal choice.[3] But what precisely is that legacy? This book offers an inquiry into one important source of our ideas about marriage, arguing that we need to understand the provenance and content of this legacy before we can assess its value. Marriage is certainly "historic," as Dobson describes it, but its history is one of constant, constitutive crisis and conflict; as a consequence, the legacy of marriage is a burdensome one.[4]

What do we even mean by "marriage"? While debate usually focuses on who can or should marry, the most basic question remains: what does it mean to *be* married? This question resonates on two levels. First, what or who determines that one *is* "married"? Second, what are the consequences of being identified as married? One way of thinking about consequences is to focus on the rights, privileges, and responsibilities attached to being married. For the purposes of this study, I am most interested in assumptions about what kind of relation marriage imposes, enables, or sanctions between spouses. Our definitions of this "fundamental" institution are contradictory. On the one hand, marriage is defined as a loving, erotic bond between two equal individuals. On the other hand, it is construed as a hierarchy in which someone, usually the husband, has to be the boss. Marriage is celebrated as the melding of two into one and as a contract between two autonomous parties. While some see the present conflict among different models of marriage as constituting an unprecedented crisis, I will argue that this conflict between incompatible models and irreconcilable expectations *is* the history of marriage. It is thus a manifestation of continuity rather than rupture.

Some would trace the history of marital conflict as far back as cave dwellers. While the institution of marriage does have deep, tangled roots, I focus on our debts to one particular cultural tradition, arguing that we have inherited three models of marriage from early modern England (1550–1700): marriage as hierarchy, as fusion, and as contract. These three models are incompatible and, to make matters worse, each is riddled with internal contradictions. Each can be understood as promoting love between spouses and fulfillment for each or as subordinating one to the interests of the other. In early modern England, a radically visionary model of marriage as a loving partnership between equals flourished in part because of the Protestant Reformation. While this ideal was not wholly new, it first found stable institutionalization, full articulation, and broad dissemination in the sixteenth and seventeenth centuries. Its promise remains unfulfilled because it never replaced a model of marriage as a hierarchy in which the husband must take the lead and the wife must obey; it also drew on the erotic and emotional appeal of a vision of marriage as the fusion of two into one without resolving the practical problems that vision obscures. Working with traditions that were already fractured and contradictory, then, the early modern period added new, equally vexed expectations for marriage. The emergent model of marriage as a contract seems to correspond to and ensure a partnership between equals; yet, as we will see, it did not escape or resolve presumptions about the unequal status of the parties to the marriage contract. Furthermore, the notion of spouses as contracting parties, each of whom acts out of self-interest, coexists uneasily with the ideal of marriage as a near mystical fusion in which one loses oneself. Each model proposes to explain the relationship between spouses. Yet, for all of the supposedly "new" emphasis on spouses as companions and partners, early modern religious, legal, and popular discourses reveal a deep distrust of equality. Associating equality with conflict, they suggest that once spouses confront one another as equals only one can win the resulting battles. Conflict can only be evaded or resolved by privileging one spouse at the expense of the other. Thus the ultimate message is that marriage only has room for one. The question then becomes: which one?

The Marital Economy of Scarcity

We can see this most clearly in three common figures for marriage. These figures do not correspond precisely to the three models of marriage I have outlined above. Rather, they attempt, unsuccessfully, to finesse the contradictions within and among those dominant models of marriage. The first is the figuration of Christian marriage as the creation of "one flesh," which at once powerfully expresses theological, emotional, and erotic union and upholds an impossible ideal. Within Christian marriage advice, the pervasive insistence that the husband stands as the head of the marital body readmits a hierarchy between the spouses into the vision of marital union. Second, the common law offered a parallel formulation, suggesting that, through a legal fiction called coverture, husband and wife should become one legal agent by means of the husband's subsumption of his wife into himself. While common law did not wholly define married women's legal status, the fiction that husband and wife achieved "unity of person" had wide-ranging influence in the early modern period and beyond.[5] Finally, a comic tradition, including plays, ballads, and jokes, would seem to mark an advance toward imagining spouses as separate and equal, since it assigns husband and wife similar claims on wit, desire, authority, and material resources. Yet it depicts this equality as a source of conflict because it compels husband and wife to war for mastery within their marriage and household, mastery figured as a single pair of pants only one can wear.

The conceptual similarity underpinning these familiar figures only stands out when one compares all three, as my study is the first to do. Taken together, the scriptural figure of "one flesh," the legal fiction of "unity of person," and popular debates about who wears the pants all suggest that marriage is an economy of scarcity in which there is only room for one full person.[6] What happens when both spouses assert their distinct and potentially opposed wills and interests? Many representations of marital conflict locate violence of one kind or another in just such moments. They then present further violence as the only way to resolve the problem of two fractious persons within the union of marriage. This definitive violence can take the form of spiritual struggles for salvation or damnation, battering and murder, or "taming." In each chapter of my book, I show how the early modern apprehension of marriage as an economy of scarcity haunts the present as a conceptual structure or plot that concentrates entitlements and capacities in one spouse, and achieves resolution only when that spouse absorbs, subordinates, or eliminates the other.

The Individual and the Couple

If marriage only has room for one "full person," then what is a full person? My argument about how marriage is conceived and described implies that an individual has boundaries, autonomy, self-awareness, desires, and volition. This is not the only way to define an individual, nor is it a definition I accept uncritically. But it is a widely prevalent definition, one that is inextricably intertwined with marriage. In various registers, from the psychoanalytic to the political, this self is viewed as defined against others. Seeking to illuminate "the genesis of the psychic structure in which one person plays subject and the other must serve as his object," Jessica Benjamin argues that the predominance of this structure "makes it seem that a relationship in which both participants are subjects—both empowered and mutually respectful—is impossible."[7] While, like Benjamin, I am interested in the conceptual challenge of imagining the relationship of two such subjects, I focus on how this "impossibility" has been produced historically. This particular definition of the self is often traced back to the early modern period; thus it is said to emerge in the same period in which the models of marriage on which I focus also rose to prominence. These supposedly "new" ideas about the individual and the marital relationship are causally related. The notion of marriage as an economy of scarcity facilitates the development of a particular kind of subject, but only one. The other spouse serves as the object to that subject. Thus for one spouse marriage and selfhood are mutually constitutive and for the other marriage and selfhood are radically incompatible.

There are many theories as to why the early modern period might have contributed to a more sharply individuated self: the Reformation promoted a direct relationship between the individual and God, as well as increased introspection and self-documentation; political change promoted an increased awareness of individual rights and responsibilities; urbanization ruptured ties to the extended family and local community; and capitalism promoted a sense of the individual as the proprietor of himself and his capacities. Scholars dispute whether a dramatic change occurred and, if it did, precisely when, why, and how. For my purposes, the issue is one of conceptual contradictions more than changing experiences, although I see the two as connected. What was the relationship between the available ways of imagining and describing the individual and the available ways of imagining and describing the union of two such individuals in marriage?

C. B. Macpherson's argument for the emergence of a "possessive individual" in seventeenth-century England has been especially influential. Macpherson connects the development of the "liberal-democratic state" in the English seventeenth century to "a new belief in the value and the rights of the individual . . . as essentially the proprietor of his own person or capacities, owing nothing to society for them."[8] Several feminist scholars have argued that this definition of individualism was not restricted to men. Focusing on writers with widely different social, political, and theological positions, Catherine Gallagher, Maureen Quilligan, and Katharine Gillespie all argue that it was possible for some women to imagine or describe themselves in something like this way.[9] Certainly, as I will show, in a winner-take-all model of spousal selfhood the wife is sometimes imagined as annexing selfhood by annihilating her rival (her husband). For my project, then, the issue is not so much whether women could be imagined as "possessive individuals" as whether *both* spouses could be so imagined.

Macpherson first defined the possessive individual so as to address the conceptual problems he, or she, posed for collectivity.

> The individual, it was thought, is free inasmuch as he is proprietor of his person and capacities. The human essence is freedom from dependence on the wills of others, and freedom is a function of possession. Society becomes a lot of free equal individuals related to each other as proprietors of their own capacities and of what they have acquired by their exercise. Society consists of relations of exchange between proprietors.[10]

Although Macpherson does not particularly address marriage, he does argue that this notion of the individual remains a problem for liberal-democratic theory. Many subsequent political theorists, especially feminists, have built on and extended Macpherson's insight. For instance, Wendy Brown examines the tension between "liberal individualism and liberal familialism," exploring how the family works to naturalize a link between equality and competition. As she points out, the "presumed nonviolence of masculine dominance in the family" is "itself made possible through institutionalized inequality. (Liberal state-of-nature theory presumes that violence inheres among equals, not between dominant and subordinate persons.)" By this logic, hierarchy resolves conflict while equality promotes it. As we will see, this assumption underpins—and undermines—many conceptualizations of marriage. If this is the case, then it becomes almost impossible to imagine functional associations among equal individuals. As Brown puts this:

The antinomy between civil self-interestedness and familial selflessness suggests that liberalism is all or nothing about selves: one group surrenders selfhood so that another group can have it. This formulation . . . also reveals the extent to which the self-interested individual is premised upon a self-less one, indeed, draws the material and sustenance of its "self" from the selflessness of another. . . . [T]he self-interested subject of liberalism both requires and disavows its relationship to the selfless subject of the household, typically gendered female.[11]

Thus, according to Brown, the kind of economy of scarcity I locate in marriage then extends from marriage into civil society, in which the "civil self-interest" of some individuals is underwritten by the "familial selflessness" of others.

The "possessive individual" is not the only supposedly "new" model to emerge in the early modern period. Lawrence Stone identifies as new what he calls the "affective individual." According to Stone, as each family member was recognized as distinct rather than as subsumed (into the head of household or into the corporate family identity), more egalitarian and affectionate relations among such individuals evolved. Stone thus assumes that individualism facilitates both egalitarianism and companionship.[12] Other historians have challenged Stone by arguing both that the "affective individual" was not new in the early modern period and that its meanings and consequences were always messy.[13] I am most interested in the line of critique suggested by political theorists like Macpherson and Brown: the individual was always defined against others, required supplementation, and was hard to accommodate to familial or democratic collectives. Many critiques of social changes in twentieth-century America suggest that women have put the family and social order at risk by demanding their own status as individuals. But, as Macpherson's and Brown's work suggests, the problem lies, instead, in the dependence of the possessive individual on the "familial selflessness" of others. In my terms, the problem is a conception of marriage that can accommodate only one "individual."

Even attempts to reconcile the individual to marriage confront the idea that one spouse must sacrifice some of the claims of the individual in order to subsidize marital union. Milton Regan describes the conflict between the individual and marriage as follows: "Modern American attitudes toward marriage reflect two competing commitments: that spouses are separate individuals with their own distinct interests, and that they are members of a community who have special obligations to promote its welfare." He names these two perspectives the "external and internal stances toward marriage, respectively." Regan suggests that spouses might occupy both stances simultaneously or oscillate between the two. While he does not want to eliminate the external stance entirely, he does argue that the law should promote rather than discourage the internal stance, which he views as crucial to the success and survival of marriages. Regan's approach casts doubt on the value of self-interest, calculation, and contracts in extremely valuable ways. Furthermore, his vision of selves transformed through intimacy and "lives lived in intimate concert" rather than in "parallel association" is inspiring. However, again and again, as Regan himself acknowledges, the wife shoulders the burden of favoring the marriage over her own self-interest. According to Regan, the external stance "represents an individual's capacity to reflect critically upon, rather than simply identify with, her commitments and attachments. It enables a person to keep in focus the extent to which any given commitment serves her interests as a distinct individual." Having so defined the external stance, Regan then acknowledges that wives might insist on occupying this stance toward their marriages because of "dissatisfaction with traditional gender roles." Later, he similarly concedes that women have often been assigned the job of preserving marriage at their own expense; "such an orientation can leave a person open to exploitation and abuse by her partner." As a consequence, he admits, "we can never feel completely comfortable about encouraging spouses to adopt the internal stance as long as there are systematic gender inequalities within marriage."[14] Although Regan is aware of the systematic gender inequalities built into marriage as well as how these inequalities undermine the achievement of the marital union he so values, he nonetheless depicts the wife as a stumbling block. She reflects critically on whether her interests are being served; she is dissatisfied with her traditional role; she is at risk of exploitation and abuse. When the wife demands the entitlements associated with being an individual, at least since the early modern period, or when these entitlements are too egregiously denied her, the fragile equilibrium of marriage falls apart.

Why the Early Modern Period?

While many historians, such as Stephanie Coontz, Nancy Cott, David Cressy, Hendrick Hartog, and Lawrence Stone, have documented the complexities of early modern marriage and the development of modern marriage, none has focused on the precise relationship between the early modern and the modern.[15] This relationship is obscured by the many changes that have intervened, including reliable birth control, the wider availability of divorce, married women's changing legal status and access to paid work, the criminalization of domestic violence, and the greater visibility and acceptance of same-sex and unmarried cohabiting couples. These changes have utterly transformed the experience of marriage and domestic life. But if we focus on them it is harder to see the continuities that persist despite them. These continuities stand out more clearly if the present and the early modern period are viewed side by side. I am freed to deemphasize historical difference by the many studies that have documented and assessed it. Rather than undertaking another comprehensive history of marriage, then, I have chosen to contrast the long twentieth century to the early modern period in order to emphasize the ways in which the problems so often lamented in U.S. culture in the late twentieth and early twenty-first century are embedded in an early modern construction of what marriage is and requires.

During the centuries sometimes grouped together as the "early modern period," huge changes occurred that affected the formulation and dissemination of particular models of marriage. These include the Reformation, as I've already mentioned and as I'll explore in Chapter 1; the English Civil War and its challenges to authority, which might or might not have extended to the household; the rise of capitalism and its consequences for notions of property and self-possession; and the thickening of boundaries around what we might call the "private."[16] Historians debate the extent to which entirely new ideals of marriage emerged in conjunction with or as a consequence of these other changes. But most agree that these dramatic changes made the early modern period in England and colonial America the crucible in which certain ideals of marriage were refined, elaborated, defended, and mass produced.

Some historians even argue that changes in marriage and the family were catalysts, rather than effects, of these other changes. Amy Erickson suggests that "the specific gender structure of English property law," by which she means coverture, "was at least part of the reason why England was early to develop a capitalist economy and also why the cash economy, the debt credit markets, and public investment apparently spread so completely throughout the society."[17] Mary Hartman stresses the importance of a late marriage pattern in England from 1500 to 1750, through which women married men closer to their own ages and therefore participated in mutual decision making and more equal partnerships than were possible between very young women and their older husbands. This marriage pattern, she argues, served as a "catalyst for industrial transformation." Hartman argues that the greater equality she attributes to late marriage was "an ongoing source of friction and conflict within marriage, especially in the early modern period"; she then concedes that such conflict persists "to this day."[18] Thus the crucial change Hartman locates in the sixteenth and seventeenth centuries has not yet been fully integrated or accepted.

Histories of marriage inform us that many enormous shifts have occurred, shifts that separate the present from the past. Marriage, we're told, has moved from patriarchal to companionate, from obedience to intimacy, from sacrament to contract.[19] Most historians agree that there is a big difference between marriage then and marriage now, although they disagree as to what the crucial shift has been, when it occurred, how, and why. I find all of the operable terms equally useful to describe marriage then or now. None of these changes is yet complete. I assume, instead, that (1) models coexisted even in the early modern period and that (2) a clear transition never was achieved. This is not just because we're feeling the aftershocks of major social change. Rather, we are still in the process of imagining, feeling, enacting, and describing those changes. With regard to marriage, we never moved past the early modern because it continues to shape our institutions, metaphors, and narratives so powerfully.

Let's consider one of these shifts as an example. The supposed shift from sacrament to contract is tied to the shifts from feudal to capitalist economies, from Roman Catholicism to Protestantism, from the unbounded self to the possessive individual. In short, it is assumed to be a sign of the kinds of "progress" sometimes said to originate in the early modern period. Why is it better to view marriage as a contract? The presumption is that a contract is between equal parties and is therefore more egalitarian and modern; and that contracts can be renegotiated or broken when they no longer meet the needs of the contractors. As a consequence, many scholars locate this crucial change in conceptualizations of marriage in the early modern period.[20] The understanding of sexual intercourse as a "conjugal debt" or "duty" that each spouse owes the other, and in the absence of which marriage was null, while not new in early modern England, can be taken to suggest a contract between equal parties. The oft-discussed lists of separate-but-equal spousal duties in conduct books also support this impression. Yet if marriage might have been construed as a contract, it was not really viewed as a contract between fully equal parties in the early modern period. For instance, Milton defends divorce on the grounds of emotional and mental incompatibility by arguing that one is not bound by a contract that does not serve one's own interests; but he assumes that the contract is between the husband and the marriage more than between the husband and the wife.[21] Historians of the nineteenth century suggest that marriage was not yet construed as a contract between equal parties even then.[22] In a contract, the two parties remain separate after the contract is transacted. But marriage claims to transform the two into one. How then are we to understand their relation to the contract? Until very recently, it was often argued that the wife freely chose to marry—to enter into the marriage contract—and then ceded her right to herself to her husband. As this logic reveals, a more contractual understanding of marriage does not invariably acknowledge both parties as equals.[23] If a shift occurred from sacrament to contract, it is not clear when it did or how much it mattered. Litigation—over prenuptial agreements and divorce settlements concerning property, custody, and alimony—would be the proof that we now view marriage as a contract. But it proves, too, that we are not at all sure what husband and wife can claim with regard to the privileges, responsibilities, and entitlements of marriage.

For the purposes of my study, the most important link between the United States today and early modern England has to do with the conjunction of the Reformation and colonialism. To my discomfort, I find myself agreeing with Samuel Huntington, whose essentialist vision of cultural identity I otherwise oppose, about one thing: "Unique among countries, America is the child of [the] Reformation. Without it there would be no America as we have known it." While I agree that the Reformation continues to exert a powerful influence on U.S. mainstream culture, I evaluate that influence entirely differently than Huntington does; I view it as a burden rather than a boon.

Huntington asserts the indebtedness of American culture to the Reformation in order to defend and celebrate what he describes as the "Anglo-Protestant" "cultural core" of the United States. "America's Anglo-Protestant culture has combined political and social institutions and practices inherited from England, including most notably the English language, together with the concepts and values of dissenting Protestantism, which faded in England but which the settlers brought with them and which took on new life on the new continent." Many historians would agree that when English colonists came to the so-called new world, many (but not all) of them carried the baggage of English law, English versions of dissenting Protestantism, English customs, English books.[24] While most colonial historians focus on the transformative impact of contact and the ways that "Englishness" immediately altered and adapted in these new and challenging circumstances, Huntington emphasizes not change but continuity. For Huntington, preserving this legacy entails anti-immigration, pro-assimilation, English-only policies. "Throughout American history, people who were not white Anglo-Saxon Protestants have become Americans by adopting America's Anglo-Protestant culture and political values. This benefited them and the country."[25] While I agree that "Anglo-Protestant" values remain surprisingly influential in U.S. culture, I think that this is to be lamented. I, too, want to expose continuity but only so as to disrupt it.

Nor do I wish to disparage other traditions. The distinctive history of marriage in America should remind us that America was never only

"Anglo-Protestant." From the beginning, various religious, legal, and cultural traditions intersected. Catholics, for instance, were among the earliest English colonists to America. Seventeenth-century Maryland was founded by George Calvert, Lord Baltimore, in 1632 as both a "haven for Catholics" and a "missionary province," and named to honor Charles I's French Catholic wife, Henrietta Maria (and perhaps the Virgin Mary, too). Yet it was also religiously heterogeneous from the start. Despite their desire to convert Indians and Anglicans to Catholicism, the Catholics who founded the colony also had an official policy of religious toleration and achieved reasonably peaceful coexistence with other Christians. In this setting, according to Debra Meyers, Quakers, "Arminian Anglicans" (that is, those who emphasized free will), and Catholics shared customs and attitudes regarding marriage. They were, however, in open conflict with English Puritans, who suspended religious toleration when they seized control of the colony in 1655–57 and who, as of 1689, excluded Catholics from civil and military offices in Maryland, just as they had been excluded from succession to the English throne.[26] This history of coexistence and conflict in seventeenth-century Maryland is a reminder that Protestantism was internally divided from its birth and that our Puritan "founding fathers," lauded in Thanksgiving myths for seeking religious freedom, sought it for themselves but did not necessarily extend it to others.

Despite their reversals of fortune in late seventeenth-century Maryland, Catholics remain a huge population in the United States today. Huntington is able to assimilate Catholics into his version of Anglo-Protestantism by emphasizing doctrinal changes that have made Catholics more like Protestants. It is certainly true that the Second Ecumenical Council of the Vatican (1962–65), also known as Vatican II, enacted many of the reforms that once defined the difference between Catholics and Protestants. Because of these changes, for Huntington, America is not a Protestant country but rather "a Christian country with Protestant values."[27] But Huntington's anti-immigration stance prevents him from acknowledging the incredible diversity of Catholics in America. While Catholics have always been here, their numbers are also continuously increased by the influx of immigrant Catholics, many of whom practice Catholicism in distinctly various ways.

The U.S. Catholic Church attempts both to honor the different traditions that parishioners bring to the community and to draw all its members under the umbrella of a church that still aspires to be "catholic and universal." For instance, all couples marrying within the Catholic church must attend required premarital counseling sessions, or "pre-Cana." Catholics may not remarry in the church after divorcing unless they get their first marriages annulled. An annulment declares that a valid marriage never existed in the first place; it is an erasure rather than a dissolution. Catholics thus have a completely distinctive relation to making and ending marriages. Yet this difference may be eroding in practice. As annulments become more readily available for American Catholics, their experience is becoming different from that of Catholics in other countries. According to one study, the easier access to annulments is diluting any claim Catholics have to being culturally distinctive (or morally superior). "By relaxing standards for nullity," Robert H. Vasoli writes, "the American [Catholic] Church has ceded an expanse of the moral high ground it held since the first Catholic colonists set foot on the shores of Chesapeake Bay. Long society's principal institutional guardian of the sanctity and permanence of marriage, the American Church now seems bent on relinquishing that honorable facet of its historical identity"—by becoming more like everyone else in mainstream America.[28] Many people who consider themselves Catholics might not bother with annulments at all. Increasingly, there is a split between what many American Catholics actually do and believe (with regard, for instance, to birth control and divorce) and the official policies of the church. This split, too, makes many American Catholics' values and choices less distinctive, less defined by their confessional allegiances. Yet, in part because of the association of Catholicism with immigrants and ethnic minorities, Catholicism retains a kind of minority status in mainstream American culture despite the fact that more than one-quarter of the U.S. population self-identifies as Catholic. To date, there has been only one Catholic president (John F. Kennedy). In short, Catholicism remains a distinct, robust strand in American religious culture. Increasingly, it is more a braid than a strand, in that it contains within itself such diverse and conflicting traditions. Catholicism only achieves its place as part of the "Christian country" that Huntington defends and celebrates to the extent that he can identify it with what he sees as "Protestant values"—and with the political objectives Catholicism shares with nondenominational "Christians" such as "defending marriage" against the encroachments of same-sex couples.

I cannot hope to do justice to the religious diversity of twenty-first century U.S. culture but let me just mention two other traditions. In both cases, these religions, like Catholicism, formed part of the first immigrations to America and cannot be viewed only as relatively recent arrivals. Historians emphasize the presence of Jews in seventeenth-century America and the increasingly important role of antisemitism in American politics from the eighteenth century on. Jews, like Catholics, have often played a negative role, galvanizing opposition to a particular candidate or position that can be associated with them. Although there were some Jews, mostly men, in colonial America, they were under particular pressure to assimilate because there were so few Jewish women. As a consequence, the history of Jews in America is, in part, a history of intermarriage. According to Walter Pencak, for instance, "between 1790 and 1840" 28 percent of Jews intermarried.[29] That history is differently interpreted by different commentators. Is it diluting or destroying Judaism, or is it a survival mechanism—and a contribution to a more open, flexible American society, a society determined by choice rather than blood and birth? Sylvia Barack Fishman presents mixed marriages as a distinctly American phenomenon, normative more than transgressive, and one that has transformed American society. In Fishman's view, "the growing prominence of mixed-marriage families has helped to create a new social reality, in which the previously pro-endogamy (inmarriage) bias of American society has given way to a largely pro-exogamy (outmarriage) ethos." Making Jewish identity a matter of choice and education rather than birth, intermarriage is a crucial part of American culture. Yet Fishman also worries that intermarriage could lead to the disappearance of Jews in America.[30] One of the many arguments for protecting a distinct Jewish tradition is that it can provide a resource for thinking outside of Christian, especially Pauline, formulations for marriage, whose long reach I discuss in Chapter 1.[31] Lawrence H. Fuchs, for instance, finds in Judaism "an example of a major paradigmatic shift in the nature of patriarchy that illuminates possibilities for creating a society in which children can obtain a continuity of authoritative, loving care from fathers or mothers or other adults whom they perceive to be responsible for them—without males appropriating power and privileges to themselves."[32] Whether or not its possibilities are as utopian as Fuchs claims, Judaism is a venerable, distinct, and highly visible and influential tradition within American culture.

If the particular problem facing Jews in early America was that Judaism is a matrilineal religion disinclined to proselytizing, so that a lack of Jewish women compelled men to marry women of other faiths (and thus bear non-Jewish children), Islam might be viewed as having a survival advantage under such circumstances since it is the father's identity that determines the child's religion. But in early America, the first Muslims may have been African slaves, who faced challenges in observing their faith both from other slaves who followed African religions rather than Islam and from slavery itself. As a consequence, the contribution of America's first Muslims has been all but erased; as one historian remarks, it is hard to "make conclusive statements concerning Islam's legacy in America."[33] What is important for my purposes here is that Islam, too, might be imagined as part of the earliest religious colonization of America rather than as a recent arrival on the scene. At present, the issues for Muslims regarding marriage are both distinct—including conflicts between parents and their second- and third-generation children regarding arranged marriages—and very like those facing other religious communities—including the prospect of interfaith marriages.[34] As the Muslim population steadily grows, it, too, will provide new resources and challenges for what marriage in America means.

All of these religious traditions place enormous emphasis on marriage as a means of solidifying a distinctive religious and ethnic identity, building and sustaining communities, perpetuating traditions, and becoming American while also staying Catholic, Jewish, or Muslim. They thus contribute to the value placed on marriage as a crucial vehicle of identity formation and assimilation. Each of these groups produces marriage advice, available online and in printed books, directly addressed to their own communities so as to compete with the much larger and more widely available discourse of nondenominational "Christian" marriage advice.

Despite the fact that these other traditions have been in the United States from the beginning, despite their diversity and dynamism today, they remain eccentric to what, for the sake of argument, I am calling the early modern legacy precisely so as to identify it as the lingering trace of one particular, formative strand from a rich tapestry. Recruited against other traditions and possibilities, this legacy now infuses highly visible and influential religious and political formulations of marriage, granting them the weight of historical precedent, the venerability of age. From there the legacy spreads out insidiously in the form of persistent figurations that can seem like common sense, like givens of marriage rather than vestiges of a very particular history. This early modern legacy shapes representations and conceptualizations of white, middle-class, heterosexual marriage; persistent figurations of what a couple is; political debates about who can or should marry; and the assumptions about the kind of marriage that needs to be defended. Samuel Huntington perceives an Anglo-Protestant legacy as embattled precisely because it is not the only legacy; it is not uncontested. Other equally venerable legacies compete with and challenge it. Earnest defenses, such as Huntington's, keep this early modern legacy at the center of American political discourse, making it a force to be reckoned with. But, in their very vehemence, such defenses concede that this legacy can be dismantled.

While Huntington's views are extreme, he is not alone in his celebration of "Anglo-Protestant" values. Marilyn Yalom, in her popular *History of the Wife*, argues that a new model of a more egalitarian, loving marriage begins in post-Reformation England, is transported and nurtured in colonial America, and can now be exported, like enlightenment and civilization, to more backward peoples. "While patriarchal structures still prevailed on both sides of the Atlantic, a new ideal of companionate marriage was taking root. Imported from the propertied class of England by the colonial elite, it would blossom and spread on a fertile shore." She thus offers a particularly crude and expansionist version of Lawrence Stone's controversial "trickle down" model of social change. In her enthusiastic narrative of cultural imperialism, the colonizing has just begun. "As world leaders, Americans and Europeans are creating a model of shared conjugal authority, which may seem foreign to much of the globe, but that much of the globe will probably come to emulate." In her book, then, Yalom tells the history of what she predicts will become the global future.[35] Just as I think our history is to be lamented because it is too much with us, I also think that it is too early to celebrate the worldwide triumph of the "companionate" marriage, an unrealized ideal riddled with contradictions. We cannot export and promote a model of marriage as new and improved when it is, instead, pieced together from the mismatched remnants of older models. Our legacy is one of distrusting rather than celebrating equality. I agree with Stephanie Coontz that couples trying to reinvent marriage in order to achieve both equality and intimacy are navigating "uncharted territory." In order to imagine, much less create, genuinely new social arrangements, we have to let go of a past that still shapes our present. My project here aspires to be just one part of a struggle that will entail economic and political changes as well.

Presentist Historicism

Many scholars working on the early modern period share the assumption that our access to the past is inevitably mediated, that the categories of analysis we employ and the questions we raise are shaped by our present concerns. These concerns motivate our inquiry; they are why we look to the past at all. As Walter Benjamin has said, "every image of the past that is not recognized by the present as one of its own concerns threatens to disappear irretrievably."[36] Michel de Certeau assumes that "any reading of the past—however much it is controlled by the analysis of documents—is driven by a reading of current events."[37] Recently, however, skirmishes have broken out on the supposed border between "presentism" and historicism, particularly among literary critics.[38] While presentism used to refer to an inability to connect to the past, or a disregard for it as irrelevant, it has recently taken on a different meaning. By most recent definitions, "presentism" involves the projection of our own assumptions onto the past so that we can only see versions of ourselves there. As Margaret Ezell puts this, "it is seductively easy when gazing at the historical past to remark with some satisfaction, 'look, *they* are just like *me*,' narcissus-like in our gaze and our desire."[39]

This critique defines presentism only in order to denounce it, insisting that it is avoidable. As opposed to those who congratulate themselves on their understanding that the past is "other," presentists, it is argued, do not get it or do not care. Presentists cannot see how a past moment or event connects to what came before it, so that, for instance, they annex the early modern as their own point of origin, seeing only its connections forward in time and wrenching it violently from its roots in the medieval period. According to such critiques, the only serious historical inquiry must emphasize that the past is "a site of something different from the present."[40] Apparently it is not "historical" to see the past as in any way continuous with the present, or to emphasize connections rather than fissures. If presentism is a nasty habit, a sloppy self-indulgence, as some of its critics contend, then one may inoculate oneself through scrupulous attention to the details of historical difference. As David Kastan advises, "history functions as some apotropaic fetish to ward off our narcissism, or at least to prevent the premature imposition of present day interests and values. (The important word here is, of course, 'premature': some such imposition is inevitable and indeed desirable)."[41] Kastan here attempts to have it both ways, as do most of those who warn against presentism. It is unavoidable, they concede, but one should not give into it without a fight. Such formulations acknowledge that a distinction between presentism and historicism is a chimera even as they police the very border they create.[42]

Historians of gender and sexuality have made the most influential and compelling arguments against "presentism"; they rightly and helpfully stress that we must avoid naturalizing our own social arrangements especially with regard to sexuality, domesticity, marriage, and the family.[43] Attending to the differences between past and present, they insist, enables us to see that social and sexual arrangements have changed and can still change. Such an awareness aspires to "rescue . . . all of us from the terrible presumption of transhistorical heteronormativity."[44] In contrast, some warn, stressing continuity and overlooking difference might suggest that change is neither possible nor advisable. But this is a rather presentist way of advising against the dangers of presentism. It might be said of such queer and feminist approaches, on which I draw here, that their "centre of gravity is . . . 'now' rather than 'then,'" as Terence Hawkes says of the kind of presentist literary criticism he proposes.[45]

Historians and theorists of gender and sexuality are also moving beyond sharp oppositions (the past as the same vs. the past as irreducibly other) and toward more supple and useful ways of thinking a relation between the two. This would lead to a practice with one foot now and the other foot then. Jonathan Goldberg and Madhavi Menon have recently urged that "we need to question the premise of a historicism that privileges difference over similarity, recognizing that it is the peculiarity of our current historical moment that such a privileging takes place at all. Why has it come to pass that we apprehend the past in the mode of difference? How has 'history' come to equal 'alterity'?" Goldberg and Menon seek to "suspend the assurance that the only modes of knowing the past are either those that regard the past as wholly other or those that can assimilate it to a present assumed identical to itself." They also observe that, "in its turn against universalism, historicism has replicated universalist assumptions; refusing, in the name of presentism, for example, the difficult task of thinking the relations between a past and present."[46] As Louise Fradenburg and Carla Freccero asked more than a decade ago, "what has to be asked is whether the observation of similarities or even continuities between past and present inevitably produces an ahistoricist or universalizing effect."[47] Surely it is possible that similarities, continuities, or connections might be excavated as part of an historical project that also uncovers differences, ruptures, and gaps.

The difficult task of thinking the relations between the past and present is one in which many other historians are also engaged, and it is important not to discount their commitments and contributions. David Halperin, who sometimes serves as a whipping boy for historicism and who makes a passionate pitch "in defense of historicism" in the introduction to his book *How to Do the History of Homosexuality*, also advocates "an approach that attempts to acknowledge the alterity of the past as well as the irreducible cultural and historical specificities of the present" and concedes that "continuities are no less crucial to take into account than historical ruptures."[48] Fradenburg and Freccero propose that we study "the history of the ways in which the past is *in* us." As they point out, "the past may not *be* the present, but it is sometimes *in* the present, haunting, even if only through our uncertain knowledges of it, our hopes of surviving and living well."[49] It is precisely because the past is in the present that, as Freccero writes more recently, we must refute "a presumed logic of the 'done-ness' of the past."[50] We can do so, in part, by writing what Foucault calls "a history of the present," which Halperin acknowledges as a "deliberately paradoxical project."[51]

Like many of these critics, I practice what might be called a *presentist historicism* that tries to denaturalize present arrangements by uncovering their roots in the past. I want to challenge the idea that a marital economy of scarcity is inevitable precisely by showing that it has a history. Critics of presentism frequently warn that we should not let ourselves feel too at home in the past; it's another country, after all. Frankly, I don't feel all that at home in the present either. As a consequence, I dwell on the connections between present and past so as to estrange the present rather than domesticate the past.

It is important to allow the past to have its say as an interlocutor in this proposed conversation between past and present.[52] My approach is grounded in historical research and indebted to the methods and conclusions of scholars on whose histories I build. Rooted in my expertise in and detailed depiction of seventeenth-century England, the project has also required me to move into areas of knowledge wholly new to me, such as colonial American history and recent debates on religion, law, and marriage in America; I have moved cautiously and respectfully into these fields so as to avoid easy generalizations. I do not ignore or erase the many disparities I uncover between the two periods I juxtapose. Rather, I ask why continuities persist despite them. Why are we still telling the same stories even after extraordinary social changes? My method here does not disregard historical and textual specificity, as my very detailed interest in particular moments and texts, and my painstaking reproduction of early modern spellings, should reaffirm. But I do venture a broad view, unexpected connections, and an openly speculative engagement with the ways in which the past makes itself at home in the conceptual and narrative structures that still inform Anglo-American representations of marriage.

I employ a synchronic juxtaposition of then and now so as to expose the striking similarity between Protestant marriage advice in the seventeenth century and today, or assumptions about the intersection of marriage and domestic work on a slave plantation in eighteenth-century Virginia and in the homes shared by two professionals in the late twentieth century. The shocking connection between the periods I juxtapose emerges precisely from our awareness of the many differences that distinguish the two. Noticing the shared vocabulary and values in two bodies of marriage advice written more than three centuries apart, we are also aware of the many ways in which the readers of these works must differ in their expectations and experiences (because our contemporaries have ready access to divorce, exposure to many other ways of imagining marriage and morality, control over their fertility, much greater equality between spouses). Exploring the differences more fully than I do here would make it harder, I think, to see the connection to which I want to draw our attention, precisely because we are reluctant to see it. That connection is the persistence of particular figurations for marriage, figurations that distrust equality, insist on hierarchy, and cast spouses in a deadly struggle for dominance. Before I embarked on this project, I assumed that certain early modern figurations for marriage would have been rendered obsolete because of, among other things, the dramatic changes in women's status and rights. But I found that this was not the case.

The economy of scarcity on which I dwell here participates in what Hélène Cixous describes as "death-dealing binary thought," a tradition in Western thought that sorts concepts into binaries or couples in which "for one of the terms to acquire meaning . . . it must destroy the other." Cixous argues that these oppositions always lead to conflict and destruction. "We see that 'victory' always comes down to the same thing: things get hierarchical."[53] Toril Moi rightly challenges the gendered essentialism of Cixous's theory, but I want to use it simply to draw attention to how figurations have a history that shapes and interacts with other histories but also follows its own trajectory so that the death-dealing binary of "the couple" might persist at the level of figuration even as it is being challenged at every other level. This is what we see in depictions of marriage.

And these figurations do have "material weight," what de Certeau calls "the weight of an endlessly present past." As Valerie Traub says of the "tropological effects" of figures she studies, such as the female friend and the tribade, "providing the terms by which social beings are interpellated through strategies of inclusion and exclusion, they are infused with psychic energies and identifications while also being productive of social consequences."[54] Indeed, the terms we use and the forms we give the stories we tell can themselves enact violence; this is the kind of violence I am most interested in here. Judith Butler argues that the presumption of heterosexuality is itself a form of violence: "this kind of categorization can be called a violent one, a forceful one, and . . . this discursive ordering and production of bodies in accord with the category of sex is itself a material violence."[55] I am making a parallel argument that a figuration enacts violence that is, in its own way, material. This claim should not be misconstrued as the assertion that all marriages include acts of physical violence.

Sharply juxtaposing similar figurations in different periods exposes the contrast of unchanging figurations and changing social practices. Yet, at a deeper level, pertinacious figurations also hint at unchanging social structures hidden beneath changing social practices and diverse experiences. When it comes to marriage, then, we might imagine what Judith Bennett describes as "a history of change without transformation." Addressing the history of women's status, Bennett invites us to think in terms of continuities that persist despite change: "a history of the many changes in women's lives that have occurred without usually transforming in significant ways the imbalance of power between the sexes."[56] I want us to see how persistent figurations contribute to preventing a transformation in the imbalance of power between the sexes; I also want to stress that these figurations are not ahistorical or transhistorical. They came down to us from a particular time and place. They are, among the various legacies we bear, the early modern legacy.

Imagining Change: Same-Sex Marriage

Obviously, the most heated debate about marriage in America today has to do with whether same-sex couples can marry. This controversy reveals just how much is at stake in debates over marriage in America. At least in the West, strenuous opposition to same-sex marriage seems to be distinctly American, in part because religious factions remain so powerful in American politics. Opposition to same-sex marriage is thus part of the early modern legacy. The fight for a constitutional marriage amendment to which I referred at the start of this introduction is an attempt to grant that legacy even greater binding force. As George Chauncey writes, "amending the constitution to prohibit gay marriage would impose the more hostile attitudes of the past on the generations of the future by writing them into the fundamental law of the land." In contrast, marriage promises to lift same-sex couples out of second-class citizenship and to include them in "the tangible rights, benefits, and protections conferred by marriage."[57] Extending the right to marry to same-sex couples as a fundamental civil right and form of legitimacy (for those who want it) is part of dismantling the early modern legacy. At the same time, it is important to accompany that bid for inclusion with a critique of marriage, as it is currently imagined, as inadequate to the task of conferring equality.

According to Chauncey, in the course of the nineteenth and twentieth centuries, "the sharp differences in the marital roles assigned husbands and wives declined, so that it became easier to imagine a marriage between two people of the same sex"; furthermore, "most of the legal rights and obligations of marriage, which once were strictly distinguished by gender, have become gender-neutral and mutual." As I demonstrate in this book, the claim that spousal roles are now conceived as "gender-neutral and mutual" is too optimistic. I agree that opponents of same-sex marriage tend to resist "marriage's evolution toward freedom and equality." In Chauncey's view, the opposition of some groups to same-sex marriage was provoked, in part, by the "fear that allowing two people of the same sex to marry would ratify the transformation of marriage over the last thirty years into an institution of legal equality and gender neutrality, in which most people expect and are expected to negotiate the terms of their own relationships free of legally mandated gender roles."[58] Chauncey insists that this transformation has already taken place. But my argument is that our figurations and plots advise us that marriage's evolution toward equality might be stalled. The many different accounts of marriage I examine here depict equality as the source of marital conflict, the problem rather than the solution. To whatever extent same-sex spouses could be imagined as more equal than cross-sex spouses that would not lift them out of the dilemmas I consider.

Moreover, as various queer activists and scholars point out, including same-sex couples in marriage will not automatically and magically make the institution egalitarian. Conflicts persist within same-sex couples, as the disturbing fact of domestic violence within gay and lesbian partnerships suggests. The existence of same-sex partner violence is sometimes taken to mean that domestic violence is not about gender difference or inequality. For Christina Hoff Sommers, if lesbians batter one another, then "battery may have very little to do with patriarchy or gender bias."[59] But that doesn't have to be the logical conclusion. The conclusion could be, instead, that battering has to do with a structure of relationship that emerged in relation to heterosexual marriage and that promotes inequality between partners, hierarchy rather than partnership. When the two persons in the position of spouses are both of the same sex this does not necessarily liberate them from these structural expectations. The assumption that equality breeds conflict, and that marriage only has room for one fully developed person, can promote violence between any two spouses. Such violence is an extreme manifestation of what same-sex couples have in common with cross-sex couples.

Nor does an economy of scarcity pertain only to what happens between partners or spouses, within couples. As Valerie Lehr argues, for instance, "although the visible presence of couples" who do not embody the most familiar "gendered power differentials" and who are "working to negotiate more equitable relationships could help to promote social and cultural change, such change likely depends on challenging inequality first."[60] Such challenges to inequality need to occur outside of marriage and would extend far beyond it. The quest for marriage has to do, at the material level, with an economic system that wants to limit rather than extend access to basic protections. Michael Warner points out that the whole debate over same-sex marriage might seem different if health coverage and other entitlements were "unbundled" from marital status. What if there were enough to go around? Warner also warns that by creating divisions between sanctioned and unsanctioned couples, marriage relies on another kind of scarcity: "Marriage sanctifies some couples at the expense of others. It is selective legitimacy."[61] Here again we find a zero-sum game with regard to marriage.

Even some proponents of same-sex marriage defend it in disturbingly disciplinary terms. William Eskridge, for instance, claims that marriage will "civilize" gay men, and one of the meanings he posits for the word "civilize" is the "provocative" one "tame" or "domesticate." Marriage will thus tame gay men, rather than taming shrews. Like the taming stories I examine in Chapter 3, Eskridge links marriage to discipline—with a twist.

According to Eskridge, "the old-fashioned marriage of breadwinner husband and housekeeper wife cannot be replicated by same-sex couples; at
least one of the husbands will be a housekeeper, and at least one of the
wives will be a breadwinner. More important, a greater degree of domes-
tication should not be rejected out of hand." Eskridge both expresses the
hope that "same-sex marriages would be more egalitarian" and assigns
them the job of domesticating or taming both spouses rather than just
one.[62] This, in his view, is an argument in favor of same-sex marriage.
Marriage is good for gay people, according to Eskridge, precisely because it imposes restrictions.

As a topic and an institution, marriage seems to produce an an-
guished awareness of scarcity and competition. Perhaps this is why so
many opponents to same-sex marriage act as if it will take something
away from heterosexual marriage. If gay people could marry, they claim,
heterosexual marriages would somehow be diminished or compromised. In fact, defenders of heterosexual marriage seem to gain by their
opposition to same-sex marriage. As I point out in the first chapter,
many of the "Christians" who most strenuously oppose same-sex marriage have also accepted enormous social changes into their own experience of marriage. As Jim Holt explains:

In some states . . . [marriage] is evidently more imperiled than in others. The
Bible Belt states, in particular, have a shockingly high divorce rate, around 50
percent above the national average. Given such marital instability, these states
are anxious to defend the institution of heterosexual matrimony, which may explain their hostility to gay marriage. The state of Massachusetts, by contrast, has
the lowest divorce rate in the nation. So its people—or at least its liberal judges—
perhaps feel more comfortable allowing some progressive experimentation.[63]

For those in Bible Belt states, or in the Christian Right more generally,
opposing same-sex marriage makes it possible to sustain their countercultural identity as the defenders of marriage without giving up the
changes they have integrated into the marriages they are defending.
Same-sex marriage becomes the line in the sand. Those who oppose it
may be divorced; they may be in dual-career marriages or ones in which
the wife is at present the only or the major earner; they may take for
granted both birth control and more widely accepted nonreproductive
sexual practices that disjoin sexual congress from reproduction. But opposing same-sex marriage allows them to consider themselves defenders
of traditional marriage without surrendering changes from which they
benefit or to which they've grown accustomed.[64] Opposing same-sex
marriage, then, is a strategy for mystifying how much heterosexual marriage has actually changed and for ignoring the problems caused by the
ways in which it has not.

Chapter 1 compares sixteenth- and seventeenth-century Puritan advice literature and late twentieth-century American evangelical books of marital counsel and inspiration in order to show how scarcity haunts even the most ecstatic visions of marital plenitude and love. In both periods, writers struggle to reconcile two biblical figures for marriage: the fusion of spouses into "one flesh" and the man's role as the head of that corporate body. At every turn, the transcendent ideal of one flesh is haunted by the prospect of the marital body as a two-headed monster. Often, the writers of Christian marital advice resolve contradiction and avert nightmare by suggesting that of the two spouses the wife must give up more to sustain the union and to shore up her husband's uncertain sense of his own status as household head, especially in the heightened social turmoil that characterizes both periods. Husbands' "headship" thus operates as a symbolic cover story for more complex distributions of power within marriage. The strategy of "nominal submission" reaches its limit, however, when a husband's tyranny threatens to obliterate his wife. Under such conditions, she must write him out of the story if she is to survive. The chapter closes with a discussion of women's texts in which a wife fantasizes her husband's death as the first step to her own achievement of happiness and salvation.

Chapter 2 examines how stories of extreme marital conflict represent enacted rather than imagined murder as the usual outcome. Several recent films, such as *Sleeping with the Enemy* (1991) and *Enough* (2002), suggest that the only way for a wife to cope with an abusive husband is to kill him. While this is a particularly dramatic and decisive way to resolve marital conflict, this plot serves deeper needs, reproducing the logic of coverture as a narrative structure that privileges one spouse over the other. We can best understand how a plot replicates a legal construction of marriage by examining two particularly heated moments of debate about married women's legal status. Therefore, I juxtapose seventeenth-century pamphlet accounts of the crime and punishment of "petty traitors," that is, women who kill their husbands, to late twentieth-century American discussions about how to defend "battered women" who kill their abusers. For the battered woman, the focus is on what has been done to her and on her victimization; for the petty traitor, the focus is on what she has done as an act of rebellion. These sharply different ways of assessing and naming violent wives have real consequences for women: "battered women" have an increased chance of acquittal, while "petty traitors" were dealt with more severely than other murderers. Yet, as I show, discourses about petty traitors and battered women share underlying similarities: both suggest that these women can only assert themselves through violence, in part because of the legal constructions of all wives, not just murderous ones. When marriage is depicted as a zero-sum game, then the wife can only assert the capacity for self-determination by usurping it from her husband, which she does in these extreme cases by killing him.

The first two chapters focus on spouses locked in one-on-one struggles with high stakes: salvation or damnation, life or death. What happens when spouses share their household—and their conflicts—with other dependents, particularly servants and slaves? In Chapter 3, I show that early modern and twentieth-century accounts of household government warn that equality between husband and wife creates fruitless struggles for the breeches. The husband can ameliorate these conflicts, however, by granting his wife equal power over their dependents, thus deflecting violence away from the couple and onto their subordinates. I explore how such a compromise might play out in Shakespeare's *The Taming of the Shrew* and in early modern diaries. As I argue, this compensatory strategy, by which the exploitation of servants shores up the apparent equilibrium between husband and wife, persists in subtler forms in twentieth-century assessments of the relationship between marriage and domestic work, such as Arlie Hochschild's *The Second Shift* (1989), a ground-breaking analysis of marriage and domestic work, and Barbara Ehrenreich's best-selling *Nickel and Dimed* (2001).

Chapter 4 addresses how popular novelists use stories set in Tudor England in order to explore the contradictions built into marriage and to entertain the possibility that marriage might not provide a happy ending. A surprising number of novels, including Susan Kay's *Legacy* (1985), Rosalind Miles's *I, Elizabeth* (1994), and Robin Maxwell's *The Secret Diary of Anne Boleyn* (1997) dwell on the exceptional cases of Anne Boleyn, whose marriage to Henry VIII ended in her execution, and her daughter Elizabeth I, who never married. Considered together, these stories suggest that assertive women are either destroyed by marriage or avoid it. The novels repeatedly depict this stalemate in terms of the marital economy of scarcity I explore in the preceding chapters. They thus popularize an insight into the very connection between past and present on which I focus. Even historical novels that are not about beheaded or virgin queens, such as Philippa Gregory's *The Other Boleyn Girl* (2001) and *The Queen's Fool* (2004), place at their centers a conflict between a heroine who makes modern claims to autonomy and the (somewhat reductive) assumption that early modern marriage robs a wife of all control over her property, her body, and her life. In novel after novel, the heroine assumes that marriage will annihilate her or lead her to destroy her husband. By associating women's subordination or even erasure through marriage with the early modern period, these stories suggest that time will resolve the conflict between spirited heroines and marriage. Yet the enduring appeal of such stories proves that this conflict remains unresolved in part because we do not yet understand our legacy from the very period they depict. Just as these novels imagine that a morbid fear of marriage is Elizabeth's legacy from her disgraced and beheaded mother, so they purvey an early modern legacy to their readers in the form of the mixed message that marriage is deeply desirable and potentially deadly.

There are other ways of imagining connection than the restrictive one on which I focus. But we cannot really clear space for them until we recognize the ties binding us to this particular past. I am interested in anatomizing this legacy and the various ways in which it bears on the present because I think the most pressing cultural challenge is not just to include more people in marriage—through, for example, the legalization of same-sex marriage—or to interweave more cultural strands with the early modern legacy or to diversify the kinds of unions that have marital prestige and privileges. We must also reconceive what we call marriage so that it has more room for whatever persons enter into it. This book offers one contribution to the wide-ranging, hotly contested effort to reimagine marriage. It aspires to help us envision change by interrogating persistent and limiting continuities.

A Note on Spelling

In order to activate an awareness of the historical distance between early modern writers and their readers today, even as I dwell on the connections between them, I have largely retained original spellings in quotations from early modern texts except when I am quoting from modern editions. However, in the interests of granting access to as many readers as possible, I have also followed the standard practice of silently expanding contractions, distinguishing i/j and u/v, and altering the long s.

Chapter One

One Flesh, Two Heads: Debating the Biblical Blueprint for Marriage in the Seventeenth and Twentieth Centuries

Writing in the early seventeenth century, William Perkins explains that a couple, whether husband and wife, parent and child, or master and servant, "is that whereby two persons standing in mutuall relation to each other, are combined together as it were in one. And of these two the one is alwaies higher, and beareth rule, the other is lower, and yeeldeth subjection."[1] This definition seems internally contradictory—how can two combine into one, even "as it were," if one remains higher? At first, it might also seem outmoded. Surely it has been supplanted by a definition like the one that Justice William J. Brennan offered in 1971: "The marital couple is not an independent entity with a mind and heart of its own, but an association of two individuals each with a separate intellectual and emotional makeup."[2] Yet despite or even because of its contradictions, Perkins's definition remains current, especially among those who ground their definitions of the couple and of marriage on the creation accounts in Genesis. There, many continue to find a powerful idealization of marriage as an all-encompassing union through which husband and wife become one flesh. While this fusion is supposed to transcend any differences between the two spouses, at least in the raptures of conjugal congress, the differences between the individuals involved bedevil conceptions of the couple. Two become one, we are told, but only by means of compromise, friction, and loss. Since equality is understood as encouraging battles of the will, only a hierarchy, according to which one submits to the other, can resolve conflicts so that the occasional or apparent achievement of union becomes possible.

Just as Perkins argues that of the two who become one "one is always higher," scripturally informed marriage instruction, in the early modern period and today, often proposes "male headship" as the solution to the inevitable conflicts that arise in marriage. These twin tenets of the "biblical blueprint for marriage" can seem contradictory: husband and wife are spiritual equals united in love, at the same time that the husband is the wife's superior and she his subordinate.[3] St. Paul, for instance, advises that husband and wife should become one flesh, and that men should love their wives as their own bodies, but also that the husband should be the head of this corporate body (Eph. 5: 22-33). Yet these formulations are contradictory only if one assumes that love requires equality. Many writers I will discuss here assume the opposite. In their view, equality promotes conflict and yields a monstrously two-headed or headless conjugal body. In contrast, hierarchy is thought to assure stability, thereby enhancing love. In turn, love ameliorates the differences in status widely viewed as essential, because marriage is expected to serve as an analogy to the relationship of Christ to his Church and because all human relations are assumed to require hierarchy.[4]

For decades, historians have debated the relationship between these two models of marriage, often described as the hierarchical or patriarchal versus the companionate or mutual models. They have also debated how these models and their interrelationship have changed over time. In an influential but controversial thesis, Lawrence Stone argues that, in seventeenth- and eighteenth-century England, companionate marriage emerged as a largely new ideal among higher status people and then trickled down the social scale, eventually being exported to the colonies. Stone argues for a gradual shift from one model to the other in the course of the early modern period.[5] Stone's book taught a broad audience that marriage had a history, drew attention to the relationship between hierarchy and mutuality on which I focus in this chapter, animated ongoing interdisciplinary debate, and set the terms of that debate.

Other historians swiftly challenged Stone's claim that the companionate model was largely new, pointing to its existence in scriptural, humanist, and Catholic traditions before the Reformation.[6] Although work on marriage and the family is so prolific and varied that it is impossible to survey comprehensively, one can perceive a compromise emerging between the extremes of Stone's argument for dramatic change and his critics' emphasis on unbroken continuity. Keith Wrightson, for instance, examines both "enduring structures" and "uneven processes of change."[7] David Cressy casts his history of *Birth, Marriage, and Death in Early Modern England* as a study of "transactions and engagements, including collisions and misunderstandings, between various sectors of post-reformation society."[8] Pamela Brown, Bernard Capp, Heather Dubrow, Anthony Fletcher, Laura Gowing, Mary Beth Rose, and Alison Wall examine the durability of gender hierarchy and patriarchal systems as well as the contradictions within early modern gender ideologies and the possibilities for resistance to them in practice.[9] From different angles and with different goals, Rebecca Bach, Fletcher, and Valerie Traub work to disaggregate the assumed

nexus of companionship, heterosexuality, and romantic love so often assigned to the "new" post-Reformation marriage.[10] I, too, examine this
nexus, focusing on how it was crafted in the early modern period and how
it persists today.

I operate on the assumption that a model of loving companionship
between spouses did not replace a harsher and more primitive hierarchical model at any particular historical moment. Male headship is, as
we will see, avidly if defensively embraced by some groups today; thus,
this is not a simple story of one model supplanting another definitively.
The transition that some historians locate in the early modern period
and others place earlier or later is not yet complete. Instead, the balance
between the two models seems to shift from period to period, place to
place, social group to social group. Like most other social changes, shifting attitudes toward marriage trickled down and swelled up and rippled
out; change unfolded in dispersed, sporadic, and uneven ways.[11] As in
Genesis itself, the two models of marriage tend to coexist (as uneasily as
spouses) in the same head, heart, or household. Surrendering a devel-
opmental model of change makes it possible to abandon the project of
dating a transition that has not yet occurred so as to focus on the continuing conflict between coexisting models.

This chapter begins with the contradictions that fracture the scriptural foundation for marital advice. I then discuss Protestant advice
printed in the United States in the late twentieth and early twenty-first
centuries followed by that printed in England and colonial America in
the late sixteenth and seventeenth centuries. In both periods, I argue,
marriage advice attributes conflict to a wife's claims to social equality
and/or a husband's failures of leadership and proposes male headship
as the solution to this conflict. Yet, as often as not, I argue, the reasser-
tion of male dominance operates as a cover story for more complex
distributions of power within marriage. This coverstory disguises but
cannot resolve the conflict between a wife's claims to spiritual equality,
on which writers in both periods agree, and the gender difference and
hierarchy they insist are crucial to the biblical blueprint for marriage.
Through a detailed examination of sixteenth- and seventeenth-century
marriage advice, I elaborate on the persistent dilemma of reconciling
spiritual equality and social hierarchy, the erotic melding into one flesh
and the tension between two potential heads of this shared body. In the
last section of the chapter, I look at three early modern women writers,
Lady Eleanor Davies Douglas, Anne Wentworth, and Abigail Bailey, who
assert their unmediated relationship to God as a strategy to justify their
independence from their husbands. As I show, these women employ
fantasies of their husbands' deaths to facilitate their assertions of themselves as separate and worthy, rather than headless fragments. These

murderous fantasies are born out of the contradictions built into biblical blueprints for marriage.

My central evidence in this chapter comes from two parallel bodies of Protestant marriage advice, eerie in their similarity, one printed in England in the late sixteenth and seventeenth centuries then transported to the colonies; the other printed in America in the late twentieth and early twenty-first centuries. While we can't be sure how widely read the early modern texts were, an extraordinary number of works were printed on the subject of marriage and family life and some particularly popular titles went into many editions—even in the eighteenth and nineteenth centuries. Today, Christian titles on marriage and the family are best sellers but tend to fall short of, say, the *New York Times* best-seller short list. In both periods under discussion here, ministers figure prominently among the writers, extending their ministry by expanding, codifying, and broadly disseminating their preaching through manuals of advice.

Why is marriage so important to Protestant writers in both periods? Just after the Reformation, the defense and promotion of marriage was one of the ways that ministers could assert the difference between Protestant and Catholic values and priorities; it was also a topic through which ministers, most of them married themselves, could forge an intimate connection to their parishioners' lives and problems distinctly different from that possible for a celibate clergy (or so they claimed). The mass production of marriage advice, as I discuss it in this chapter, remains largely a Protestant phenomenon, written mostly by married ministers. In recent American politics, the linked projects of defending (heterosexual) marriage, prohibiting same-sex marriage, and restricting access to divorce prove that defining and defending marriage is central to the Christian right's larger moral and political agenda. Today, there are certainly Catholics in the "Christian right." In England in the century or so after the Reformation, such coalitions were rare. That the marriage advice I examine is largely a Protestant phenomenon, broadly conceived, suggests that the Reformation was a paradigm-shifting event not because it ushered in wholly new social arrangements or attitudes but because it produced such prolific and urgent defenses of what was also asserted to be traditional. It is still true that Christian writings on marriage claim to recover and reform values, not to invent them. In this emphasis, they seek to naturalize particular ways of imagining and figuring marriage, claiming that this is how God intends us to structure our intimate lives. Yet the proliferation of Christian marriage advice itself reveals that the model of marriage it promotes is not natural, not a given.

The abundant Christian literature on marriage and the family available today seeks to persuade couples to marry and to help them survive their conflicts in order to avoid divorce. It operates on the assumption that, as one popular guide puts it, "becoming married is for most people a process rather than a single event," and that people need guidance through that process.[12] Early modern conduct literature similarly works to guide readers through the process of marriage: persuading readers to marry yet also warning them about the inevitable problems they will face in marriage. Both bodies of advice strive to offset the disappointment they attribute to unreasonable expectations, expectations they suggest have recently changed or inflated. As William Whately warns in his grimly pessimistic *A Care-Cloth: or a Treatise of the Cumbers and Troubles of Marriage: Intended to Advise Them That May, to Shun Them; That May Not, Well and Patiently to Beare Them* (1624), "none doe meete with more crosses in marriage, or beare their crosses more untowardly, then those that most dreame of finding it a very Paradise."[13] Many historians agree that such dreams were increasingly invested in marriage from the early modern period onward. Writers in both periods advise readers on how to fulfill some of their expectations, while resisting cultural pressure to expect too much from marriage.

For both periods, it is unclear exactly how to categorize the writers' confessional identities. Are they Puritans or dissenters in the early modern period? To read the new *Dictionary of National Biography* entries on the sixteenth- and seventeenth-century writers is to learn in detail the widely varied doctrinal and political views, and consequently careers, of those grouped together as "Church of England clergymen." In the late twentieth and early twenty-first centuries, are the ministers who publish their marital advice fundamentalists, evangelicals, or Christians? I often use the word "Christian," as these writers themselves do, to indicate a large, nondenominational group. The strategic use of that term works to obscure important doctrinal differences within Christianity and Protestantism so as to secure an enormous readership, market, and voting bloc. In my own usage, it works as a reminder that this is a large, amorphous group rather than a fringe one.

However we might name them, these writers present themselves as morally authoritative but as culturally marginal, fighting to reform and reclaim the cultural center. "Christian" defenders of marriage identify "secular humanism" as the galvanizing threat that provokes staunch defenses of "traditional" arrangements; they privilege male headship as "one of *the* most defining and differentiating features of couples subscribing to a conservative Christian worldview."[14] Ministers writing in the century or so after the Reformation most often argue against Catholic or pre-Reformation assumptions that celibacy is superior to marriage. In both periods, the groups on which I focus present themselves as responding to a crisis they have not caused but must try to solve. That's one reason why they defend their positions so strenuously, presenting the stakes as very high and, for all of their moral certainty, not taking the outcome as determined.

In both eras, these authors of marital advice repeat and repackage themselves; they also quote and plagiarize from one another. Many writers in the United States in the late twentieth and early twenty-first centuries expressly connect themselves to the predecessors they call Puritans.[15] Reaching back before the "founding fathers," they stake a claim to a conjoined church and state as the ideal state of affairs in America. Above all, Protestant writers in both eras rely heavily on the same biblical passages, citing and glossing them repeatedly.[16] This reliance on the Bible is one of the chief links between the bodies of Protestant marriage advice produced in the two periods; it also poses a challenge to an historical understanding of these discourses by collapsing the distance between past and present. Does one begin in the beginning or does one start in the present? It's sometimes hard to tell the difference.

Fantasies of Past Fantasies

The Bible remains one of the most crucial terrains of struggle over gender roles and relations in late twentieth- and early twenty-first-century America. As one rich sourcebook on interpretations of creation accounts asserts: "in no previous century has concern for establishing men as the 'head' of women been more pronounced" than in the twentieth.[17] This concern has intensified both because of the perception that male headship is newly threatened by changing attitudes and conditions and because the commitment to male headship, whatever that may mean, has become a "strategic boundary," the crucial means of defining a countercultural group identity "in the face of broad cultural acceptance of ideological egalitarianism."[18]

Nevertheless, the precise meaning of male headship remains ambiguous. The Southern Baptist Convention clearly proclaims that women should not take leadership roles within the church and should submit themselves at home. As the president of the Southern Baptist Theological Seminary announced in an op-ed piece in the *New York Times*, "Southern Baptists experience family trouble like everyone else, but at least they know how God intended to order the family," that is, as they declared at their convention in 1998, through the wife's submission. Yet what she is supposed to "submit herself graciously to" is called, paradoxically, "the servant leadership of her husband."[19] The Danvers Statement (1987) by the Council on Biblical Manhood and Womanhood similarly qualifies its terms in an otherwise bold reinforcement of gender hierarchy, advocating "the humble leadership of redeemed husbands and the intelligent, willing support of that leadership by redeemed wives."[20]

Ken Abraham, an apologist for the Promise Keepers (PK), a Christian men's movement that, in the early 1990s, attracted huge numbers of men eager to recommit themselves to Jesus and to reclaim a role in their families they felt they had lost, counters the charge that the organization teaches men "to dominate and manipulate women" by claiming that, instead, the Promise Keepers teach men to lead.[21] As PK preacher Tony Evans notoriously urges in his *Seven Promises of a Promise Keeper*, men who have surrendered the leadership role in their families must not ask for it back but rather "take it back": "there can be no compromise here. If you're going to lead, you must lead. Be sensitive. Listen. Treat the lady gently and lovingly. But *lead.*"[22] For many men, the leadership role available to be seized is the rather thankless one of earning a wage and sharing child care and domestic work. Evans himself explicitly urged men to embrace the "second job" at home. Perhaps this is why the call to seize the reins is cast in terms of service.

According to Abraham, the complex relationship that PK proposes between husband and wife is only confusing

> to those who do not understand the biblical basis upon which the organization operates. At the same time Promise Keepers teaches that husbands and wives must submit to each other (Ephesians 5:20), it also advocates the position that the husband-father should be the head of the household, that the man should be the family leader. The essence of the Promise Keeper's leadership, however, is not dictatorial, but rather is earned through serving his wife and children.[23]

But the platform message from the Promise Keepers was even more equivocal than this. They rarely mentioned male headship at press conferences, in endorsed publications, or at stadium gatherings. This enabled them to occupy a middle ground, seeming to please everyone.[24] This is a middle ground that many evangelicals attempt to stake out between symbolic endorsement of male headship and a pragmatic acceptance of more equal or mutual relations. The doctrine of "mutual submission" was first articulated by evangelical feminists, but has gained wide currency—among Promise Keepers and even the most conservative Christian writers about marriage and the family—because it allows writers to have it both ways: to acknowledge social changes such as dual earner households while preserving an idea of marriage in which, at any given moment, someone must lead and someone follow.

Resorted to as a bedrock on which men can reclaim leadership, biblical texts offer a mixed message whose contradictions must be finessed through oxymorons such as "servant leadership" and "mutual submission."[25] This mixed message emerges from a scriptural foundation that is itself fractured because, as has been much discussed, the Hebrew

Bible contains two creation accounts. In the first, briefer account, God creates man and woman simultaneously—"male and female he created them"—and grants them joint dominion over other creatures. In the second account, God creates man first and then woman as a helper and partner for him and from him. The word often translated "help-meet" is *kenegedo*—companion, partner, helper—and can carry various connotations, including "less than," "parallel with" or "corresponding to," "greater than," "against" or in "opposition to," or simply "complementary," with no comment on the relationship.[26] Upon the creation of woman, man greets and accepts her, proclaiming: "This is now bone of my bones and flesh of my flesh; this one shall be called Woman, because she was taken out of Man" (Gen. 2: 23). Adam's words express love, kinship, and ownership, describe origin, and predict destiny—just as two came from one flesh, they will again become one flesh in marriage. Various relationships have been posited between the two terse creation accounts in Genesis: the second can be seen as an elaboration of the first or as either contradicting or supplementing it as an alternative way of imagining the creation of humankind. When considered together they have always been read as grounding gender relations in both equality and hierarchy, in a tension between difference and sameness. The history of translation, commentary, interpretation, and revision of Genesis 1-3 shows how many possibilities have been found in these texts; they have provided a rich ground for contestation but a very unstable foundation for gender roles and relations. Because biblical Hebrew does not spell out any "categorical difference between 'woman' and 'wife,' 'man' and 'husband'" and describes a rich array of relationships between men and women whose complexities are obscured under the one word "marriage," it might be argued that English translations of the Old Testament impose definitions of marriage on the text rather than derive them from it.[27]

Considerable debate centers on whether Genesis presents the subordination of woman to man as part of the original creation or as a punishment for the fall. Is the curse or prediction to Eve that "your desires shall be for your husband, and he shall rule over you" "a disruption of, or a return to, the divine intent for male and female relationships"? Is hierarchy between husband and wife paradisal or a punishment for sin?[28] Some theologians contend that hierarchy was ordained from the beginning. Calvin, for instance, argues that Eve "had, indeed, previously been subject to her husband, but that was a liberal and gentle subjection; now, however, she is cast into servitude." God punishes Adam "because you have listened to the voice of your wife," suggesting that he should have led or ruled even before the fall (and thus have prevented it) and that woman's leadership in marriage is inevitably disastrous.[29]

Across the centuries, the view that God imposed hierarchy as a punishment seems to be more persuasively and widely argued. Chrysostom (a "church father" writing in the fourth century) paraphrases God's response to Eve in this way:

In the beginning I created you equal in esteem to your husband, and my intention was that in everything you would share with him as an equal, and as I entrusted control of everything to your husband, so did I to you; but you abused your equality of status. Hence I subject you to your husband. . . . I want you to have yearning for him and, like a body being directed by its head, to recognize his lordship pleasurably.[30]

Chrysostom builds from his description of the paradise Eve lost to the injunction she take pleasure in her submission; this emphasis on pleasure will become the centerpiece of evangelical idealizations of marriage. In the sixteenth century, Luther argues that

Eve has been placed under the power of her husband, she who previously was very free and, as the sharer of all the gifts of God, was in no respect inferior to her husband. . . . The rule remains with the husband, and the wife is compelled to obey him by God's command. He rules the home and the state, wages war, defends his possessions, tills the soil, builds, plants, etc. The woman, on the other hand, is like a nail driven into the wall. She sits at home. . . . If Eve had persisted in the truth, she would not only not have been subjected to the rule of her husband, but she herself would also have been a partner in the rule which is now entirely the concern of males. Women are generally disinclined to put up with this burden, and they naturally seek to gain what they have lost through sin.[31]

Later commentators continue this elegiac approach to gender relations, even if they can't match the power of Luther's description of the wife's transition from "sharer" to "nail driven into the wall." In 1645, John Brinsley argues that after the fall, Adam's "Patent was inlarged, and her liberty somewhat abridged."[32] In her unequivocal essay "The Head of the Woman Is the Man," published in 1989, Susan T. Foh says that

The battle of the sexes is the result of sin and the judgment on it for the woman. The woman's willing submission is replaced by a desire to control her husband. Consequently, to maintain his headship the husband must fight for it. Sin has ruined the marital dance, the easy, loving lead of the husband and the natural following of the wife. In its place are struggle, tyranny, domination, and manipulation and subterfuge.[33]

In Foh's interpretation, there is no possibility of sharing either before or after the fall. Before the fall, the woman submits willingly (at least until her great act of disobedience). After the fall, she creates the battle of the sexes because she fights not to be her husband's equal but to be his master; he in turn must fight to stay on top.

Some commentators on the resurgence of fundamentalism and evangelicalism at the end of the twentieth century in America argue that the "biblical basis" for marriage endures not because it is stable but rather precisely because it is contradictory and dynamic. Biblical figures and plots regarding marriage can adapt to new circumstances because they articulate desires rather than describe conduct, operating as a resource for working-class people, and serving different needs for men and for women.

For instance, Judith Stacey examines the appeal of a small Pentecostal church in the Silicon Valley, focusing on what it offers to wives with feminist sympathies. The women Stacey interviews turn to evangelicalism as "a strategy for achieving heterosexual intimacy, one facilitated by the surprisingly feminized view of a loving marriage" articulated by their churches. Many of these women associate feminism with autonomy and self-assertion, and therefore assume that it is at odds with the compromises and codependencies required of intimacy. To assert oneself, the logic goes, is to oppose one's husband and resist union. As a consequence, the women Stacey interviews use the scripturally inflected language of hierarchical marriage to express connection.[34] Judith Newton, too, argues that the rhetoric of a patriarchy "more mythic than actual" helps men to limit "the anxiety or 'gender vertigo' that attends undoing the protective strategies of maintaining distance or control in domestic relationships with women." As a result, she speculates, this rhetoric of patriarchy "may in fact sustain the willingness and, indeed, the very ability, of some Promise Keepers' husbands to be more open, more vulnerable, more humble, more giving, and more intimate with their wives."[35]

Barbara Brasher similarly finds that women in two Christian fundamentalist congregations she studied in southern California in the 1990s promise submission as part of a courtship strategy and depict submission "as a tactical approach employed by both husband and wife to encourage more just interactions than their parents had." These women also emphasize male leadership to enjoin their husbands to a responsibility and probity that they view as in their own best interests.[36] John Bartkowski, working in the 1990s with members of the Parkview Evangelical Free Church, "a conservative Protestant congregation located in a large metropolitan area of Texas," finds that wifely submission is assumed but that its meaning is "embattled" and that many members of the church combine "egalitarian terminology" such as "mutual submission" with "recommendations for a patriarchal family structure." He also finds women describing submission as a means of getting what they want: one woman says "submission is the oil in the lock and the grease in the gears of your marriage." Another wife says that submission "puts a lot of responsibility on them, but it makes them act better"; as

Bartkowski points out, this woman "argues that it is the deficiencies in men rather than the inferiority of women that makes wifely submission the key to marital success," and interlaces her remarks "with various types of quid pro quo exchanges." He too finds wives strategic: "Far from being passive doormats, many of these women portray themselves as active strategists who have generously decided to defer to husbands whose fragile egos could not withstand the onslaught of women's overt assertiveness."[37] A fiction of male headship provides a mask of dependency and subordination behind which woman can be assertive and competent, and a mask of authority behind which men can be emotionally responsive and even dependent. Thus women engage in what Stacey calls "nominal subordination" in the service of enjoining their husbands to a leadership that is being increasingly redefined.

In his book *Soul Provider*, for instance, Tim Elmore defines a spiritual leader as "one who assumes responsibility for the health of the relationship or group."[38] Sally Gallagher finds that a majority of the "religiously committed Protestants" she surveyed define "headship" as "spiritual leadership" rather than being the family's breadwinner or final decision-making authority. According to Gallagher,

> headship plays a strategically important yet largely symbolic role in the lives of ordinary evangelicals. While husbands retain the status of head of the household, the roles of evangelical men and women in decision making, parenting, and employment demonstrate that, for the most part, evangelical family life reflects the pragmatic egalitarianism of biblical feminists while retaining the symbolic hierarchy of gender-essentialist evangelicals.[39]

In many households that espouse the ideal of "male headship," wives earn wages, make most of the decisions regarding material life, and pay the bills.[40] In such cases, male headship is a fiction that conceals women's financial contributions to, perhaps even sole responsibility for, the family income.

Susan Faludi, an astute commentator on the Promise Keepers movement, argues that "servant leadership," whatever that would mean, is a fantasy designed to compensate men for what they feel they've lost—including the material basis for a leadership role in the home. In response to declining economic opportunities and social power, she suggests, the members of Promise Keepers "are clinging to a phantom status" or an "honorary post" as the "figurehead" of the household.[41] A similar claim has been made for how some heterosexual men use "pornographic fantasy as compensation for their powerlessness in the real world"; from this perspective, "pornography is therefore not so much an expression of male power as it is an expression of their lack of power," which they redress by consuming *depictions* of themselves as extremely powerful.[42] The fable of male headship may operate in a similar way, as a narrative in which men can view themselves as dominant. David Savran identifies a similar compensatory strategy at work in films from the last two decades of the twentieth century, associating it explicitly with middle-class white men attempting to "recoup the perceived losses of the past twenty years."

No longer the sole breadwinner in most households, he [the white male viewer/consumer] is obliged, on the one hand, to be more responsive both economically and emotionally to an increasingly fluid family dynamic. On the other hand, this very occupational and emotional instability simultaneously inspires him—if only in his fantasies—to enact a hypermasculinized heroism, as if in compensation for his perpetually misplaced virility.[43]

In such representations (for Savran, a crucial example is Rambo), the white male is always simultaneously aggressor and victim. Savran's emphasis on whiteness provides a possible insight into the downsizing of the Promise Keepers, which seems to have been undermined not by feminist resistance (many women apparently encouraged their husbands to join) but rather by unease about the organization's commitment to racial integration. Perhaps the mixed race brotherhood the group began to promote undermined its ability to feed what Savran calls "white male backlash." Whereas controversy has focused on the Promise Keepers' call for men to "take back" their leadership in the home, a call issued by an African American preacher, perhaps the more challenging call was the one issued by another African American minister in 1996 for white members of the organization to "give up" white privilege in the interests of interracial brotherhood.[44]

For the working-class people in recent studies of evangelicalism, then, figurations of the couple as one flesh and the husband as his wife's head provide a cover story that cushions couples against the shock of changing domestic relations such as two-earner couples or female breadwinners. Yet, at the same time, this buffer or disguise also sets limits on spouses' ability to confront, discuss, embrace, or resist such changes consciously. Male headship is a fantasy of domination that persists despite changing material conditions and, indeed, takes on new functions precisely because of those changing conditions. It is no less "real" for being a fiction. It is precisely because certain figures for and formulations of marriage were always fictions that they can outlive the material conditions under which they first flourished, proving adaptable and tenacious, and supporting, constraining or facilitating new kinds of social arrangements.

When male headship is tacitly supported only so that more egalitarian relations can flourish behind its back, marital hierarchy is accepted as having cultural usefulness. Furthermore, what the rhetoric of headship covers is sometimes another form of headship. All seem to agree that the pressing questions in marriage are the ones Douglas Brouwer articulates in his marriage manual *Beyond I Do*: "Who's in charge? Or, to put it another way, who has the final word? In a marriage, whose opinion is finally going to carry the most weight?"[45] According to James Walker, in his book *Husbands Who Won't Lead and Wives Who Won't Follow*, "we are told that in marriage 'two shall become one.' Our problem is *which one*?"[46] It's hard to imagine a more explicit statement of the marital economy of scarcity I explore in this book. A zero-sum game underpins these visions of marriage, despite their variety, creativity, and flexibility. Someone has to be in charge. The one flesh formed through marriage requires the enlargement of one spouse and the eclipse of the other. In the various ethnographic studies I've been citing those interviewed usually come down on one side or the other. The wife is really the one but she lets her husband think he is. The husband is, of course, the one in charge, but by conceding this the wife ultimately gains. Or they take turns being the one in charge. In such cases, the ideal of "mutual submission" winds up sounding more like "serial submission." One spouse or the other must be in charge at a given moment, but it isn't necessarily the same one every time.

The enormous Christian marriage literature of the late twentieth- and early twenty-first century, of which Brouwer's and Walker's books form a part, constantly circles around the conceptual problem of scarcity at the heart of marital plenitude. Elisabeth Elliot assures readers of her book *Let Me Be a Woman* that "God is not asking anybody to become a zero." She and many other writers of marital advice suggest that the problem with feminism is that it has led women to suspect that they would be the ones assigned zero status.[47] One of the women interviewed by Susan D. Rose in a community of "independent charismatics" in upstate New York in 1982-83 claims that men's strength in the community has "not been without a cost—the death of women. . . . We had to step down in order to let them (men) step up to their 'God-appointed' positions. We had to relinquish some of our power." Rose argues that these women gained men who were actively involved in parenting and with whom they participated as decision makers. But these gains "demanded a denial of personhood" from the wives.[48] Defenders of male headship counter such perceptions by arguing that all Christians must embrace submission and that losing is gaining for everyone—but especially so for women. As Beverley LaHaye explains,

Oh, that we could just grasp the attitude in the heart of Jesus—the willingness to be humbled, to be obedient unto death, and to be submissive. It is the principle of losing oneself to find oneself. As the woman humbles herself (dies to self) and submits to her husband (serves him), she begins to find herself within that relationship. . . . [T]he wife who truly loves her husband will make his happiness her primary goal. With this kind of motivation, they both are winners in the end![49]

The Christian paradox of losing to gain pervades these texts. In *Hidden Keys of a Loving Lasting Marriage*, the prolific author Gary Smalley tries to outwit the economy of scarcity in a chapter entitled "If Your Wife Doesn't Win First Place, You Lose!" His advice shows how instrumentality creeps into these texts, as it does into the advice of their early modern predecessors. Smalley relates a personal anecdote in which he responds to his wife's request for more help at home by asking his boss for a less demanding job, gets the demotion, spends more time with the family, and finally gets an even better job a few months later. His wife shows no resentment for this promotion because she is "now so secure with me." Smalley concludes, "I gave in and gave up at first, but I won in the long run. That's almost exactly how Christ explains the principle of exchange in Mark 8:34–37."[50] As James Walker, warns, "to win at the battle for control is, finally, to lose."

The struggle for personal identity in marriage can easily become an undercover brawl. Frequently, after the luster of a new marriage and the excitement of the honeymoon has worn thin, one partner or the other silently asks, *Can I be the real me and still stay married to you?* If the answer to the question is *no*, the wife may choose to hide her "real" thoughts, desires, and personality. A Christian woman may actually believe that in doing so—in nearly erasing herself—she is living the biblical lifestyle of the submissive wife.[51]

This, he goes on to explain, is not the case. The wife can become or fulfill herself through dynamic, engaged submission. Note the shift in Walker's passage from "one partner or the other," who fears the consequences of marriage, to the wife who chooses to hide her real self. The doctrine of male headship may offer a ready answer to the question of who is in charge or which one the two shall become, but the specter of the erased, dead, or zero wife haunts that happy ending.

These books are committed to their readers' happiness; they also take seriously the wrenching pain of marital failure. James Dobson, for instance, comments that the "easy-out concept" of marriage "underestimates the power of sex and marriage to make us 'one flesh,' and fails to anticipate the ripping and tearing of that flesh at the moment of disintegration."[52] Again and again, these writers insist that recent changes in attitudes and practices cause or exacerbate the problems facing married couples; they advise their readers to return to a biblical blueprint or foundation whose internal contradictions they do not acknowledge. Yet most of these writers are also attentive to social changes they embrace as beneficial or accept as inevitable; their advice has changed over time as they appeal to an audience that increasingly includes readers who are divorced individuals or couples whose need for two full-time incomes has transformed their management of money, decision making, housework, and child care. Changing social conditions place pressure on the ideal of marital hierarchy—pushing it into abstraction—even as they compel the reiteration of its importance. Yet spiritual equality is a greater conceptual challenge to marital hierarchy than two incomes, and it was recognized as a problem long ago, in the immediately post-Reformation period. The perception that more is asked of women in the process of forging the one flesh of marriage, and that the process might, for them, involve some level of violence, is connected to the perception that wives have their own consciences. It precedes their having their own incomes and emerges from *within* Christian marriage discourses rather than from a clash between Christian ideals and a changing secular culture.

Spiritual Equality and Gender Difference

Just as Genesis presents the relationship between Eve and Adam in multiple, conflicting ways, so it depicts Eve's claim to spiritual equality in ambiguous terms. Spiritual equality qualified Eve to be the sort of helpmeet to Adam the other animals could not be.[53] Her capacity for independent choice and action was then crucial to her role in the fall. By casting Eve as the spouse who chooses to eat from the tree of forbidden knowledge, Genesis both assigns Eve a role as a leader rather than a follower and condemns her for playing that part. Yet while Eve's precedent was an ominous one, many wives since have interpreted their disobedience or difference of opinion as justified and godly.[54] Furthermore, Eve's special status and ruinous choice place the wife's conscience at the center of Christian marriage advice—as both a given and a potential problem.

How could spiritual equality and social inequality, submission and conscientious judgment, coexist? In 1609, Robert Pricke, otherwise unequivocal in his defense of male headship, states in no uncertain terms that, if the husband "doeth commaund anything contrarie unto the will of God, she is not to obey him." In 1620, Thomas Gataker enjoins that "though the husbands will shall be crooked, so it be not wicked, the wives will is not straight in Gods sight, if it be not pliable to his"; yet he also insists that the wife's submission cannot extend "to any thing against the will and word of God."[55] The wife must thus check her husband's will against God's as she understands it; her own relationship to God requires that she assess her husband's commands before obeying them. Such a practice threatens to render the wife's duty "precarious and liable to be subtracted upon every pretence of demerit," that is, conditional.[56] A wife for whom every act of obedience is a judgment call is not a cipher; she has not been erased. This insight that submission is an unending sequence of judgments persists in recent Christian marriage advice. In 1988, for instance, Gary Smalley explains to women that they need not be doormats: "God gave you a mind and feelings that He never intended your husband to trample underfoot." Yet he enjoins them to "a willingness to hear him [your husband] out and yield, *if you can do so without violating your own conscience.*"[57] Thus, from the start, Protestant discourse contained within it justifications of male dominance and limits placed on that dominance, justifications of female subordination and limits on that subordination, an idealization of loving union and an insistence on the warring interests and fallen attitudes that would fracture that union. The spiritual equality that prepared spouses to love one another also threatened the very union it made possible.

The idea that husband and wife are spiritual equals raises the possibility of warring consciences, or two heads to the marital body. The advice offered in the two periods explains this problem in related but distinct ways. The emphasis in the twentieth century falls on gender difference as the reason not to overemphasize equality. If two equal souls might create conflicts over authority and judgment, then gender difference is supposed to resolve those conflicts by proposing male headship as the inevitable solution. To avoid marital conflict, Laura Doyle advises her readers to "abandon the myth of equality."[58] For, as Elisabeth Elliot reminds her readers in a chapter entitled "Equality Is Not a Christian Ideal," "marriage is not a political arena. It is a union of two opposites. It is a confusion to speak of 'separate but equal,' or 'opposite but equal' in referring to this unique union of two people who have become, because they were made different in order that they might thus become, one flesh."[59] Many apologists for so-called Christian marriage seek to enhance perceived gender difference and gendered "specialization" of roles and tasks as a means of strengthening marriage.[60] For example, James Dobson insists that between husband and wife "there should be a clear delineation between maleness and femaleness, exemplified by clothing, customs, and function."[61] The assumption that marriage requires sharp gender contrast is remarkably widespread. Laura Doyle, whose references to "faith" and a "higher power" are considerably more ecumenical than the other writers I am discussing, asserts that "high gender contrast in a marriage is what makes things exciting in the bedroom. It means that instead of striving for agreement and sameness, you highlight and appreciate each other's unique characteristics and special traits."[62] Far from being obvious, gender difference must be amplified and displayed. Yet it must also be bridged because, while marital advice heralds gender difference as the biblical blueprint for marriage, it also advises readers on how to overcome it as what might almost be called a design flaw.

For instance, in the first of his many books of marital advice, Tim LaHaye—now fairly well known as one of the authors of the best-selling "left behind" series of Christian apocalyptic thrillers—explains that "God designed the opposite sexes to complement each other. He wanted a man and woman to be joined in marriage so that they might each give to the other what each one lacked. But these differences that can complement and blend two unique individuals into one can also be incompatibilities that divide and cause separation instead of oneness." Perhaps this is why LaHaye calls his book *How to Be Happy Though Married.* He goes on to reassure his readers that "differences between partners need not be fatal!"[63] Gary Smalley opines, "I would venture to say that most marital difficulties center around one fact—men and women are TOTALLY different. The differences (emotional, mental, and physical) are so extreme that without a *concentrated effort* to understand them, it is nearly impossible to have a happy marriage."[64] James Walker assures his readers that "maleness and femaleness were not created by God in order to drive couples apart; there are two halves to a marital whole. They can be fully understood and appreciated only when they are in the presence of each other." Yet, "our sexual contrasts come up in virtually every conversation. When we are not meshing, not attached to each other in a positive, building, strengthening way, our sexual differences will begin to grind, to wear us down and even, eventually, to destroy personality."[65] Such contradictions structure the thought in these books from the late twentieth century: sexual attraction thrives on difference; marriage creates completion by joining together opposites; and yet men and women are so utterly different as to be incompatible. Gender difference is a defining feature of marriage and its structural flaw. Most of these writers address this paradox by arguing that only Christians can overcome the sheer impossibility of marriage in order to reap its rewards. They have to write their books because heterosexual marriage, while fundamental and, they insist, natural and divinely ordained, also needs to be defended, promoted, and supported.

In the early modern period, marital discourses similarly have a quality of special pleading, as if they are asserting as inevitable something that people also need to be talked into or talked through. Much of the work I've cited on evangelical communities in the 1990s emphasizes a gap between a rhetoric, myth, or fantasy of male headship and the more complex daily negotiations of marriage. Turning now to a more sustained discussion of sixteenth- and seventeenth-century marriage advice, I want to emphasize that this gap was just as great in the early modern period. It is not that social change snapped a tether that once tied fictions and experience together; no such tether ever existed. Instead, the discourses themselves were always internally fissured, embattled, out of synch. Increasingly, scholars of the early modern period emphasize that conduct literature in that period, too, functions as a kind of cover story. Alison Wall avers that Elizabethan women recognized that the marital ideals articulated in prescriptive literature were drawn "from fantasy," constituting a "rhetoric of submission" that required "lip service" more than internalization. Zachary Lesser argues that William Whately's defense of marital hierarchy and male headship was already "a rear-guard action" in the seventeenth century. Tim Meldrum explains that "the script for patriarchal household mastery was a rhetorical resource" available to household heads in the late seventeenth and eighteenth centuries.[66] Susan Faludi's description of the Promise Keepers' reliance on "fantasies of past fantasies" captures a spiraling regress in which returning to those past fantasies never enables us to reach a patriarchy more actual than mythic.[67]

This is especially evident with regard to the problems posed by the yoking of spouses of different genders, problems that are not at all new. As early as Augustine, male writers have suspected that if God had wanted to make a companion for Adam, then surely he would have created a male friend for him, rather than the deeply problematic Eve.[68] If gender complementarity *is* the biblical blueprint for marriage, then its rationale is difference and not equality. Yet at the same time, writers in the sixteenth and seventeenth centuries recognize the deep appeal of equality, an equality they associate not with marriage, where it causes rather than resolves problems, but with friendship, especially between men. As several scholars have recently reminded us, early modern English culture idealized friendships between members of the same sex and the same status as the most equal, consensual, and precious relationships. In friendship, the self is lost in order to be enhanced. Neither submits himself to the other; rather, each is remade in the crucible of intimacy.[69] In contrast to idealizations of the union achieved through male friendship, Laurie Shannon argues, early modern discourses understand marriage as the joining of those who are unlike and unequal. All marriages, by this logic, are "mixed." "Though heterosexual coupling—it goes without saying—is a sine qua non of social reproduction and so draws support from a range of other cultural imperatives, its merger of disparate, incommensurate kinds, especially in marital or celebratory forms, poses something of an intellectual problem. However normative it may be as hierarchy, it contradicts the likeness topos at the center of positive ideas about union." Perhaps, Shannon suggests, marriage is so constantly discussed and enjoined in the early modern period because a special case needs to be made in favor of directing one's affect toward marriage, toward the opposite sex, and, in men's case, towards an inferior. Marriage's apologists had to argue, then, not just against a tradition of valuing virginity and celibacy over marriage but a "same-sex economy" that "explicitly eschews or downgrades cross-sex association."[70] The idealization of relationships between those who are alike suggests that cross-sex couples face a particular challenge in bridging the enormous gap of difference to recover their prelapsarian union. As a consequence, marriage discourses proliferated to make the case for marriage. Valerie Traub speculates that perhaps in the late sixteenth and seventeenth centuries, "heterosexual desire was constructed in order for marriage itself to remain socially desirable," that is, as an incentive.[71]

Many early modern writers praise marriage as an incomparable boon precisely because of the ways in which it overcomes difference and individuation, making one of two. George Whetsone claims that "the Maried, hath a Companion of his owne flesh, of his owne wyll, and of his owne Spyryt, so wrought to his owne Affection: that between them, there is seene two bodies, and but one thought, perceived: The Maried joy alike, sorrow alike: are of one substance, one concord, one wealth, one povertie, Companions at one Boorde and in one Bed."[72] Ann Fanshawe writes of her own marriage: "Glory be to God, we never had but one mind through out our lives, our souls were wrapped up in each other, our aims and designs one, our loves one, and our resentments one."[73] While this statement verges on a confession that husband and wife had only one brain between them, it also expresses Fanshawe's own sense that she and her husband stood together against the world. Daniel Rogers rhapsodizes that a wife "is one with [her husband] in all things, one in flesh, one in generation and posterity, one in blessings and welfare, copartner also in all crosses and wants: All these are in common: the husband shares with the wife, and suffers in all her diseases, paines, trials spirituall and bodily."[74] As Henry Smith advises, "let all things be common between them, which were private before." Nathaniel Hardy and Matthew Meade use the same imagery to describe this communion. Hardy asks of husband and wife, "what are they, but as two springs meeting and so joining their streams that they make but one current, so that the water of the one and the other cannot be severed. . . . Indeed so close and near is the communion, that as to use they have all things common, bodies, children, houses, conditions of prosperity and adversity." Meade reminds his readers: "Remember you trade in a joint Stock; as two Springs, joining their Streams together, make but one Current. Your Interests are the same; you are equally Sharers in Profit and Loss."[75]

It was thus possible to imagine a wife as an equal sharer with her own stake in the couple's "joint stock" and marital property as held in "common." As Natasha Korda has shown, wives were responsible for "keeping" household goods "as if" they were their own.[76] Yet, at least in printed marital counsel, a disparity between these sharers inevitably reasserts itself. While paeans to sharing, trade, and joint stock emphasize the common property of marriage, the prime possessor, we are often reminded, is the husband. In their hugely popular text, John Dod and Robert Cleaver, who have enjoined that husband and wife are to share "an uniforme agreement of mind, and a common participation of body and goods," also state that "the husband ought not to be satisfied with the use of his wives body, but in that hee hath also the possession of her will and affections."[77] Edmund Tilney suggests that this possession is best accomplished through theft.

In this long and troublesome journey of matrimonie, the wise man maye not be contented onely with his spouses virginitie, but by little and little must gently procure that he maye also steale away hir private will, and appetite, so that of two bodies there may be made one onelye hart, which she will soone doe, if love raigne in her . . . the man that is not lyked, and loved of his mate, holdeth his lyfe in continuall perill, his goodes in great jeopardie, his good name in suspect, and his whole house in utter perdition.[78]

A husband must steal his wife's will defensively, then, so that she will not steal his goods, reputation, or life. The wife, too, is enjoined to various forms of deception: one sermon reminds her that "a good Wife, by obeying her Husband, rules him."[79] In *Counsel to the Husband, to the Wife Instruction*, S. B. drives this message home: "Surely her subjection shall get her government, and her obedience rule; the more subject, the greater power shall shee obtaine; and the more humble in her obedience, the more libertie shall she win."[80] Here we see a sermon advise a wife to undertake the covert strategy of performative submission that some modern evangelical women ascribe to themselves. Such advice suggests that marriage can only accommodate one will; the presence of two wills—private rather than conjoined—means war. In many other contexts, too, an unsubmissive or "private" will was feared as, in Richard Allestree's words, "the grand incendiary which sets Kingdoms, Churches, Families, in combustion . . . a kind of anticreative power, which reduces things to that Chaos from whence God drew them."[81] In marital advice, love quells this fire. It does so not by joining two wills but by enabling one will to possess or steal or rule the other.

Again and again, marriage discourses written in the first centuries after the Reformation associate marital conflicts and compromises with the fall while struggling to find in marriage something more than a reminder of our fallen state. According to Calvin, for instance, "marriage cannot be so wholly spoiled by man's sin that the blessing with which God hallowed it by his word is entirely abolished and no longer exists.

Therefore in spite of the many troubles of married life, which arise from our degenerate nature, there remains a residuum of divine good; in a fire which is almost smothered, some sparks still glow."[82] Luther also describes a falling off but also "a kind of faint image and a remembrance" of paradise in marriage. For women, there also "remain remnants, like dregs" of their paradisal "dominion."[83] They find these remnants in their power over children, servants, and slaves, as we will explore in Chapter 3. Apologists for marriage must grant it some vestigial relationship to paradise if they are to compel men and women into this as the sanctioned, fundamental relationship "ordained by God."

Thus the promise that "they two shall become one flesh," derived from *Genesis*, repeated in Paul, and inscribed into the very language of the marriage ceremony, is a promise of reparation, a myth of lost union, equality, and harmony restored. This Christian notion of the couple as yearning toward and dimly approximating "paradise lost" resembles other traditions in which man and woman were once parts of one androgynous creature, since split. These include Plato, Midrash (a tradition of early rabbinical commentary written in the third to seventh centuries), gnosticism (early Christians who approached Genesis 1-3 as myth rather than history), and Kabbalah.[84] This conceptualization of the couple could suggest that man and woman are incomplete without one another and that the unmarried person is partial, unfinished, and unfulfilled. According to Calvin, Adam "lost, therefore, one of his ribs; but, instead of it, a far richer reward was granted him, since he obtained a faithful associate of life; for he now saw himself, who had before been imperfect, rendered complete in his wife."[85] Of a man alone, Henry Smith writes in the seventeenth century:

Thoughts, and cares, and fears will come to him because he hath none to comfort him, as thieves steal in when the house is empty; like a turtle which hath lost his mate; like one leg when the other is cut off; like one wing when the other is clipped; so had the man been, if the woman had not been joined to him; therefore for mutual society, God coupled two together, that the infinite troubles which lie upon us in the world might be eased with the comfort and help one of another, and that the poor in the world might have some comfort as well as the rich.[86]

Such a view can work to naturalize, even divinely sanction, heterosexuality.[87] Even as it expresses completion and attachment it also suggests that a person alone is partial, disabled.[88] Marriage is thus the finishing school of creation. As William Heale argues,

no sooner were these of one divided into two, and made distinct and personal: but streight waie againe they were of two contracted into one, and made the same and Individuall. Their creation was presently accompanied with institution of their marriage; wherein *Adam* received his owne againe with rich advantage.

Hee lost (as far as we read) but a bare bone: He received it againe branched into many bones, bewrapped up in tender flesh, . . . ful of lively spirits . . . lovely to be seene, lovely to be talk'd withal, *like in al things.*[89]

For Adam, in this account, the investment of his "bare bone" yields the "rich advantage" of his wife, loss with a return estimated from his perspective. Still, such passages view marriage as surplus rather than scarcity because each spouse becomes more by means of it.

Puritan writers frankly acknowledge sexual intercourse as the wellspring of marital plenitude, the primary means by which two become one, and yet each is more rather than less.[90] Through sexual congress, the ideal of "one flesh" might be constantly recrafted and a primal unity restored through the temporary transcendence of hierarchy. Thomas Gataker argues that husband and wife are closer than parent and child precisely because their bodies come together in marriage rather than separate through birth: "For children indeed are *part of their parents*, because *they come out of their bowels*: they are *part of their flesh*, but severed from them. But man & wife, they are *one flesh*, conjoyned not severed."[91] William Gouge writes that "the use of the body is a proper act of the matrimoniall bond, wherein the difference betwixt superioritie and subjection appeareth not: the wife hath as great a power over the husbands body as the husband over the wives." But, he hastens to add, this equal power does not pertain to their control over "the goods." For Gouge, sex resolves the dilemma of how fellowship and subjection can "stand together": "There may not only be a fellowship, but also an equality in some things betwixt those that in other things are one of them inferiour and subject: as betwixt man and wife in the power of one another bodies: for *the wife* (as well as the husband) is therein *both a servant, and a mistresse, a servant to yeeld her body, a mistresse to have the power of his.*"[92] As Angus McLaren puts it, "from the sixteenth to the eighteenth centuries the commonplace assumption was made that the bed was one place at least in which men and women were more or less equal."[93] Such more or less equality overcomes the discord that, after the fall, defines heterosexuality. What, then, of the partner whose desires do not conform to expectation? As Valerie Traub points out, this new emphasis on sexual compatibility makes "erotic desire for a domestic partner . . . *a requirement for* (not just a happy byproduct of) the bonds between husband and wife."[94]

However visionary or prescriptive these idealizations of conjugal sex might be, they also acknowledge that, even under the best of circumstances, the moments of ecstasy in which husband and wife achieve "equality in some things" and share equal power over one another's bodies are evanescent. Such passages celebrate the transforming power of love and the ecstatic, if temporary, loss of boundedness. But when sexual union is connected to other daily practices of sharing it becomes more clear that of the two spouses, the wife must always give up more to sustain the union and to shore up her husband's uncertain sense of his own status as household head. Just as the cover story of male headship is often treated as a compensatory fiction, the promise of erotic fulfillment is described as an ameliorative interlude, a "time out" from unequal relations.

According to early modern marriage advice, the union temporarily achieved in sexual congress had to be reknit laboriously through more visible and constant practices. First, the wife had to take her husband's name so as to signal to others the corporate identity formed through marriage. As Gervase Babington argues,

Hee called them both Adam, saith the Text, both the man and the Woman: by that one name noting unto us, that inseperable, holy, and misticall union, that is made by marriage of two persons to become but one fleshe: the lyke in some sorte remayneth still in use amongst us, in that the wyfe is called by her husbands name, her owne name ceassing, and being used no more, as if it should be sayde, now that you are married, though before you were two, yee are become one, and therefore fitte that one name should serve you bothe, to note so much both to your selves and others. The man is the worthyer person, and therefore by hys name shall you both bee called, and the womans name shall cease to bee as it was, since now shee is changed, and become one fleshe with him, whose name shee injoyeth.[95]

In his justification for sharing a name, Babington thus celebrates an "inseperable, holy, and misticall union," and emphasizes that it is also a hierarchy in which "the man is the worthyer person."

In addition to sharing a bed and a name, husband and wife must share a household. William Whately is particularly insistent about this widely accepted point. Whately argues that it is no wonder that the wealthy and powerful often have unhappy marriages, since "how ill then doe they provide for themselves, that must dwell asunder, fare asunder, lye asunder, and have two houses, two tables, two beds for one couple, that should bee but one body." If love can accomplish "a pleasing combination of two persons into one home, one purse, one heart, and one flesh," it does so not just through the mystery of marriage but through a daily practice understood as required and onerous.

Let one house and one bed hold them constantly; let them be as much in each others presence, as businesses of their callings will permit; let them often talke together, and be sorry together, and be merry together, and communicate their joyes and griefes each with other; and this will surely knit them, if any thing will. And let them never suffer any jarre to worke so dangerously upon their affections, as to make them so much as for one night, in froward or sullen angrinesse, to part beds for any occasion of dislike.[96]

Whately depicts a fragile union, imperiled by even a night apart. His contemporaries similarly dwell on the dangers of separation. John Brinsley warns that "the unnecessary absence of Husbands from their Wives oft times exposeth them to many dangerous temptations, which otherwise might either be prevented or frustrated." Matthew Meade advises, "they have one *Name*, and therefore should have but one *Nature*. They are one *Flesh*, and therefore should have but one *Soul*. They have one Bed, one Board, one House, one Purse, and therefore should have one *Heart*. What they say of [the twins] *Castor* and *Pollux*, is true of Man and Wife: If they are divided, it is ominous." Thomas Gataker explains, "they make but one body; and it is against nature for one body to bee in two places at once. For the man is the head, the woman is as the body: for head and body to be sundered, it is present death unto either."[97] Thus living apart or withholding any part of one's self from the marital union effects a decapitation, a fatal division. I want to stress both these early modern writers' vivid evocation of daily life—of the fabric of marriage woven in beds, tables, and purses shared—and their threat that separation would be fatal. Whereas the single person lacks a limb or a wing, separated spouses are not viable.

Violence and Individuation

Since fusion is depicted as the inadequate but sustaining reparation of the lost ideal, then the partner who individuates, who acts against the union, compounds the fall and recloses paradise. As Dod and Cleaver explain, "it is not said, marriage doth make one man, or one minde, or one body of two, but clearly one person." William Gouge insists that since marriage binds two into one, they cannot "make themselves *two* againe." Daniel Rogers explains that "to affect a singularity, a privacy in so close an union, and for the husband to be a man by himselfe apart, from her who is one and the same flesh with him, what a podigious [sic] selflove is it? union breedes love, and love, sympathy and compassion; but where selflove abides, union and love are absent."[98]

Marriage forges two into "one flesh" through two processes of surrender. First, both husband and wife surrender themselves to their union and to God. Their union is more important than the self-interest of either individual. Second, the husband becomes so identified with the union of marriage, as its head, that the wife must submit herself to him. The two achieve a harmony, but it is one, according to Dod and Cleaver, "as when in a Lute, or other musicall instrument, two strings concurring in one tune, the sound neverthelesse is imputed to the strongest and highest: so in a well ordered houshold, there must bee a communication and consent of counsell and will betweene the husband and the wife, yet such, as the counsell and commandement may rest in the husband."[99] Writers on marriage recognize that both partners venture or risk themselves. For instance, for William Whately it is the husband who is unnecessarily absent; for Daniel Rogers it is the husband who "affects a singularity" and is "a man by himself apart." Given the emphasis on male autonomy, it makes sense that men might have particular trouble surrendering their independence to marital union and responsibility. According to some of the studies of evangelical communities I discussed earlier, "Christian" marriage discourse still strives to reconcile men to the interdependencies, constraints, and obligations of marriage. In contrast, the early modern emphasis falls on convincing the wife of her inferiority. Husband and wife achieve a union in which counsel and commandment rest in the husband, a "common participation of body and goods" in which yet the husband should achieve "possession" of his wife's "will and affections." The wife takes the husband's name rather than he hers because he "is the worthyer person" and "shee is changed" as he is not.[100] These texts suggest that marriage depends not on the wife's inevitable subordination but on convincing her to submit herself willingly and apparently. If she does not, marital harmony cannot be sustained. The problem is not only her active resistance to her husband and her role, although these texts frequently imagine such a possibility. The subtler and more insidious problem is her individuation. Having her own will, her own ideas and interests, constitutes a withholding of herself from the union, a withholding that renders that union nonexistent. When one flesh devolves into two fractious persons, as it constantly threatens to, the prospect of two selves threatens the very concept of the couple and of marriage. To forestall the dreadful prospect of her private will the wife must weave, like Penelope her shroud, the fiction of her husband's headship. Whatever she feels secretly, she must perform her subordination and her husband's dominion for his benefit. She must underwrite the fantasy of plenitude by making her self scarce.

The intimacy praised as the solder of marital union is also feared as the occasion of one devolving back into two. After his praise of cohabitation, Whately somewhat illogically mentions that "it is societie that most times choketh the love of the married, they grow weary each of other." Because of the challenges of close quarters, Daniel Rogers writes, "marriage of it selfe . . . will try of what mettall you are made."[101] John Wing offers a particularly detailed description of what a bitter curse a bad wife is: because of "the nearnesse and propinquity of an evill Wife to a man, being *by* him, *of* him, and *one with* him, no evills are, or can be comparable to those that are so *close* to us, that cleave to us, the *farther off,* the *lesse felt,* but *nearnesse* and *vicinity* makes an evill *superlative.*" As Wing explains, a husband is most vulnerable to his wife precisely because of her intimacy with him: "Who but *Delilah*," he asks, "could have undone *Sampson*?" He elaborates: "to have our deadliest, and most desperate evill in the *house*, at boord, at *bedde*, and lying in his bosome, who can measure (somuch as in imagination) this mans misery[?]" Worse still, in a culture in which divorce is not readily available, there is no end except death: "shee is a *crosse* in *coppi-hold*; during life there is no *end* of date or expiration of her evill."[102] The conflict between spouses, which Wing so vividly imagines and concentrates in the figure of the "evill Wife," is a consequence of both insubordination and betrayed intimacy. These depictions of marital breakdown achingly dwell on "nearness and propinquity," high expectations and lost love. With characteristic vividness, Milton claims that without a "fit union of their souls . . . such as may even incorporate them to love and amity," husband and wife, "instead of being one flesh, . . . will be rather two carcasses chained unnaturally together, or, as it may happen, a living soul bound to a dead corpse."[103] Milton forces his reader to imagine what happens when the ideal of one flesh decays into the inescapable yoking of carcasses. He writes his way toward the most disturbing image—the living soul bound to the dead corpse. For again, unnatural chaining is understood not as the fault of marriage itself but rather of one spouse who is "evil" and "dead" and who thereby not only infects the couple's corporate body but entraps and degrades the more wholesome spouse—whom Wing and Milton both imagine to be the husband.[104]

Regina M. Schwartz's brilliant analysis of monotheism provides a way to connect this notion of an economy of scarcity within marriage to a larger pattern that shapes relations of love and power in Judeo-Christian thought. Schwartz shows how, throughout the Old Testament, we find "a conception of identity as something that is won in a competition, at someone else's loss, an identity born in the rivalry and violence that unravel from scarcity," that is from a God who can accept the sacrifice of only one of two brothers, Cain or Abel, a father who can grant a blessing to only one of two sons, Jacob or Esau. "Scarcity, the assumption that someone can only prosper when someone else does not, proliferates murderous brothers and murderous peoples. And it seems that even God, the very source of blessings, does not have enough to go around." Under a notion of love that presupposes scarcity, "once you start loving, either you lose your identity or else the loved one does: someone loses."[105] In the terms of my argument, there is not enough personhood—interiority and agency, self-love and will—to go around. Scarcity in this case proliferates murderous spouses.

Although Schwartz is most interested in the formation of collective identities, her insights apply to the relationship of husband and wife—as she suggests but doesn't explore at length. She argues that "imagining identity as an act of distinguishing and separating from others, of

boundary making and line drawing, is the most frequent and fundamental act of violence we commit. . . . Violence is the very construction
of the Other."[106] I do not want to perpetuate such violence by naturalizing or defending a notion of a rigidly bounded, possessive self. I simply
want to point out that this idea of the self is incompatible with the idea
of marriage as fusion. When identity is understood as separation from
others, and marriage requires union, then there is a conflict between
one's identity as self and one's identity as partner. That conflict produces violence, whether figural or enacted. This violence takes the form
of one spouse annexing or eliminating the other, even if only metaphorically, or much less often, the two forming a corporate self that excludes
and forsakes all others. An extreme consequence of this way of thinking
is that one spouse imagines the other's death as the condition of her
psychic and spiritual survival or salvation. Wing's description of an evil
wife in "coppi-hold" creates an urgent hope for the wife's death. If "during life there is no end of date or expiration of her evill," then her death
becomes the only means by which her husband can escape, can *be*. Milton's description of the coupled carcasses invites the squeamish desire
to release the living soul from its bondage to the dead.

In the next chapter, I will explore how early modern writers link
the appeal of murder to the absence of any other means of escaping
marriage (such as divorce). As I show there, seventeenth- and twentieth-
century accounts of battered women who kill their abusive husbands
suggest that murder is an extreme means of individuating from one's
spouse. In accounts of life or death struggles between husband and wife,
the wife asserts her agency at her husband's expense and over his dead
body. In contrast, when early modern works of marital advice directly
address violent spousal conflict they hint that spouses must defend the
union of marriage even at the cost of their lives. Here it is usually the
wife's death that marks the horizon of acceptable sacrifice. The good
wife would die rather than set herself apart.[107]

In England until the nineteenth century, divorce was harder to obtain
than in any other Protestant country. As a consequence, the ways out of
marriage remained fairly consistent before and after the Reformation,
for Catholics and for Protestants. Marriages could be annulled but only
on limited grounds (such as bigamy or nonconsummation). Church
courts could grant separations, but these did not free women from the
restrictions imposed at common law by coverture and did not enable
the estranged spouses to remarry; furthermore, some husbands were
remiss in paying the mandated maintenance to their wives while others
exploited coverture to gain control of their estranged wives' earnings.
Women sued more often for separation than men did, and their grounds
were distinctly gendered: men accused their wives of adultery, while

women accused their husbands of cruelty. Women's suits alleging men's violence were considerably less successful, and they declined in the course of the seventeenth century, perhaps because cruelty was difficult to prove.[108] According to Martin Ingram, because wife beating was not exactly illegal, "the church courts had perforce to interpret cruelty in a strict sense; and plaintiffs normally claimed that they had suffered abuse sufficient to endanger their well-being or even their life."[109] In the 1690s, Parliament granted what were arguably the first true divorces, that is, allowing for remarriage, but this option was available only to peers on grounds of their wives' adultery.[110] Desertion was often an unofficial solution to irreconcilable differences, but it was hard on women, especially those with children, since it left them without financial support. As a consequence, men tended to desert their wives, more than wives did their husbands.[111] Yet mortality rates were so high that, as Lawrence Stone and others have argued, death often did the work then that divorce does now in cutting marriages short.[112] Even those spouses who refrained from giving mortality a little push must sometimes have greeted the death of a spouse with, shall we say, mixed emotions.

As in England, in colonial America "disease, disaster, and old age were more likely than the courts to release a woman [or a man] from an unsatisfactory union."[113] Yet divorce was far more widely available in America than in England, at least in those colonies that viewed marriage as a contract broken by the misbehavior of one of the spouses. In New York and Virginia, which closely followed English practice, divorce was available on roughly the same terms as in England. South Carolina did not grant divorces. But the colonies of New Haven (before it was absorbed into Connecticut), Connecticut, and Massachusetts Bay heard divorce petitions on the grounds of adultery, male impotence, and confirmed desertion as early as the 1630s, and granted full divorces that allowed for remarriage; in these colonies, the majority of petitioners were women. Connecticut maintained an especially liberal divorce policy and heard petitions based solely on cruelty. "Cruelty" was strictly defined as requiring repeated abuse over a long period and threatening permanent bodily harm or death.[114] As Cornelia Hughes Dayton has argued, cruelty, not a refusal or failure of husbandly obligation but an abuse of husbandly power, was a particularly risky basis for a divorce petition: "wives who petitioned for divorce on cruelty grounds were asking the state to inspect the way in which a man governed his family and to declare illegitimate certain actions over which the husband had traditionally in English law been given wide discretion." As a consequence, cruelty pleas became more restricted in the eighteenth century, when the bench stopped granting child custody and the majority of marital property to wives divorcing irresponsible or immoral husbands, and began to view a wife who left the family home to escape a husband's cruelty as deserting, "rebellious," and therefore guilty.[115] Thus, even Connecticut moved toward punishing women's independence and protecting men's authority, except when men abdicated their roles as household governors through desertion.

Perhaps because of the difficulty of escaping a marriage, violence everywhere inflects early modern descriptions of the struggle that is marriage. These texts portray marriage as a perilous adventure with high stakes: As Richard Allestree puts it, "marriage is so great an adventure, that once seems enough for the whole life."[116] Mary Beth Rose has shown that early modern writings on marriage consistently rely on "military metaphors of conquest and self-defense."[117] This language often explicitly addresses the household as a battlefield from which any retreat would be ignominious. According to Whately, spouses, like good soldiers, must stand their ground: "This is my place . . . , here God hath set me, here I will be, this ground I will make good, though I endure tempests, stormes, railings, blowes, wounds, and death it selfe."[118] These texts enjoin husbands to patience just as much as their wives. William Gouge reassures his readers that a bad wife can be "a schoole of vertue" to her husband: "As a skilfull pilots sufficiency is tried and knowne by tempestuous seas, so a mans wisdome by a troublesome wife."[119] Socrates' wife Xanthippe is the most often cited example of a wife who served as her husband's trial, in this case teaching the master-teacher the lesson of patience. One writer even suggests, tongue in cheek, that "'Tis Heroical to suffer, and Heroical Actions always breed an inward pleasure and satisfaction. And therefore he that dyes Matrimonies Martyr, has no reason to blame his wife that is the occasion of such a noble Inscription upon his Monument."[120]

But if the advice that spouses must despair of escape and stand their ground applies to both husband and wife, it becomes especially troublesome with regard to abused wives. Gouge advises that "howsoever their husbands may deale roughly and untowardly with them, yet God will graciously respect them, if they shall patiently in obedience to his ordinance beare their husbands unjust reproofs."[121] Whately argues that a woman may ask her friends or the magistrate to help her "bend her husband to more mildnesse" but she may not talk back, strike back, or run away, all of which "can never agree with subjection which God requireth at her hands."

If it bee said, that some men are so violent, as the wife may be in danger to have her braines knocked out, and may she not refuse to dwell with such an one? The answer is: shee may decline the present brunt, but she may not forsake the matrimoniall society: she may flie to the Magistrate, and seeke safetie, with a purpose of returning upon such securitie: but she may not flie quite away from him, with a purpose of not returning: for as it is no warrant for a souldier to quit his standing, because the case falls out so, that hee must either die or leave it, so neither must a Christian in any place depart from his place for feare of death: for how can one spend his life better, than in keeping the place where God hath set him, or die with more comfort, than when he knowes that in loosing his life, he shall find it, because he chuseth rather to loose it in doing his dutie, than to save it by omission thereof.

Here Whately explicitly claims that a wife is better off dying in the place where God has set her—that is, in her marriage, beside her husband— than leaving in order to save her life. He thus makes literal the praise Cotton Mather will later offer the good wife: "She is a dove, that will sooner die than leave her mate."[122] Yet the midpassage shift in the pronouns from feminine to masculine records an unease about the extremity of this specifically feminine form of self-sacrifice. At the very moment when Whately compares the battered wife to the soldier, she disappears, wholly replaced by the Christian who must not depart from *his* place. As Whately builds toward his extreme endorsement of dying rather than leaving, he downplays the fact that the particular Christian about whom he is speaking is not a soldier but a wife whose life-threatening enemy is her own husband.

Writers do not justify such advice only in terms of how it benefits the husband or protects the institution of marriage. The assumption that a wife should stay even with an abusive husband can lead to the claim that a wife might actually benefit, spiritually, from having the worst imaginable husband. As Robert Wilkinson writes, "by how much it is more difficult, by so much it is more praise-worthy." A wife earns little credit in living with a gentle, caring husband.

But she that is yoak'd with a *Nabal*, a Churl, a Fool, as *Abigail* was, and bears that patiently, she may say, with *Deborah* [in the fifth chapter of *Judges*] *O my Soul, thou hast marched valiantly!* And there shall more true Honour grow to you by such Patience, than if, Soldier-like, ye did prevail by Fury and Violence; and the worse your Husbands be, the more shall your Virtue shine, which in Affliction shineth most, like Stars twinkling in the Night; and if it be grievous to find Matter of Patience, there where ye look'd for Comfort and Protection, yet it shall have, in the End, a Reward, and in the Interim a singular Admiration.[123]

Wilkinson's allusion to Deborah undercuts his advice, since the events Deborah celebrates in her song, "O my soul, thou hast trodden down strength," include Jael's decidedly impatient and "soldierlike" assassination of Sisera by nailing his head to the ground (Judg. 5:21). Despite his own unsettling example, Wilkinson insists that a miserable marriage earns the greatest long-term rewards, first, in the social world outside the marriage, where others singularly admire the stalwart wife, and then in eternity, when the wife enjoys her hard-earned rewards (and one assumes, the husband pays the penalty for his churlishness). Thus, marital suffering pushes the wife into a spiritual life beyond the tyrant's grasp; misery detaches her from her husband in a way that undermines marital union while sustaining the appearance of marital continuity. As Wilkinson's own allusions show, the Bible has its Deborahs and Jaels as well as Abigails.

It isn't simply male authors who try to talk wives into submission by praising suffering. Many women writers make similar claims. For instance, Mary Astell, in her *Some Reflections upon Marriage* (1700), praises "Affliction" as "the sincerest Friend, the frankest Monitor, the best Instructor, and indeed, the only useful School that Women are ever put to"; "the Husband's Vices may become an Occasion of the Wife's Vertues, and his Neglect do her a more real Good than his Kindness could." Astell suggests that women avoid marriage if at all possible. She assumes that once they have committed themselves, they cannot leave or improve their situations. After they are married, they can make the most of a bad situation not by resisting but, paradoxically, by submitting completely:

she who marries purely to do good, to educate Souls for Heaven, who can be so truly mortified as to lay aside her own Will and Desires, to pay such an intire Submission for Life, to one whom she cannot be sure will always deserve it, does certainly perform a more Heroick Action, than all the famous Masculine Heroes can boast of, she suffers a continual Martyrdom to bring Glory to God, and Benefit to Mankind; which Consideration, indeed, may carry her through all Difficulties, I know not what else can, and engage her to Love him who proves perhaps so much worse than a Brute, as to make this Condition yet more grievous than it needed to be.[124]

Here we see the language of adventure, conflict, and conquest that Rose identifies in conduct books and sermons reaching its apotheosis in a heroism achieved through marriage to a brute, a heroism that surpasses that of "famous Masculine Heroes."[125] Sara Mendelson and Patricia Crawford argue that many women in early modern England made this bargain, shifting their focus from "a degrading struggle for the breeches" to spiritual withdrawal, internal mental reservation, and even a sense of moral superiority.[126] In later periods, too, women draw on Christian valorizations of suffering to grant dignity and purpose to their marital unhappiness. Anna Clark argues that "neither religious tracts nor chapel discipline" offered women in eighteenth- and nineteenth-century England any material redress against abusive husbands, but that religious faith did give women in violent marriages "a sense of self-esteem as martyrs and fed fantasies of divine rescue."[127] Nancy Nason-Clark claims that modern Christian women's tendency to link suffering "to some ultimate good, such as personal growth or the ability to help others in a similar situation" informs how the abused women among them depict their especially severe marital suffering.[128] Religious discourses consistently help women to endure suffering yet in so doing, they also end up foreclosing alternatives to suffering, and valuing women for "standing their ground."

Imaginary Widows

Some women writers have found ways to use religious discourses to justify leaving their abusive husbands. These writers tell stories that suggest that it is possible to detach oneself from the one flesh of marriage without physical force, by shifting the struggle to the level of the spirit rather than the flesh, and by operating within, rather than defying, the conventions of Christian marriage. Yet, at the level of fantasy, violence continues to haunt these texts. A surprising number of autobiographical accounts of heroic wifely endurance position the husband's death, whether corporeal or spiritual, desired or experienced, as an enabling event. I will examine three cases here: Lady Eleanor Davies Douglas, Anne Wentworth, and Abigail Bailey.

In an autobiographical text she published in 1646, Lady Eleanor Davies Douglas depicts her accurate predictions of her two husbands' deaths (one in 1626 and one in 1644) as crucial moments in her own development as a prophet. In her narrative, *The Lady Eleanor Her Appeal*, she grants considerably more importance to her predictions, and the provocations to which they responded, than to the actual deaths, which seem important only as confirmations of her own foresight—and of her vengeful power. When her first husband, John Davies, threw her manuscript into the fire, she prophesied that in three years he should "expect the mortal blow" and immediately donned her "mourning garment" in anticipation of her impending bereavement.[129] Her husband did indeed die in December 1626, less than a year after her prediction and three days after Eleanor spontaneously began weeping at the dinner table. Because other people had learned about her prediction, they were shocked by her husband's death. She reports that Charles I had interrupted a consultation between his wife, Henrietta Maria, and Eleanor about the queen's chances of becoming pregnant by remarking that he had "heard how I foretold my former Husband of his Death some three days before it" and scolding her because such a prediction "was the next way to break [her husband's] heart" and thereby hasten his death (188). Other sources suggest that the king became increasingly uneasy about her after that. At least according to her own account, Eleanor's prophesying continued to cause her conflicts over authority closer to home.[130] Her second husband, Sir Archibald Douglas, was "so much vext" at her predictions—"wimzees, as he termed it" (especially about members of

the royal family to whom he claimed to be related as James I's illegitimate son)—that he "ventured (at my motion) to lay the Breeches"
(188), that is, to lay down the law that he was the one who wore those
breeches. Eleanor introduces him into her narrative as already doomed:
"another Husband, who escaped not scot-free: likewise burning my
Book, another Manuscript" (187). In the presence of others, who
deemed her actions "want [ing in] affection," Eleanor "declare[d] sentence" on her husband: "Not so happy to be as to dye, nay worse than
death should befal him." Eleanor signed this statement before witnesses
in March 1631. Three months later, Douglas had a stroke or breakdown.[131] Just as Eleanor describes the king as scolding her for predict-
ing her first husband's death, she reports that her second husband's
uncle accused her of turning him "into his long Coats indeed" (190)—
that is, turning the man who threatened to seize the breeches into an
"unbreeched" infant. The couple then lived apart until Douglas died in
1644. By Eleanor's account, authoritative men attribute to her the power
of life and death, even if they condemn her use of such power. Eleanor
responds to her own grievances not by directly threatening her husbands, or even by confessing to care whether they live or die; rather, her
predictions seem to express a desire to escape and avenge their opposition, and she uses their deaths as proof that her predictions come true.

One cannot help but notice how many nobles and royals crowd Lady
Eleanor's autobiography. Yet Eleanor defines her identity not in terms of
who her father or husband is but in terms of what she has to say. This
strategy is equally useful to women farther down the social hierarchy.
Anne Wentworth is also a prophet and she, too, claims that her writings
foment marital conflict. She does not predict her husband's death and,
inconveniently, he does not actually drop dead. But she claims that, for
all intents and purposes, he's dead already. In 1677, Wentworth published a *Vindication* of herself for having "unduly published things to the
prejudice and scandal of my Husband" and having "wickedly left him"
after eighteen years of "Severe and Cruel persecutions . . . and unspeak-
able Tyrannies of an *Hard-hearted Yoak-Fellow*."[132] Wentworth describes
her husband as "him that has wounded and oppressed me for 18 years"
by means of "his fierce looks, bitter words, sharp tongue, and cruel
usage" (13, 5). According to Wentworth, God's love enables her to find
meaning in her sufferings; these sufferings have helped to empty her into
a more suitable vessel for the Lord's work: "my *oppressions* and *deliverance*
had a *Publick Ministry* and *meaning* wrapt up in them" (12). Attempting to
justify her decision to leave her husband, Wentworth first articulates an
argument that she will ultimately repudiate. She *could* argue that self-
preservation was sufficient grounds for her leaving him: "Forasmuch as
the Natural constitution of my mind and Body, being both considered,

He has in his barbarous actions towards me, a many times over-done such things, as not only in the *Spirit* of them will be one day judged a murdering of, but had long since *really* proved so, if God had not wonderfully supported, and preserved me" (4). But she refuses to make this argument, since she has learned from God "not to be afraid of him, who can only kill the *Body*, but can do no more" (4). She argues instead that "I was forced to fly to preserve a life more precious than this natural one; and that it was necessary to the peace of my Soul, to absent my self from my earthly Husband ... to undertake and finish a work, which my earthly husband in a most cruel manner hindered me from performing, seizing, and running away with my Writings" (4-5). Properly considered, she explains, "I have not left my Husband, but he me" (5).[133] She would be willing to receive her earthly husband back as a "new-man, a changed man, a man sensible of the wrong he has done me," "provided I may have my *just* and *necessary* liberty to attend a more then ordinary call and command of God to publish the things which concern the *peace of my own Soul*, and *of the whole Nation*" (6). Wentworth's writing matters because it expresses not her own will but God's; indeed, she has written against her own will. Thus, in a strategy frequently used by prophets in seventeenth-century England, Wentworth asserts herself largely as God's instrument.

Katharine Gillespie argues that Wentworth's belief in her soul's distinctness and worth endows her with a sense of a "sovereign" and "essential" self that enables her "to construct a subjectivity and a voice that is separate from her husband's but which does not entail her murdering him."[134] Achieving separation without recourse to murder only seems remarkable when considered from inside the logic by which, as we have seen, only one spouse can achieve subjectivity and voice and must usually do so at the expense of the other. As Gillespie, Hinds, and others show, dissenting women in seventeenth-century England, such as Wentworth, were already putting pressure on no-exit, economy-of-scarcity models of marriage (and of political obligation). Given that these alternatives emerged so early, why did this confining model persist nonetheless? Under its purview, a sovereign self can only be created through the conceptual violence of repudiating the other self, the husband. Even if Wentworth manages to individuate herself without access to divorce or recourse to murder, a conceptual economy of scarcity reenters her text at the metaphorical level. The logic is still the same: to be separate as a married woman with one's own conscience is to be a widow. The husband's imagined death is an opportunity.

For my purposes, what is most remarkable about Wentworth's account of her marriage is how, for her, violence constitutes both intimacy and separation. She presents her marriage as a life or death, salvation or damnation struggle in which there can be only one winner. Yet she also claims that she is the victor or survivor of this contest, despite the fact that her husband is not dead, and Wentworth does not have the responsibility of killing him. He is dead to her and dead to God; she must be preserved for a cause larger than herself. Leaving her husband is so scandalous that Wentworth defends herself in print. Yet her self-defense is metaphorically murderous, suggesting that she recruits a fiction of her husband's death as less shocking than her own willful defection.

Understanding her husband's metaphorical death as the precondition of her own union with Christ and consequent salvation does not mark Wentworth as eccentric. Richard Rambuss situates her in a tradition in which "an allegorized application of a biblical stricture of monogamy" requires a violent repudiation of earlier attachments because "the soule hath but one husband." As Rambuss points out, Francis Rous, in his *The Mysticall Marriage* (1631), insists that "the Christian's previous spouse (by which Rous means one's past unregenerate way of life) 'must be slaine, and by death, put off,' if, 'Christ Jesus, the new and true husband of the soule shall be put on in regeneration.'" Similarly, Rambuss argues, "the poet An Collins declares that Christ will betroth himself only to those whom 'their former mate, / Doe quite exterminate.'"[135]

Wentworth also adopts violent metaphors that conflate her bodily and spiritual experience. For example, in *A True Account of Anne Wentworths Being Cruelly, Unjustly, and Unchristianly Dealt With by Some of Those People Called Anabaptists* (London, 1676), she describes her husband's supporters as "men sheathing their swords in my bowels" and complains of their "violent misusing and abusing of me" as well as the threat they pose of a "rape of my Soul."[136] Wentworth's vividly corporeal description of spiritual trial and trauma blurs the difference between her old and new husbands. As Rambuss argues, "unsettlingly imitative of her past spouse's battery of 'fierce looks, bitter words, sharp tongue and cruel usage' (*Vindication*, 5), not to mention the threat of physical violence he embodies, Christ himself ultimately proves to be no less the domestic tyrant when his new bride would willfully follow her own mind. . . . Domestic violence evidently has its place even in the marriage to God."[137] Wentworth explains that God has been for years "*breaking* me all to peices in my self, and making me to become as *nothing* before him; and . . . has by many and great Tribulations been *bowing* my own will, and fitting me for his service" (*Vindication*, 3). Thus, Wentworth imagines that her husband's metaphorical death is necessary for her to be able to commit herself to a new spiritual union; yet she construes this new marriage as equally violent, its violence again a matter of bowing her will, breaking to pieces, becoming nothing.

The construction of God as a violent husband plays an equally complicated role in other women's accounts of their difficult marriages and wrenching separations. My third case occurs about a century later, in New Hampshire rather than in London. The three cases differ in the details of the marital conflict described and in the response and beliefs of each couple's Protestant community. Yet this wife, too, launches herself into a separation from her husband in part by imagining that he is dead. Abigail Bailey's *Memoirs* of her life in late eighteenth-century New Hampshire narrate the process by which she separates from and ultimately divorces Asa, her husband of twenty years and the father of her fourteen children, on the grounds that he committed adultery with servants and then with their sixteen-year-old daughter. Bailey's *Memoirs* were written some time after the events based on diaries she kept during the years in which she came to know of the incest and struggled to decide how to respond. First published in New England in 1815, the year of Abigail's death, the *Memoirs* present a quite sensational story of sexual and physical abuse, abduction, and confinement.

Abigail's reluctance to leave or prosecute her husband fuels the struggle at the center of her memoirs. While her four-year delay in leaving her husband or redressing his misconduct could be read as conformity to the advice we've been examining—that a wife stand her ground no matter what—the response of her contemporaries suggests both that such advice was coming into question and that the particular circumstances of the Bailey case altered the morality at stake. The first editor of the memoirs, Rev. Ethan Smith, comments that "her forbearance does indeed seem to have been carried to excess. . . . After all, it will be difficult to resist the conviction which will be excited in the course of these memoirs that Mrs. B. did truly err, in not having her husband brought to justice" upon discovery of the incest.[138] For the Reverend Smith, Abigail's obligations as a mother were at odds with her obligations as a wife. Abigail Bailey herself constantly defends her hesitation. "I thought the more I was chastened, the more I longed to live near to God, and could truly say, with Job, 'Though he slay me, yet will I trust him'" (109). What seems to provoke her contemporaries' doubt is not Bailey's willingness to trust her own slayer, but her willingness to expose her children to injury and exploitation.

Hendrick Hartog reads Bailey's story as an early version of one that becomes standard "in fiction as well as in autobiographies and memoirs and trial transcripts" in nineteenth-century America, a story that details "a wife's discovery of her capacity for disobedience and resistance, of a less coverture-encumbered self."[139] By a "less coverture-encumbered self," Hartog means a self understood as distinct from both her husband and her marriage, a bounded and discrete self—what Gillespie identifies in Wentworth's writings as a "sovereign self"—whose separation from and even opposition to her husband is justified rather than transgressive. For Hartog, it is faith that enables Bailey to claim this self. Yet, according to Bailey, her faith is also what keeps her with her husband even when others question her decision.

Bailey claims that she assumes a subordinate role in every relation, human and divine. She approaches marriage as the substitution of one master for another, husband for parents. "As, while I lived with my parents, I esteemed it my happiness to be in subjection to them; so now I thought it must be a still greater benefit to be under the aid of a judicious companion, who would rule well his own house" (56). She found her husband "very unreasonable": "it was the sovereign pleasure of the allwise God to try me with afflictions in that relation, from which I had hoped to receive the greatest of my earthly comforts" (57); "before one month, from my marriage day, had passed, I learned that I must expect hard and cruel treatment in my new habitation, and from my new friend" (57). Because she views her suffering as providential, deserved, and instructive, she can imagine no appropriate response other than endurance: "God had seen fit to make use of Mr. B. [her husband] as a rod for my awful chastisement. He had seen fit to suffer him to go on from one act of singular cruelty to another. And it was now impressed on my mind that God's anger was not yet turned away, but his hand was stretched out still. But I thought I could truly say, The Lord is righteous. I have sinned. I deserve all this, and infinitely more from God. Yea, I need it for my good" (120). Throughout her text, Bailey conflates God and Mr. B., chastizer and rod. "As to my own person, I thought little or nothing of any tortures, or miseries, that Mr. B. might inflict on my mortal part. If he should kill the body, he could do no more" (125). Wentworth similarly argues that she does not care about her bodily life and disdains her husband's power to inflict physical injury or death; but Wentworth does not have a child. Embracing submission and suffering, Bailey focuses confidently on herself: what she has done, deserves, and needs. The nagging question, of course, is what the daughter her husband molests deserves and needs. If Abigail is the object of a chastisement inflicted by God through her husband, then what role does her abused daughter play?

Given the value Bailey finds in her own suffering, she struggles to justify ending or at least ameliorating this deserved chastisement. Ann Taves, editor of a recent edition of Bailey's memoirs, emphasizes the process by which Abigail comes to see her own story in the terms of a captivity narrative. When she can say of her husband, "I felt myself in the hands of a cruel tyrannical enemy" (136), then she can resist and leave him. Bailey asks herself the following question: "But O, I thought to myself, who is this cruel oppressor? this grievous rod in the hands of the High and Lofty One, by whom I am thus sorely chastised?" She finds her answer in Psalm 55, which she alters by replacing the word "acquaintance" with the word "husband," as Taves points out. "It was not an enemy; then I could have borne it. . . . But it was the man mine equal, my guide, my friend, my husband!"[140] As Wentworth had written two centuries earlier, "all my afflictions, sorrow, suffering, heart-breaking grief was from my nearest Relation."[141] Both of these cries of anguish emphasize the pain of proximity. The husband can afflict precisely because he is simultaneously cruel tyrant and intimate.

For Hartog, Bailey's crucial sentence comes at the end of this same passage: "He has broken his covenant" (73). By viewing her husband as having obligations to her, their family, and God, obligations that he has not fulfilled, Bailey can justify ending her own obedience to him. He rather than she has broken the covenant. He did so by exceeding the bounds of his authority, bounds being renegotiated in the seventeenth and eighteenth centuries. By separating from her husband, Abigail Bailey made public "both his misconduct and her moral separation from his sinfulness." "Her claim offered no challenge to his ordinary legal authority over her; indeed, it rested on the same normative assumptions that underlay his conventional assertions of authority. He had changed, had abused his legal rights; thus, she had to claim her right to separate, else she would be complicit in his abuse. She would separate not in order to end her marriage, but so she could remain a good wife."[142] Like Wentworth, then, Bailey leaves the traditional understanding of the good wife unchallenged, even as she leaves her husband. Whereas Wentworth claims that she leaves her husband to preserve her writings rather than her own life, Bailey belatedly turns to her responsibilities as a mother to motivate her opposition to her husband.

While I find persuasive Hartog's argument that Bailey construes separation as the ultimate expression of marital union, I also find it significant that she prepares herself for this separation by a slow recasting of her husband as enemy. Hartog's and Taves's readings are compatible because each emphasizes that, for Bailey, conceptual separation was more challenging than physical separation (despite the fact that her husband went so far as to kidnap her) and each isolates a strategy Bailey uses to justify her separation from her husband. Even if her first editor suggests that what requires explanation is how long Abigail stays with Asa, Abigail herself, even in retrospect, feels she must defend her departure. She faces various obstacles: her sense that God is the agent behind her chastisement and thus that anything she suffers is deserved; her sense that her husband is not her enemy; and her assumption that she is so joined to her husband that their interests must coincide. Ultimately, she overcomes these impediments to divorce by recasting her husband as her captor and enemy, and by shifting the onus onto him as the covenant breaker whose transgressions release her from her obligations to him, from her "coverture encumbered" self.

For my purposes what is most important is her willingness to imagine him as dead so as to imagine herself as separate. In one confrontation Mr. B. tells her that he so trusts in her goodness that he doesn't suspect she'll do him an injury. "I answered that he had no reason truly to think that I should ever injure him by laying any violent hands on him. But if no other way should appear for me to be delivered out of his cruel hands, and God should see fit to cut him off by death, my goodness, (of which he spake,) if I had any, would lead me to view such an event as a merciful interposition of Providence in my behalf. And I added, that I should cheerfully acquiesce in whatever God should see fit to inflict upon him for his most uncommon sins" (135). Here Bailey imagines God's wrath turned toward her husband, not herself, and embraces the fantasy that she might survive him. As she sweetly points out, his death could only be viewed as deserved. Furthermore, just as she has "cheerfully acquiesce[d]" in God's affliction of her, she will as cheerfully accept her husband's death. Here again, a woman's text imagines and welcomes the possibility of her husband's death as part of a narrative of her own survival. Yet the husband's death takes place only at the level of fantasy.

Abigail and Asa Bailey's marriage is an extreme case of violent conflict and total breakdown; Abigail Bailey's account of her marriage and justification of her divorce is, by its very nature, an unusual document. Yet what motivated Abigail Bailey to write was the challenge of reconciling her roles as a person of conscience and as a wife, a challenge that even wives in somewhat less straitened circumstances also faced. Furthermore, the strategies she chose to use, especially her fantasy of her husband's death as the solution to her own dilemma, are on a continuum with other more mundane ways of imagining and figuring marriage.

One work of marital advice printed in the late seventeenth century seems to suggest that the prayerful desire not to be married, and its violent implications, were widespread. *The Honourable State of Matrimony Made Comfortable, or an Antidote against Discord* admonishes female readers: "And when thou dost wish that thou hadst never been related to him as thy Husband, thou dost in truth desire God to break thy Relation to him by his death: but know that God seldom gratifies the desires of such humoursom persons, and commonly those that long for the death of another, do die first themselves."[143] This author exposes the murderous longing and vengeful entreaty behind a woman's wish that she had never met or married her husband. He also warns readers of a punitive God, who will punish them for such desires. But Lady Eleanor, Anne Wentworth, and Abigail Bailey survive (and publish) their humorsome desires; Lady Eleanor survives not just one husband, but two.

Reading these three women's texts, one wonders whether more readily available, socially acceptable divorce might lessen the imaginative appeal of death as the way to "depart" from one's husband. Yet the fantasy of the dead husband persists even in what has been called a "divorce culture."[144] In a 1975 issue of *Aglow*, the magazine of Women's Aglow Fellowship International, a charismatic Christian organization, R. Marie Griffith finds the story of a woman who "wishes her husband could be someone different" and "became obsessed with the thought that my healthy, happy, needed-to-be-changed-in-my-sight husband was going to die." He was not ill. Just as Lady Eleanor wore mourning for her husband following her prophecy of his death, this woman began to grieve for her husband and even to plan his funeral service. She would later describe "this time as one of great illness in which she 'subconsciously' wished for her husband to die." According to Griffith, this apparently remarkable story fits into the magazine's conventions; most contributors' stories follow an arc from resistance to their marital roles and resentment of their husbands toward final submission to their husbands' leadership. As Griffith is careful to point out, submission has complex meanings in Aglow literature, meanings that shift over time. Still, at the level of narrative, the storytellers in *Aglow* magazine achieve happy endings through their own surrender. Thus surrender becomes the narrative trajectory of the stories. These stories in turn produce a by-product that is not all that surprising when we connect them back to Lady Eleanor Davies Douglas, Anne Wentworth, and Abigail Bailey. Many narrators imagine one possible release—the death of one spouse or the other—before embracing another (submission).[145] Either plot—the fantasy of death or the happy ending of submission—requires the annihilation, suppression, or erasure of one spouse. Thus, in *Aglow* magazine we find the continuation of a Christian tradition in which the assumption that one spouse, usually the wife, must sacrifice herself to achieve perfect union breeds fantasies of miraculous release through death, fantasies the good wife must repudiate in favor of submission.

In 1997 at a Promise Keepers conference, preacher and author Gary Smalley recounted that, two years into a troubled marriage, he became so shocked by his self-centeredness and the problems it was causing that he staged a mock death of his demanding self in order to clear the way for a new man and a new marriage. In other words, he claimed to have done what Eleanor Davies Douglas, Anne Wentworth, and Abigail Bailey longed for their husbands to do, except that he recovered. He celebrated his death and resurrection every year and at the Promise Keepers meeting he passed a bucket or symbolic casket into which other men could inter cards on which they'd written forms of self-centeredness they were willing to relinquish.[146] Smalley did not mention the attitude of his grieving widow to his death—or to the fact that it wasn't permanent. Smalley is reborn as a better husband when he imagines himself as dead, so that his wife won't have to.

Many short stories about women's experience of marriage suggest that the husband dwarfs or stifles his wife, however unintentionally, and his death consequently liberates her. The heroine in Kate Chopin's well-known and often-taught "The Story of an Hour" (1894) describes marriage as a "powerful will bending hers in that blind persistence with which men and women believe they have a right to impose a private will upon a fellow-creature."[147] Although the heroine's husband was often kind and tender, she rejoices in the news of his death because of the space it creates into which she can expand as a person. She so eagerly anticipates this opportunity that when she learns that he is not dead, she dies herself, in an interesting twist on the "die or kill" pattern we will see in the next chapter. Once she's admitted to herself how much her husband stifles her, marriage isn't big enough for the both of them. In Mary Heaton Vorse's "The Quiet Woman" (1907), Eunice Gaunt, a widow, confides that she

could never tell when he [her late husband] would swoop down on her and extinguish her. What he did to give her this impression she could not for the life of her have told; but with him she felt she had to fight for her life or cease to be; the irritating part of it was that he was largely and serenely unaware of the effect he produced, and it was a humiliating thing to be fighting for life with a force which doesn't even realize that there is a fight.[148]

Interestingly, in both of these stories, a husband's death, actual or alleged—but not at his wife's hand!—provides the occasion for her to consider what marriage has cost her, and what she might regain as a widow. Both stories take care to specify that these were not brutal husbands. Their annihilations and impositions are simply enactments of what their culture tells them it means to be a husband. The subtle forms of violence described in these stories are a consequence not of what's wrong with men but of what's wrong with marriage. In this context, the love that is assumed or expected to grow up between husband and wife is not an alternative or solution to the problem of the engulfing husband. It is, instead, another aspect of this problem. The fear of one's own annihilation and the fantasy of the other's death are complements built into a particular way of imagining, figuring, and narrating marriage that the "Anglo-Protestant" strand of American culture shares with its early modern past.

Chapter Two

Battered Women, Petty Traitors, and the Legacy of Coverture

In the film *A Perfect Murder* (dir. Andrew Davis, 1998), a woman who is beautiful, brilliant, and heiress to 100 million dollars kills her sinister husband (who has hired someone to kill her so he can get her money) in the midst of a struggle (in which she has struck the first blow). While the main character, played by Gwyneth Paltrow, is far more active than the character Grace Kelly played in the original *Dial M for Murder* (dir. Alfred Hitchcock, 1954), her proactive approach to the problem of the murderous husband is to kill him. After she does so, a sympathetic policeman reassures her: "what else could you do?" What interests me here is: why do stories about spousal conflict so often come to this?

Not all films depicting violent spousal conflict end in the death of one party or the other. But many do. A classic of the genre is *Sleeping with the Enemy* (dir. Joseph Ruben, 1991), in which the wife, at last, must murder the husband who has been stalking her ever since she left him. Her act is presented both as premeditated—she calls the police to report the murder before she shoots him—and as self-defense. I'd like to move quickly through just a few other films. In *Break Up* (dir. Paul Marcus, 1998) and *Double Jeopardy* (dir. Bruce Beresford, 1999), wives are unjustly suspected of murdering their husbands. Ultimately, both wives do kill their husbands in self-defense; neither is either tried or punished for the murder (one has already served her time). In *The Rainmaker* (dir. Francis Ford Coppola, 1998), a young lawyer who has befriended a battered wife ends up beating up her abusive husband in self-defense. She then stops him when he is at the point of killing her unconscious husband, saying "get out, you were never here," and finishes off the husband herself. Almost parenthetically, the lawyer later remarks that the district attorney decided not to pursue the case, and the film ends with the lawyer and the widow embarking on a new life together. In *Enough* (dir. Michael Apted, 2002), the resourceful wife stands up to her abusive husband from the start, leaves him, taking their daughter, and changes her identity several times. When a lawyer advises her that she will never be able to stop her husband's harassment through legal channels, she hires a trainer, bulks up, entraps her husband, and beats him to death. When she momentarily hesitates to finish him off, he turns the tables and she must finally kill him in self-defense. A policeman advises her that she is "one of the lucky ones," and the film closes with happy images of her with her daughter and new boyfriend.

I would like to make several observations about this small sample. Most obviously, the wives are the killers in all of these films. If you relied only on newspapers, TV movies of the week, true-crime fiction, novels, and films, you would think that women commit murder constantly. Yet women who kill their husbands or partners are relatively rare, despite the fact that they dominate the popular imagination.[1] By various accounts, roughly half the women who are murdered in the United States or the United Kingdom are killed by their husbands or boyfriends. In contrast, as few as 4 percent of male homicide victims are killed by a current or former wife or girlfriend. Several studies show that, in murders between spouses, two-thirds of the victims were wives and one-third of the victims were husbands. According to R. Emerson Dobash and Russell Dobash, "no matter who dies, the antecedent is often a history of repeated male violence, not of repeated female violence."[2] In other words, male violence is at the center of most cases of spousal murder, no matter who does the killing. While these films might suggest a sudden rash of murderous spouses, spousal murders in the United States actually declined 52 percent from 1976 to 1996. Furthermore, if these films were your only evidence, you would think that murderous wives were largely, even exclusively, white and affluent. Statistically, the majority of victims and perpetrators of spousal murder in the United States are poor African Americans; one survey found that it was only among African Americans that "wives were about as likely as husbands to be charged with murder of their spouse."[3]

Thus, the popular story of the prosperous white (or in one case Latina) murderous wife does something more or other than document what really happens. The story of a man who beats his wife to death, and is charged with manslaughter because the record of a history of beatings suggests that he did not intend to kill her this time, does not have much to recommend it to our attention, while the story of the wife who responds to a history of abuse by calculatedly killing her husband can at least make it to the Lifetime channel.[4]

At first glance, this kind of inversion seems unremarkable. Stories of killer women, perennial favorites, are both shocking in their inversion of one set of gender expectations—women are weak, nurturing, nonviolent—and reassuring in their confirmation of another set of equally venerable gender conventions—women are evil, sneaky, and dangerous. Interestingly, the films I mentioned above do not depict women as monstrous. All of these films have happy endings, ensuring the suffering heroines a promising future in several ways. (1) They evade the charge of male bashing by including exceptionally sympathetic male characters, often in the role of a detective investigating the husband's murder, who help the women; the films usually gesture toward a future romance between the woman and this rescuer, just to reassure us that she has not been discouraged from heterosexual coupling by having to kill her husband. (2) They erase the ways in which race, ethnicity, or class might foreclose options, presenting husbandly tyranny as an excess of privilege rather than a response to social desperation, and the heroic wife's horizons as unlimited once she escapes him. (3) Although anger or passion are traditional and still viable mitigating factors in murder, these films, except for *Enough*, muffle the women's rage. (4) They present the wife's murder of her husband as inevitable. Because the husband forces her into murdering him, he is ultimately the one responsible, and therefore the wife obviously should not have to pay for an act of which her husband is presented as the instigator. This is a phenomenon that criminologists call "victim precipitation." Thus, while these female characters are presented as threateningly active, responsibility is also shifted off of them, and onto various men, stalkers and saviors.

One might conclude that we tell stories of spousal conflict that end in death because, in fact, this reflects how these relationships all too often play out in real life. Reassuring us that these husbands will not blight their wives' future lives, these endings might be read as a response to research suggesting that women are more likely to be killed after they leave.[5] We can only imagine a happy future for these female characters if we know that the husband cannot reappear later. But while domestic violence does often end in death, it does not invariably do so. Spousal conflicts have many shapes, textures, and outcomes. Although the resources and options available to conflicting spouses have changed, the stories have, for the most part, remained the same, suggesting that spouses in conflict have only one way out of their struggles: dominate or submit, kill or die. Sometimes this occurs at the metaphorical level; sometimes it is depicted as literal. Too rarely do these stories imagine that *both* spouses survive a violent marriage—despite the fact that women and men do leave unhappy unions and form new lives, and that some always managed to do so, one way or another. Certainly murder is a particularly dramatic and decisive way to resolve a plot. However, as stories about women who leave are becoming more widely told, they are proving to be just as dramatic and compelling as those about women who kill or die.[6] As a consequence, the narrative trajectory ending in death seems to serve deeper needs than closure.

This chapter argues that many legal and popular depictions of violent spousal conflict are indebted to a legal construction of marriage that American culture has inherited from early modern England and colonial America. This notion assumes that, by entering into marriage, two become one, and the husband subsumes or "covers" the wife (through the legal process known as "coverture"). Obviously, the lived experience of marriage was always more complicated than this. While we cannot really know what happened in early modern households, or what is happening next door, we can assume that couples often negotiate their relationships in ways for which legal and moral prescriptions cannot account. Furthermore, there were always other ways of construing the relationship between spouses; and the legal force of this notion of the "unity of person" between husband and wife has been gradually, if unevenly, dismantled in both the UK and the U.S. Still, as I will show, the assumption that marriage only has room for one full person persists, even as the original legal structure recedes into the past and domestic arrangements diversify. I will begin by looking at recent debates about battered women who kill their abusers, and then use the present to motivate an inquiry into the past, in particular the relationship between married women's legal status and depictions of women who killed their husbands in the early modern period.

The Battered Woman

At the level of plot, the films I cited above point to the conundrum that is at the heart of legal debates about battered women who kill their abusers: the extent of their agency in committing a violent crime in response to a history of violence, and their accountability for that action. A woman who has been hit becomes a "battered woman" through repetition and through the ministrations of the helping professions; medical personnel and social workers do much of the cultural work that transforms a woman with an injury and a complaint into a victim of a syndrome.[7] Although debate surrounds the value and connotation attached to this label, little controversy attends whether there are "battered women," that is, women who sustain repeated, long-term psychological and physical assault. The question that attracts the most attention is how women's interiority and agency are shaped by this experience, an experience that is, after all, summed up as being the object of another's action: "battered." The agent who takes this defining action often disappears from the story,[8] as does a broader political context for domestic violence.[9] Erasing the story that follows from, rather than precedes and defines an identity as "battered," the term itself conveys hopelessness; the battered woman's past defines her identity and determines her future.

The "battered woman syndrome," which was named and defined by psychologist Lenore Walker in 1979, argues that some women who have endured long histories of abuse are so transformed through terror and suffering that they perceive and respond to the world very differently than would someone who does not share both their gender and their experience of abuse. One component of "battered woman syndrome," in Walker's view, is what she calls "learned helplessness," that is, an acquired sense that one cannot control what happens or intervene effectively in the course of events.[10] Julie Blackman has argued of three severely battered women that "their psyches were fully products of the violence they endured. It is as if there was nothing left—no part of them had been shielded from the ravages of the violence."[11] Examining battered women's statements, Robin West argues that "the redefinition of self as giving in an abusive marriage is the literal death of a woman's liberal subjectivity. She learns to consent for the satiation of the other's desires"; "for the gain of controlling fear, you give up your subjective life."[12] In the trial of Francine Hughes for the immolation of her husband, an expert witness, Dr. Arnold Berkman, who helped make the case that Hughes acted out of temporary insanity, argued that, when her husband made her burn the books she needed to attend college, he "was forcing her to kill that part of herself which was on the threshold of independence . . . to symbolically kill herself and all that she had invested and suffered in trying to be a person."[13] All of these statements present battered wives as psychically erased or murdered by their experience of prolonged domestic violence.

Yet these statements also acknowledge persistent if circumscribed agency: these women *learn* helplessness; consent, give up their subjective lives, symbolically kill themselves. Many feminists resist the notion of a self wholly lost or erased—who then is left to survive? They argue instead for a more tactical response to trauma. Therapist Judith Herman, for instance, argues that concepts such as "learned helplessness"

tend to portray the victim as simply defeated or apathetic, whereas in fact a much livelier and more complex inner struggle is usually taking place. In most cases the victim has not given up. But she has learned that every action will be watched, that most actions will be thwarted, and that she will pay dearly for failure. To the extent that the perpetrator has succeeded in enforcing his demand for total submission, she will perceive any exercise of her own initiative as insubordination. Before undertaking any action, she will scan the environment, expecting retaliation.[14]

From a perspective such as Herman's, insisting that a battered woman is empty or absent colludes in the project of abuse itself, which is often to deny a woman a separate existence, a will of her own.

Debates about why some battered women do not leave their abusers focus on the problem of recognizing and defining the woman's agency. When this question arises in court, it shifts the emphasis onto her conduct, rather than his, on staying rather than beating. Some see staying with an abuser as a sign of dysfunction that, while caused by abuse, becomes an impediment in itself. Others point out that requiring that the woman leave ignores the fact that leaving is likely to escalate rather than end domestic violence. According to Sally Engle Merry, the law offers the battered wife a difficult choice between agency and marriage, a liberal self and the position of wife: "She is offered, instead of subordination to patriarchal authority in a violent relationship, the promise of liberal legalism; a self protected by legal rights, able to make autonomous decisions, as long as she is willing to sever the relationship with the man, or at the least, risk making him very angry by filing charges against him or testifying against him."[15] Christine Littleton argues that some women choose to stay, rather than being unable to go.[16] Littleton's reminder that staying is as much an action and a choice as leaving could help to address a problem sometimes created by testimony on "battered woman syndrome." By provoking the question "why didn't she leave?" and then attempting to answer it, expert testimony sometimes evades the more central issue: why did the woman act as and when she did in killing her abuser? If her defense presents staying as a result of her defects and incapacities created through violence, then it disables its own ability to account for the action (rather than inaction) that occasions the criminal trial.

Critics of the legal relevance of "battered woman syndrome" question both the origins of the theory—Walker derived her idea of "learned helplessness" from research that was first conducted with dogs—and its consequences. While expert testimony about a "battered woman syndrome" has led to acquittal for some women, it may have reinforced attitudes toward women that, in the long run, will impair their chances for equal justice. By emphasizing women's weakness and incapacity, these defenses confirm the most conventional and damaging ideas about women, undermining their claims to adulthood and citizenship.[17] Such critiques of the consequences of emphasizing battered women's victimization come from feminists such as Elizabeth Schneider as well as those, such as Alan Dershowitz, who condemn all discussions of prior abuse as legally irrelevant "abuse excuses."[18]

Legal discussions of domestic violence and its redress remain focused on the woman. As one critic points out, "rather than examine standards of conduct that allow the aggressor to behave as he has, we must instead examine our client's actions to see whether she is a worthy victim."[19] A "worthy victim," one whose story will be most compelling to judge and jury, is one who invites sympathy and protection through her helplessness.[20] Women have gained protection from domestic violence, and have earned acquittals when they have defended themselves or retaliated against their abusers, largely to the extent that they have been acknowledged as victims. In both England and America, the depiction of women as the suffering victims of male brutality helped fuel attempts by organizations such as the Society for the Protection of Women, Societies for the Prevention of Cruelty to Children, and the Women's Christian Temperance Union to enact legislation that would impose harsher penalties for wife beating. These protections were not without their costs for both men and women. Men, especially working-class men, were more subject to surveillance and control, while women had to appeal to one kind of male authority (the courts) for protection against another (their husbands). They were most likely to get this "protection" if they emphasized their own weakness and dependency, rather than demanded freedom from domestic assault as a right.[21]

Many argue that this stress on women's victimization has gone too far. On one hand, the feminists discussed above emphasize women's strategic response to trauma; on the other, some researchers insist that men are often the victims of domestic violence. Work such as Suzanne Steinmetz's controversial essay "The Battered Husband Syndrome" confers on women a kind of equality: they "give as good as they get." Much of this research, as well as the enthusiasm with which it is embraced, depends on the kind of reversal that simply restores an earlier status quo rather than challenging the categories themselves: women aren't passive, they're threateningly active; they're not on the bottom, they're on the top. However, such studies have been widely criticized for paying too little attention to the outcomes of violence. Male violence often does more damage. The fights may not be one-sided, but the husbands usually "win" because they are bigger and/or stronger.[22]

Obviously, emphasizing the defendant's agency raises its own problems. Some feminist theorists point out that insisting on the murderous wife's agency, even celebrating it as a form of resistance to gender inequality and oppression, naively ignores that such agency will lead to conviction and possibly even execution. To view battered women who kill as resistant, in Catharine MacKinnon's view, is to argue that their violence is not determined by the violence that precedes it; it is also to argue that these women should be held individually accountable for their actions. To be constructed as an agent on the condition of death or imprisonment costs too much. As MacKinnon points out, when battered women kill, they are still acting within a defeating logic: "I think it parodies autonomy to say that someone pushed to the wall who lashes out and is imprisoned for life as a consequence acted autonomously, even in the single moment of lashing out. It ignores why she needed to act and what she paid for it, neither of which she chose."[23]

In contrast to those who praise or blame a "battered woman syndrome defense," still other feminist legal theorists emphasize that battered women need not and should not be viewed as "a separate class of defendants who require legal reforms to accommodate their circumstances."[24] Expert testimony about "battered woman syndrome" was originally imagined to help judges and juries understand why a battered woman, given her experience, might have acted reasonably in perceiving her husband as an enemy who required counterattack with extreme force. By this logic, testimony does not then excuse or justify her conduct, but rather helps to explain it as the action of a person constituted rather than erased through violence, who therefore reasonably uses violence. But this approach is threatening in itself. As Elizabeth Schneider points out, "it is simply impossible for many judges—not to mention lawyers, legal scholars, and the public at large—to imagine that women are acting reasonably when they kill their intimate partners."[25]

Schneider argues powerfully against the insistence that women must be either innocent victims or guilty agents. In the view of judges, lawyers, and juries, she writes, "a battered woman supposedly cannot be victimized if she has acted in any way that suggests agency or if she is a survivor; in contrast, if she is a victim, she cannot be considered reasonable." Still, as Schneider insists, "battered women who kill are simultaneously victims and agents; they are abused but they also act to protect themselves."[26] Yet the binary logic lingers, and is often invoked at women's expense. Many popular justifications of "women who kill" remove the woman from intention, motive, calculation, and accountability in the period leading up to and during her murder of her abuser, then argue that she becomes a full and autonomous self by means of murder. Thus, the batterer is responsible for the woman's act, but after she has committed it, and eliminated him, she emerges as an agent and reclaims the subjectivity that she is understood to have lost or buried in the course of the relationship. As Donald Downs summarizes: "Up to and including the fateful act, the defendant is defined as an extension of the oppressor; only after this act is he or she an independent self capable of self-determination."[27] The transitional moment—the act of aggression through which the torch of personhood is seized—poses a conceptual conundrum. If a "battered woman" has been beaten into doing anything to please, or at least not provoke, her abuser—if she has been forced to suppress her will and her desires—then how does she come up with the idea to kill? As Mark Kelman puts it: "her act—killing a perceived oppressor—could hardly be seen as the introjection of the oppressor's desires."[28] The logical sleights of hand in many of these discussions occur largely because of the need to treat women as agents while shielding them from criminal accountability. The claim that a battered woman emerges fully into a responsible and rational self *after* she kills (but not *as* she kills) implies that marriage entails an economy of scarcity with regard to interiority and agency. While the husband is alive, he monopolizes full personhood. When the wife kills him, she can usurp that personhood—stand in his shoes, wear the pants. In this zero-sum game, one of the spouses can be a person, but not both.

Studies of battered women suggest that they experience their options in terms of dying or killing. In her interviews with battered women, Angela Browne found that most of them "began to look toward death as the only solution to the escalation of violence and their inability to escape the abuser, and either considered taking their own lives or assumed that their partner would soon do it for them." These women assumed that, if one of the two partners died, they'd be the casualties.[29] Under such circumstances, murder is not an irrational act but rather a calculated response to a realistic assessment of the options and prospects. According to Kathleen Kreneck, of the Wisconsin Coalition Against Domestic Violence, "those who kill do so because they know if they don't they will die."[30] Such reports on the outlook from inside an abusive relationship suggest that murder is inevitable within the zero-sum structure of a violent marriage.[31]

The emergence into selfhood through violence is precisely what we see in countless early modern texts, in which the decision to kill is a wife's first self-owning act, in part because recognizing or asserting herself as separate from her husband is construed as conceptually violent in itself. These limited options—die or kill—and the economy of scarcity with regard to agency assumed to operate within marriage, are both the legacy of coverture, the common law construction of married women's legal status.

The Feme Covert

Under the common law, an unmarried woman (or "feme sole") had approximately the same legal rights and responsibilities as a man; she could own and sell property, bequeath her property by will, make contracts, sue and be sued. In consenting to marriage, a woman conferred many of these rights and responsibilities onto her husband, who exercised them for her, presumably in the best interests of both, and on the assumption that these interests would never conflict. Marriage thus transformed two independent legal agents into one agent—the husband—by means of the husband's "subsumption" of his wife into himself.[32] In this process, the wife became a "feme covert," meaning that she was figuratively "veiled, as it were, clouded and over-shadowed." As a consequence, she had the legal status of "either none or no more then halfe a person."[33] Her husband, in turn, became an enlarged person with broadened powers. Thus coverture refers both to the many restrictions imposed on married women under the common law and to the idea of the wife as being under her husband's cover—that is, both protected and obscured.

There are many formulations of coverture. Although it oversimplified common law and overstated its significance within the broader and evolving landscape of English law, Blackstone's eighteenth-century articulation became highly influential in both England and America:

By marriage, the husband and wife are one person in law: that is, the very being or legal existence of the woman is suspended during the marriage, or at least is incorporated and consolidated into that of the husband: under whose wing, protection, and *cover*, she performs every thing; and is therefore called in our law-french a *feme-covert;* is said to be *covert-baron,* or under protection and influence of her husband, her *baron,* or lord; and her condition during her marriage is called her *coverture.* Upon this principle, of an union of person in husband and wife, depend almost all the legal rights, duties, and disabilities, that either of them acquire by the marriage.[34]

In theory, a feme covert's conditional state was ended, and her legal existence reanimated, when her husband ("her stern, her *primus motor,* without whom she cannot doe much at home, and lesse abroad") died, abjured the realm or was banished, or deserted her. In his end was her beginning. A married woman also emerged into legal accountability through committing treason or murder. Whereas a married woman was not liable for most misdemeanors she might commit, she stood accountable when she committed a serious crime on her own. This is one legal reason why the murderous wife is so culturally visible. Her felony and her husband's death simultaneously un-cover her. Thus even at the theoretical level, the wife's legal agency is understood as suspended, covered, or delegated rather than as erased; when the cover is gone she can pop back into view.

It has sometimes been argued that coverture participated in a process by which marriage made the wife into her husband's property. After all, in the Book of Common Prayer marriage ceremony, the father *gives* the bride to her husband "in a silent but potent symbolic transfer of authority"; the wedding ring, which the bride wore but the groom did not, could also be viewed as "a tag, a mark of ownership" or "a symbol of purchase."[35] The husband's supposed ownership of his wife might also be seen as manifested in his sexual access to her, and his right to sue her lover for "criminal conversation."[36] Yet the fiction of unity of person argues that wife and husband become one person, not one owner and his property. Whatever coverture effected it was not quite the transformation of married women into chattel.

Furthermore, beneath the legal fiction of coverture, married women achieved considerably more control of property than was once thought. In their magisterial nineteenth-century history of English law, Pollock and Maitland acknowledge that "we cannot, even within the sphere of property, explain the marital relationship as being simply the subjection of the wife to her husband's will. He constantly needs her concurrence, and the law takes care that she shall have an opportunity of freely refusing her assent to his acts."[37] Wives managed their moveable goods, a significant form of wealth in the early modern and colonial period. In England there were coexisting and distinct legal systems, of which common law was just one. Married women could get around the restrictions of coverture with regard to property, at least to some extent, via equity law through the Courts of Chancery and Exchequer. As Margaret Hunt argues, because equity courts "were capable of recognizing that husbands and wives might have separate and antagonistic interests, they quickly became the venue of choice for settling many kinds of marital disputes."[38] Records of women's litigation, especially in equity courts, suggest that married women of widely different social and economic status assumed and asserted a right to maintenance and to some control of the property they brought into their marriages.[39] Although, according to Timothy Stretton, devices such as uses, trusts, and jointures "usually released women from the shackles of coverture only by transferring reliance on husbands to reliance on family members or trustees," they nevertheless enabled women to protect their interests and to curb their husbands' "wholesale rights of bounty and possession."[40] Given that coverture never was "the only law in town," it is especially telling that it had such enduring and far-reaching imaginary resonance.[41]

While the material constraints imposed on wives by coverture could be crushingly real, even if they could be cleverly evaded, the corporate legal personhood of husband and wife was always understood as a strategy "designed to overcome (in the husband's favour) the dilemma of who should have legal responsibility within the partnership of marriage" and as a legal fiction to which there were exceptions in both theory and practice. According to Hendrick Hartog, for instance, "lawyers and judges used marital unity as a legal fiction, that is, as a set of imaginary 'facts' created to achieve a legal result. It was a tool, not an explanation: existing only for particular purposes, to be discarded when no longer useful."[42] Furthermore, married women always acted: as helpmeets who had to engage in financial transactions in order to fulfill their duties as housewives and domestic managers; as "deputy husbands" who took their spouses' absences as opportunities to act in their stead;[43] as "fictive widows" when their husbands "for one reason or another, were unwilling or unable to govern them."[44] According to nineteenth-century American jurist Tapping Reeve, for instance, despite her "suspended" existence, we find the wife "often an active agent, executing powers, conveying land, suing with her husband, and liable to be sued with him, and liable to punishment for crimes."[45] At the level of legal theory, then, jurists struggled to come to terms with "the contradictory presence of the independent female human being in the unitary legal fiction of the matrimonial couple."[46] Literate women's diaries and letters reveal that many women did not experience themselves as erased or subsumed.[47] Finally, coverture protected women as much as it constrained them, helping to make "the structured inequality that was marriage morally acceptable" by requiring the husband to provide for and protect his wife—and concealing various forms of agency from view.[48] My focus here is not what women actually felt or were able to do, which exceeded the bounds of coverture, but rather the contradictions within the idea of unity of person and the extended reach of that idea, despite its contradictions and even after it had been superseded. Precisely because it always was a fiction, the story of marital unity could survive its contraversion in practice and, ultimately, its demise as law.

Outside England, coverture was not the usual arrangement. Coverture also took a while to take hold in the different circumstances and commitments of colonial courts, where it had to jockey for position with the legal systems that immigrants from other countries knew and assumed. Some historians argue that the common law became more influential later, as the colonies became more interested in forging connections to England and aping English fashions and tastes.[49] Gradually, however, coverture was dismantled, as jurists in both countries moved to curb powers that were abused, especially with regard to property. In England, the Married Women's Property Act of 1870 enabled a working woman to control her own earnings; by 1882, a married woman had achieved something like a single woman's (or a man's) control of property, but even then it was of separate rather than marital property. In the United States, most states had passed acts granting married women control over their own earnings and their separate property by the late nineteenth century. Here, too, wives were acknowledged as the owners only of wages they managed to segregate as separate property. Thus, the wife who could demonstrate her financial and even physical separateness from her husband and the marital assets was the wife who could lay claim to her own earnings.[50]

Paradoxically, as Hartog shows in his study of separation cases in nineteenth-century America, "courts were precisely the arena where a wife's separate identity was most easily and commonly recognized. Legal doctrine created coverture. Legal processes provided public recognition of the separate legal identities of wives." The process of contracting a separation redefined the wife:

the act of drawing up an individual contract would have given a wife a sense of herself as an individual with individual needs and wants and an individual history. Marital unity was torn apart, the identity of a wife replaced by the self of a contractually capable actor in the world. In place of the nearly unbounded relationship of husband and wife, in which a wife might experience herself as open to her husband, as unable to resist or control his power, a separation agreement posed a limited and mutually agreed-upon list of rights and duties. . . . A separation was thus, regardless of its ultimate enforceability, an enormously important performance.

The increasing availability of separation agreements, and then divorce, actually helped to define marriage and its rights and obligations more clearly, so that the ideal of "unity of person" was most fully articulated in the face of its dissolution; subsequently, in "the imagined world of casebooks" in the 1890s, coverture was redrawn as a back-formation, an exaggerated view of the powers men used to have. Even the changes in women's legal status were often understood within "a zero-sum universe where what husband had, wife did not, and vice versa," a universe, I would emphasize, operating under the logic of coverture. Thus when "wives were understood as having gained public rights that necessarily meant losses of rights for husbands."[51]

Coverture not only set the conceptual contours of married women's domestic role and legal status, but also their relation to public life, which was, by definition, understood as less important than their obligations to their families and households. Through a system of analogies between the household and commonwealth, which have been widely assessed and which were exported to the colonies, as the husband stood subject to his king, so the wife stood subject to her husband.[52] But did this mean that the wife was doubly subjected, or did her subjection to her husband somehow eclipse her relation to her sovereign? Writing in the mid-seventeenth century, Margaret Cavendish suggested the latter:

And as for the matter of Governments, we Women understand them not; yet if we did, we are excluded from intermeddling therewith, and almost from being subject thereto; we are not tied, nor bound to State or Crown; we are free, not Sworn to Allegiance, nor do we take the Oath of Supremacy; we are not made Citizens of the Commonwealth, we hold no Offices, nor bear we any Authority therein; we are accounted neither Useful in peace, nor Serviceable in War; and if we be not Citizens in the Commonwealth, I know no reason we should be Subjects to the Commonwealth: And the truth is, we are no Subjects, unless it be to our Husbands, and not always to them, for sometimes we usurp their Authority, or else by flattery we get their good wills to govern.[53]

Cavendish here tellingly claims that what authority women have they "usurp" from or flatter out of their husbands. Having pointed out women's enslavement, she proceeds to soften that insight by claiming that nature granted women beauty precisely so that they could "oftener inslave men, than men inslave us." Women's situation was more ambiguous than Cavendish admits here. For instance, uncertainty surrounded whether married women could offer sworn testimony or should swear oaths, such as an oath of allegiance to the government, separately from their husbands.[54] But Cavendish accurately articulates the way in which women were related to the state through their husbands. The priority placed on women's domestic responsibilities was sometimes understood as a freedom from obligation, sometimes as a denial of rights—or, as in the above passage, as both.

This situation prevailed in America. According to Linda Kerber, for instance, "from the era of the American Revolution until deep into the present, the substitution of married women's obligations to their husbands and families for their obligations to the state has been a central element in the way Americans have thought about the relation of all women, including unmarried women, to state power."[55] Married women's citizenship was often determined not by birth but by marriage. Beginning in 1844 in the UK and 1855 in the U.S., alien women who married citizens were naturalized. But this logic also applied in the reverse and was ultimately made explicit through new laws. Between 1870 and 1948 in the UK and between 1907 and 1934 in the U.S., women who married aliens lost their citizenship, no matter where they resided. In a parallel development, as freedmen and immigrants slowly claimed the entitlements of citizenship, they often did so as husbands and fathers, that is, at the expense of their wives' own claims to citizenship.[56]

Women did not, of course, accept this without protest. In the course of revolutionary changes in both countries, many women asserted that justifications of resistance must be extended to the home; that wives had as great a right to resist tyrannical husbands as male subjects had to resist tyrannical rulers. In 1776, Abigail Adams famously urged that husbands' privileges be curbed: "Remember all Men would be tyrants if they could."[57] Men, too, made these arguments. The "revolutionary" events from 1536 to 1776 could be seen as precedent-setting divorces of the Church of England from the Church of Rome, of Parliament from the king, of the colonies from England. John Milton and Thomas Paine, both estranged from their wives, argued that imprisonment in unhappy marriages restricted the very independence for which they were writing and fighting. Yet Milton and Paine both emphasized the importance of *men's* liberties, especially with regard to escaping unsatisfying marriages.[58] As Mary Astell pointed out in England in 1700, even the most radical men ultimately retreated from extending revolution to gender roles. "How much soever arbitrary power may be disliked on a throne, not Milton, . . . nor any of the advocates of resistance, would cry up liberty to poor *female slaves* or plead for the lawfulness of resisting a private tyranny."[59] Furthermore, marriage proved highly adaptable as a model for political relations precisely because of the contradictions inherent to it: it was a model of hierarchical yet affectionate relations, as well as of contractual, egalitarian ones. As a consequence, the idea of marriage might be mobilized to distinctly different political ends, while the practice remained the same. Even at the level of the ideal, coverture and "concord," submission to one's husband and submission to the goal of marital harmony might play out the same way.[60]

During the course of the seventeenth and eighteenth centuries, according to Carole Pateman, "the mere subject, bound by, and governed through, personal loyalty to monarchs and lords, and tied into a network of kinship, would be replaced by equal citizens who consented to be governed, and enjoyed rights, including the right to participate in government"; women, however, even those who actively participated in the political processes of rebellion, did not earn these new rights and obligations.[61] Rather than being wholly excluded, women were, instead, included on different terms. Yet women's relations to political life in England and America from 1600 to 1800 were more diverse and complicated than we once thought. Recently, scholars have shown that women had a potential for political stature and engagement—left open by omission in theory, if not often manifested in practice—that was defined out of existence as a public sphere they had helped to shape was closed against them.[62] At the same time that women's relation to the state was restricted by being more clearly defined, women also gained symbolic prominence in the visual and verbal iconographies of public life, and crafted roles (such as Republican Mother or Republican Wife) for themselves that were unthreatening enough to allow them access to civic participation.[63]

Changes in women's relation to the state and to public life would happen more slowly and subtly than through an immediate extension of revolutionary political principles to domestic life. In that process, many early feminists insisted that the position of the wife was analogous to that of the slave—a person excluded from political membership and self-ownership. One supporter of both abolition and women's suffrage put this particularly bluntly: for Emily Collins, the "stultifying effect of subjection, upon the mind" of women was "exactly paralleled by the Southern slaves." Elizabeth Cady Stanton asserted that "the rights of humanity are more grossly betrayed at the altar than at the auction block of the slaveholder."[64] This analogy obviously obscured crucial differences between white wives, who, to the extent that they were ever viewed as property, were inalienable, and slaves, who were freely bought and sold.[65] It was also available to apologists for slavery, who could defend that relation by its analogy to other relations of dominance and subordination in the household.[66] Yet this analogy enabled feminists to state their case in bold terms, and to argue that the available vocabularies for describing political status did not apply to married women. Feminist abolitionists could also displace their discussions of free women's circumscribed ownership of their own bodies in marriage onto the figure of the slave woman vulnerable to sexual assault.[67]

As Pateman puts it, "criticism of the rule of husbands as despotic, absolute monarchs over their wives, is one of the central themes in feminist political argument from the early modern period onward."[68] This insight that the "personal is political" was based on the same analogy between the household and the commonwealth that sometimes worked to limit women's civic role to the family. This analogy also made wives' obedience a cornerstone of all social and political order. While the law only gradually acknowledged that husbands could be tyrants, it had long asserted that wives could be traitors.

Running from Cover: Petty Traitors

A statute of 1352 (25 Edward III) acknowledged the special threat of the murderous wife by distinguishing her crime from other murders. This statute defined killing one's husband as petty treason, that is, as analogous to high treason—any threat to or assault on the monarch and his or her government. When servants killed masters or curates the ministers under whom they served, they might also be charged with this aggravated form of murder.[69] In each of these cases, the murderer is "one that is in subjection, and oweth faith, duetie, and obedience, to the partie murdred." Although there was some dispute, when a female servant killed her mistress her crime might also be considered petty treason. According to Blackstone, even a wife divorced "a mensa et thoro"—that is, legally separated—could be found guilty of petty treason because "the *vinculum matrimonii* subsists" between the spouses; similarly, a servant who has left a master and kills him "upon a grudge conceived against him during his service" can be guilty of petty treason because "the traiterous intention was hatched" under relations of both intimacy and subordination. The "violation of private allegiance" defines the crime.[70] Women convicted of petty treason were sentenced to the same punishment as those convicted of high treason: they were burned at the stake. The law thus conferred on this "domestic" act enormous political significance. As late as the eighteenth century, some notorious murderous wives were burned; not until 1790 in England did the female traitor's punishment become hanging rather than burning. Petty treason was not formally abolished as an offense distinct from murder until 1828.[71]

Although petty treason remained in colonial statutes, it was not much enforced with regard to wives. For Kerber, the reluctance to prosecute murderous wives for petty treason reveals a tacit recognition that "the fact of women's citizenship contained deep within it an implicit challenge to coverture." Catherine Bevan may have been the only white woman to be burned at the stake for petty treason in colonial America (in 1731). The punishment for petty treason was more often used on servants and slaves. Most notoriously, Paul Revere, on his famous ride to Lexington, passed the body of Mark, a slave convicted of petty treason and hanged in chains twenty years earlier (in 1755). Phillis, the female slave with whom Mark had allegedly conspired to poison their master, and who was burned at the time that he was hanged, was not on display. Reduced to ashes, she does not have even Mark's rather ignominious place in history. In America, petty treason laws were first intensified in their application to slaves (in the eighteenth century), and later repealed state by state (in the nineteenth century).[72]

In early modern England, many texts about petty treason circulated. I want to focus on those that link the wife's violence to a history of contention and abuse. Although these texts present this history as reflecting badly on the husband and setting the limits on his authority, they are reluctant to present it as in any way mitigating a murderous wife's guilt. During this period, as various scholars have shown, men's use of violence in the household was being questioned and monitored.[73] As long as a male head of household did not kill, maim, or seriously endanger his subordinates, or disturb his neighbors, he was not legally accountable for how he treated those in his care.[74] Because he stood responsible for his subordinates' conduct, he could use reasonable force, when necessary, to keep them in line.[75] What constituted reasonable force or "moderate" correction, was, of course, unclear. Furthermore, a wife was not quite the same as apprentices, servants, or children. She occupied a double position as both an authoritative mistress and a subordinate.[76] Although a wife's misbehavior might sometimes require that she be treated like a child, that is, beaten, in most cases "that small disparity which . . . is betwixt man and wife permitteth not so high a power in an husband, and so low a servitude in a wife, as for him to beat her."[77] From the pulpit and in print, ministers stepped into this gray area to negotiate the limits on a husband's power to discipline and control his wife through force. The discourse they produced prescribing domestic conduct was usually published in England, but it crossed the Atlantic to circulate in the colonies as well, in effect creating a transatlantic "republic of letters," "collective mentality," or shared culture of print if not necessarily of conduct.[78]

Early modern reformers of personal conduct did not argue that the husband had no right to beat his wife, or that doing so is unfair, immoral, or illegal. Instead, they argued that refraining from violence is more dignified, authoritative, and expedient than resorting to it. Thus, in contrast to arguments that wife beating in the nineteenth and twentieth centuries was "instrumental," a successful way to achieve domination and control, these reformers argue that wife beating does not work. In their view, domestic violence is counterproductive because it promotes rather than subdues resistance. In a hefty collection of his sermons on "domestical duty" that went through three printings, William Gouge, a popular London preacher, warns that since a wife has "no ground to be perswaded that her husband hath authority to beat her," his doing so will lead her to "rise against him, over-master him (as many do) and never do any duty aright." Robert Snawsel has one of the characters in his dialogue *A Looking Glass for Married Folkes*, a translation and expansion of a work by Erasmus, advise that "the wife would bee made more unruly and outragious by beating."[79]

The argument is also made, in these conduct books and elsewhere, that a husband should not beat his wife because "they two are one flesh" and "no man but a frantike, furious, desperat wretch will beat himselfe."[80] According to William Vaughan, "he that injureth his wife, doth as if hee should spit into the aire, and the same spittle returne backe upon his owne selfe."[81] Of course, people do injure themselves, fail to love themselves, spit in the wind. But this argument insists that the husband's conceptual subsumption of his wife grants him more authority and motivation to protect her, and renders him less liable to hurt her. For instance, in *A Bride-Bush. or, a Direction for Married Persons*, the controversial Oxfordshire preacher William Whately argues that loving and caressing a wife's body and injuring it cannot go together: "with what face can he come to kiss and embrace the same person whom he hath laid upon with his fist, or with a cudgell? How doth he cherish her as his own flesh, whom he thus opprobriously putteth to griefe and smart? . . . Is this to erre in her love, to smite her on the face, or to fetch bloud or blewnesse of her flesh?"[82] In his *Apologie for Women*, vicar William Heale uses the language of love poetry to suggest the absurdity of bruising one's wife: "Who could quarrel with her cheekes so purely mixt with Lilies and Roses? Who could violate those eies the spheares of light and loadstars of affection? Who could wrong those lips such rubies of value, and rivers of delight? Who could not imagine those ivorie armes fitter for imbracing then buffeting?"[83] Henry Smith, a popular preacher in London in the late sixteenth century, puts it more bluntly: "Her cheeks are made for thy lips, and not for thy fists."[84] Whately, Heale, and Smith do not acknowledge the complex eroticism of violence, nor the ways in which it might emerge from intimacy itself. As Gouge argues, a wife is more vulnerable to abuse than a servant because she sleeps in her husband's bed, she has no redress against him, and, perhaps most of all, because he can inflict greater emotional damage than a master could: "the neerer wives are, and the dearer they ought to be to their husbands, the more grievous must stroakes needs be when they are given by an husbands hand, then by a masters."[85]

The notion of husband and wife as "one flesh" could also offer a justification for physical chastisement as a form of self-care—"a sharpe medicine for so festered a sore."[86] As some writers point out, men do injure themselves in the course of some medical treatments. In a letter to his wife, Sir Francis Willoughby justified his treatment of her by saying "in usinge some severite I sought reformacion & not revenge; to punish was a punishment of my self."[87] Whately offers the most sustained and ambivalent endorsement of this approach.

But for blowes, for strokes with hand or fist, nothing should drive an husband to them, except the utmost extremities of unwifelike carriage, unlesse shee bee peremptory and wilfull in cursing, swearing, drunkennesse, &c; unlesse shee raile upon him with most violent and intollerable termes; unlesse shee out-face him with bold maintaining, that she will doe as she doth, in despight of him; unlesse she begin the quarell, and strike or offer to strike; an husband no doubt should hold his hands, and not forget himselfe to be an husband, till she have cast off all shewes of remembring her selfe to be a wife: but if such extreame putrefaction shall fall out in any mans case, I see no cause of forbidding to cut or seare ones owne most tenderly beloved flesh.

The exceptional circumstances under which violence is justified sidetrack Whately, who lists them in passionate detail. Yet throughout his lengthy discussion of wife beating, a more vexed topic for him than for some writers, he returns to his insistence that these brawling spouses share one flesh: "the husband must ever remember, to use no more roughnesse, than is fit to his owne flesh"; "To strike ones wife, is to make an incision into his own flesh." Whately confides that he has been reluctant to authorize "the lawfulnesse of an husbands using such a medicine." But he decided that, even if this remedy could be abused, it must be made available to those husbands in desperate straits who have tried everything else. Unable to leave the topic, Whately repeatedly succumbs to the temptation to list the offensive behavior by which wives provoke their husbands. Yet he does not want to endorse "the mad violence of those tyrannous husbands, with whom there is but a word and a blow, and which use their wives in more rude and rough manner, than a man ought to use his slave or bondman. Such outragious husbands are worthy to bee hissed out of the societies of mankind. Who is not ashamed to strike a woman?" Nothing can justify a husband leaping on his wife "as a Mastiffe on a Beare." Throughout, Whately addresses the ambivalence that defines his text through the image of the physician: "There is great difference betwixt the carriage of a tender-hearted (though resolute) Chirurgion, comming to cut off the arme of his patient (because the whole body must else perish), and of a valiant souldier in the field, fighting with his foes, and cutting off their leggs and armes."[88] The wife, as patient rather than foe, loses one limb but not all four.

Gouge counters the analogy to the physician by pointing out that most men cannot administer painful remedies to themselves, but must instead submit to a physician's help. As a consequence, Gouge advises that a particularly recalcitrant wife should be handed over to a magistrate to be beaten so that "shee may feare the Magistrate, and feele his hand, rather then her husbands."[89] William Perkins, a respected and popular teacher and preacher, as well as a prolific writer whose collected works saw numerous printings in the seventeenth century, similarly advises: "Nevertheless, if she grow to extremities, and be desperately perverse, so as there be no hope of amendment, then the Magistrate may be informed; who to prevent scandalls, and to provide for publike peace, both ought and may assigne unto her necessary correction, and punishment according to her desert."[90] For Gouge and Perkins, any violence against a wife should not be "domestic" unless the wife forces her husband to act in self-defense. This notion was, briefly, enacted into law in Massachusetts, where the "Body of Liberties of 1641" advised that "Everie marryed woeman shall be free from bodilie correction or stripes by her husband, unlesse it be in his owne defence upon her assalt. If there be any just cause of correction complaint shall be made to Authoritie assembled in some Court, from which onely she shall receive it."[91] The "Body of Liberties," like Gouge's and Perkins's proposals, attempts to displace the husband's discipline onto magistrates, so as to redefine the husband's role as a more loving and equitable one.

Yet recourse to the magistrate also exposed the husband to greater surveillance and regulation. Convincing men to police themselves was an important, if not necessarily successful, step in the attempt to change attitudes toward wife beating. As greater responsibility was placed on men as providers and protectors, some men—such as working men in the cities or recently freed slaves—became particularly vulnerable to the charge that they abused their authority, neglected to govern themselves, or failed in their responsibilities. Wife beating became a way to distinguish one person, class, race, or nation from another; it was persistently constructed as a practice of the past, of the lower classes, of immigrants, of other countries or peoples.[92] What has been called an attempted "reformation of manners" thus asserted that there was a conceptual limit on a husband's power over his wife, while also announcing that limit as variable and negotiable.[93]

A network of informal surveillance discouraged husbands from abusing their power.[94] Those who intervened most often—to complain to husbands, to protect women, to come into court—were other women. When women sued for separation on the grounds of cruelty, they were most likely to bring other women as their witnesses. Women were not only protected by other women's watchfulness, of course. Women also policed other women, censuring their adultery, nagging, and violence. When shaming and scrutiny weren't enough, neighbors might play important roles in getting a couple into court or in testifying. In England, church courts meted out fines or imposed separations between husbands and wives. In New England, justices did so as well; in addition, they sometimes sentenced those found guilty of spouse abuse to whippings, although they imposed this sentence more often on abusive wives than on husbands.[95] In short, while it is impossible to tell whether the rate of physical violence in the household actually changed, prescriptive literature and law were gradually redefining wife beating as a failure of control, a lapse in good household government, a derogation rather than an affirmation of manhood.

The printed accounts of petty treason that interest me here make most sense in the context of this debate about wife beating. Many of these texts narrate a history of domestic violence preceding the murder, and present this history as reflecting badly on the husband. In *The Adultresses Funerall Day*, Henry Goodcole, minister of Newgate, describes the violent marriage of a couple, "shee being young and tender, he old and peevish." The husband "used not onely to beat her with the next cudgell that came accidentally unto his hand, but often tying her to his bed-post to strip her and whippe her, &c." Goodcole concludes that "her injuries, and harsh and unmanly usage spurred on by the instigations of the divell, *almost compeld* her to what she did." He then proceeds to tell the story of Alice Clarke's relation to her husband, Fortune. When Fortune, justifiably angry at his wife's infidelity, "outragiously" falls from "words unto blowes with his wife, the smart whereof she feeling, incontinently begot in her dislike, and resolution of revenge on her Husband Clarke for the same, a fit humour for the devill to worke on." When Fortune finds his wife with her lover, "he freshly fell foule upon her, and so cruelly added blowe upon blow upon her body, that the markes thereof were very visible on her body at this present," that is at the time that she is apprehended and examined for killing her husband.[96] Goodcole suggests some connection between those bruises and the murder, but cannot articulate exactly how the law might account for it.[97]

The numerous printed accounts of Sarah Elston's murder of her husband suggest that she killed him in a fight. According to *A Warning for Bad Wives*, "he having beat her very severely, she with a pair of Sizzars gave him a wound on the left part of his breast"; according to the printed assize proceedings, the husband "was seen by some of the opposite Neighbours to strike her with a Fire shovel" and was "catching up a Frying-pan to beat her again" when she held up her sewing scissors "to keep him off."[98] While these two texts record what sounds like self-defense, they also report the testimony of witnesses who claim to have heard Sarah Elston threaten her husband's life. This is the emphasis in *Last Speech and Confession of Sarah Elestone*, which claims that Sarah's drunkenness and profligate spending drove her husband "to beat her out of this wicked course, and to that end [he] did sometimes chastise her with blows, which she was not wanting to repay." "Troubled and disturbed" by being forced to use violence, including "thrusting" his wife "downstairs" on the night she killed him, the husband was heard to "wish himself dead, or that he had been buried alive that day he was married to her, and she wicked and graceless soul would many times in cold blood threaten him, that at one time or other she would kill him; which proved to be too true."[99] J. M. Beattie describes Elston as using "on the face of it a plausible plea of self-defense"; in contrast, Garthine Walker argues that a "self-defense plea was inappropriate in the context of husband-murder" because "in law, wielding a knife or pair of scissors against a man who used mere bodily force or a blunt instrument indicated excessive retaliation," not legitimate self-defense.[100] Indeed, while the fullest pamphlet account depicts Sarah Elston as insisting that she lacked "any murderous intention or designe to kill him," it assigns her the motive not of protecting her own life but rather doing him "onely . . . some slight Mischief in *revenge* of his Cruelty in beating her" (emphasis mine). The author of *A Warning for Bad Wives* concedes that, because of the couple's history of discord and "frequent wrangling," "some now would *partly excuse* the woman, and alleadge the man as the principal Cause of their Differences by his ill husbandry, cross carriage, ill company, and other provocations, not here to be mentioned" (emphasis mine). Yet the pamphlet also depicts Sarah as asserting her own responsibility. She confesses that her "rage, unquietness, and evil communication . . . had often provoked her Husband to be more violent and cruel towards her than probably he might otherwise have been." At the stake, she confessed that "notwithstanding all his Abuses," she still felt that "she had done very ill in lifting up her hand against her Husband, and offering to revenge her self of him." Obviously, this case became a topic of some controversy and debate at the time and its meanings have been debated by historians since.[101] This controversy is interesting in itself since it demonstrates a struggle to come to terms with how a history of domestic violence might lead to an act of petty treason. Yet the relevance of this history is acknowledged and documented only to be denied. Those who wrote about Elston's case, like Henry Goodcole in his account of Alice Clarke, grant some significance to the couples' violent history and the women's bruises. Yet, having acknowledged the woman's victimization, *A Warning for Bad Wives*, like *An Adultresses Funerall Day*, comes down squarely on the side of the wife's accountability. Each wife's bruises "almost" or " partly" excuse what she does, but not quite.

A history of domestic violence might even exacerbate rather than mitigate a woman's guilt. In her study of Cheshire quarter sessions records in the late sixteenth and seventeenth centuries, Garthine Walker finds that a documented history of domestic violence "could undermine a woman's claim of self-defence against her husband's life-threatening violence" by indicating that he had "beaten but not killed her before," and therefore that she might be acting out of revenge not self-defense. Furthermore, according to Walker, the predominant assumption that husband murder was always a form of self-assertion worked to foreclose self-defense as a "feasible plea" for women accused of killing their husbands.[102] Yet some sources suggest that at least some aristocratic commentators were beginning to imagine that women might kill their husbands in self-defense. John Chamberlain wrote to Sir Dudley Carleton regarding Anne Wallen's murder of her husband that "if the case were no otherwise than I can learn it, she had *summum jus*; for her husband having brawled and beaten her, she took up a chisel, or some such other instrument, and flung at him, which cut him into the belly, whereof he died."[103] One source even suggests that Henrietta Maria attempted to intervene with her husband, Charles I, to pardon a battered woman turned murderous. This woman "poisoned her husband who was a most barbarous and cruwell man to her and," given his violence, "his own nearest of kindred . . . were suitors for her pardon," so that "the Queen laboured earnestlie for it, but howsoever the woeman was much pitied of all, yet the king thought it dangerous to spare hir, soe that he would not pardon her."[104] Both of these women were ultimately burned at Smithfield, one in 1616 and one in 1631.

Accounts of a notorious murder vividly articulate how seventeenth-century culture both recognized and could not assimilate the relevance of past abuse to husband murder. Mary Aubrey or Hobry was a French, Catholic midwife who emerged into prominence in late January 1688, when the head, torso, and limbs of her husband Denis were discovered one by one around London. Body parts usually provoke speculation and alarm. These body parts immediately became a focus for the anxieties surging through London at a time of particular upheaval, anxieties that often attached to those who, like Mary Hobry, were both foreign-born and Catholic. Pamphlets, broadsides, ballads, and even playing cards all depicted Hobry's crime and punishment.

Once the heap of body parts was identified as Denis Hobry, his wife Mary was apprehended at the house of one of her clients. At the time of the murder, Mary had been married to Denis for four years. She pled guilty at her arraignment for petty treason and murder at the Old Bailey, and was burned to death at Leicester Fields on March 2, 1688.[105]

Most accounts of the murder suggest that the marriage had been contentious and violent.[106] The couple "lived together in continual strife." They fought about Denis's extravagance, especially his seizure and waste of what Mary earned through her "industrious Care" as a midwife; his drunkenness and dissolute life, which Mary claimed had infected her with a sexually transmitted disease; and his insistence that she "submit to a compliance with him in Villanies contrary to Nature."[107] The couple alternated between separations, when Denis returned to France; brief reconciliations, during which he would promise to amend his ways; and open hostility. Whenever they lived together, Mary's life was in danger.

The fullest account of the events of January 27 appears in *A Hellish Murder Committed by a French Midwife, on the Body of Her Husband, Jan. 27, 1687/8*; other printed versions seem to have been based on this lengthy pamphlet prepared by Roger L'Estrange, which includes the detailed "confession" he secured in a private interrogation with the help of a translator. In L'Estrange's account of her examination, Mary claims that, at one point, she made Denis sign a declaration before a priest and witnesses that "he would be another Man."[108] Yet he did not become a new man, and the conditions under which Hobry lived are presented as promoting violence: "This Informant finding herself without Remedy, in a Distraction of Thoughts, and under the Affliction of Bodily Distempers, contracted by her said Husband's dissolute Course of Life, her Frailty was no longer able to resist the Temptations of dangerous Thoughts." As a consequence, "finding herself in this hopeless Condition, and under frequent Temptations of putting some violent end to her Misfortunes," she was tempted "to think of Extremities either upon her Husband or upon Her self." Although the text is presented in the third person, Mary Hobry's dialogue with her husband is quoted, as are her thoughts; most of her "I" statements respond to provocation and articulate resistance and violence: "This Examinate spake to her Husband to this effect: 'Hobry . . . if you Treat me as you did formerly, I do not know what Extremities you may Provoke me to."[109] Yet, as we have seen in other seventeenth-century accounts of petty treason, a history of abuse cannot be taken as justifying or even explaining a wife's murder of her husband. In *A Cabinet of Grief*, another pamphlet account of her crime and execution, Mary Hobry is twice made to say that her husband's abuse is no excuse: "but yet the sorrows and sufferings that I underwent I own to be no Argument that I should make my self guilty of his Blood"; "Though he to Wickedness was bent, / and show'd himself so cross and grim, / I own this was no Argument / that I, alas! should Murder him."[110]

In her examination as presented in *A Hellish Murder*, Mary Hobry recounts numerous moments when she had contemplated murdering her husband and openly threatened him. On the night of the murder, her husband "attempted the Forcing of this Examinate to the most Unnatural of Villanies, and acted such a Violence upon her Body in despite of all the Opposition that she could make, as forc'd from her a great deal of Blood, this Examinate crying out to her Landlady, who was (as she believes) out of distance of hearing her."[111] By presenting Denis's sexual demands on Mary as "unnatural," "villainous," and forced—and as a catalyst to her violence—*A Hellish Murder* emphasizes how he oversteps his authority and creates the conditions for his wife's transgression. Perhaps it was easier to depict a foreign husband with "unnatural" sexual appetites as so inflating himself that his subsumption of his wife—his unrestricted access to her earnings and her body—threatened her obliteration. As *A Hellish Murder* presents it, Mary Hobry's testimony aligns her sense of self with her rage and her decision to fight back against her husband's excessive and destructive demands. In the "winner-take-all" situation created by Denis, Mary can only articulate and assert a self against Denis and through violence. After Denis rapes her, beats her, and bites her "like a dog," Mary asks him "Am I to lead this life for ever?" to which he replies:

"Yes, and a worse, too, ere it be long, you had best look to your self," and upon these words he fell asleep.

Upon this Respite the Examinate lay in Torments both of Body and of Mind, thinking with her self, "What will become of me? What am I to do! Here am I Threatned to be Murder'd, and I have no way in the World to Deliver myself, but by Beginning with him"; and immediately upon these Thoughts, this Examinate started up and took one of his Garters.[112]

She strangles Denis with his garter and then lops off the extremities of the man who drove her to "extremities," subjecting him to treatment curiously resembling the dismemberment of traitors. In asking "what will become of me?" Mary Hobry imagines herself as not only separate from but in conflict with her husband. To preserve her own life, to achieve her own future, to deliver herself, she must "begin with," that is, murder, him.

Having recounted Hobry's story in grisly detail, L'Estrange yet retreats from claiming that it casts her conduct as reasonable or as self-defense. "In the Womans Story, I have done all the Right that Honestly I could to the Compassionable Condition of an Unhappy Wretch, but without Extenuating the *Horror* of the *Wickedness.*" He goes on to say that his subsequent inquiries confirm that Denis Hobry was "a *Libertine* and *Debauchee* to the *Highest Degree*, but *Drunk* or *Sober*, without any *Malice.*"[113] This claim that Denis Hobry lacked malice certainly runs counter to his wife's portrayal of him in her examination.

The details of Mary Hobry's story are gory, and the process by which her crime came to be widely represented and invested with political meaning was complex.[114] Still, I take Hobry's formulation—"I have no way in the World to Deliver my self, but by Beginning with him"—as a summary of sixteenth- and seventeenth-century English representations of murderous wives. A wife in one pamphlet decides that "she should never be in quiet until by some way or other she were shifted of him." The unnamed battered wife discussed by Goodcole in *The Adultresses Funerall Day*, "weary of so wretched a life, which she would have bin glad to be rid off, and loath in her modesty to acquaint any friend or neighbour with her desperate purpose . . . pondered with her selfe how she might end both their lives by poyson." Ambivalently, she too decides to "begin with him," in Mary Hobry's phrase.[115] Margaret Osgood, who lived with her husband, "as it were in continual brawling for seldom a day or night passed but they had a falling out," attempted "often to make away with her self, but had not the power; yet, though the Devil could not bring her to destruction one way he effected it by an other as prodigious as the former might have been if Acted," that is, by prompting her to kill her husband as he slept. After butchering her husband with a hatchet Margaret told the proprietor of an alehouse nearby that "she thought it was better to *Kill than be Killed.*"[116] As the wife in each of these texts articulates herself as having a life distinct from and in competition with her husband's, she asserts a self and simultaneously manifests this self as violent and criminal. The logic shaping these accounts resembles that shaping the depictions of the "battered woman's" sense of her alternatives and assertion of herself *against* her husband.

The options for Hobry and other battered women in early modern England are understood as so fatally limited—kill or die, me or him—in part because there were so few real ways out of marriage, as I discussed in Chapter 1. Many early modern people linked violence to the limited access to divorce. Conceding that no man in scripture "cudgelled his wife," William Whately attributes this omission to the fact that Mosaic law allowed for divorce: "No doubt that remedy made it needlesse to strike. No man would be pestered with a woman of shrewd disposition, that should enforce him to fighting, if with a dash of his pen, he might turne her packing."[117] The author of *The Passionate Morrice* warns that when couples marry for money, "Hee will practise her ende; she will wish his death . . . but howsoever they two speede, . . . she will speede

worse . . . until her hart breake; which happie day must ende her mis-
erie."[118] In *A Godly Forme of Houshold Government*, one of the most popular
early modern conduct books, John Dod and Robert Cleaver argue that
the horror of realizing one is permanently and intimately tied to someone hateful leads to "so great ruines, so wicked and vile deeds, as
maymes, and murthers, committed by such desperate persons, as are
loth to keepe, and yet cannot lawfully refuse, nor leave them." As a consequence, "the husband that is not beloved of his wife, holdeth his goods
in danger, his house in suspition, his credit in ballance, and also sometimes his life in perill: because it is easie to beleeve that shee desireth not
long life unto her husband, with whom she passeth a time so tedious and
irksome."[119] In *Matrimoniall Honour*, Daniel Rogers asks his readers to
contemplate the violent consequences of incompatible matches: "how
many have beene the cursed attempts of poisoning each other, to be rid
of the loathed party, husband or wife? What one Assizes passes without
such presidents?" In *Conjugall Counsell*, Thomas Hilder blames parents
who force their children to marry against their inclination as "acces-
saries" to the consequent "brawlings and contentions . . . poysonings, or
other bloudy plots to take away the naturall lives of either person."[120] All
of these statements suggest that spousal murder is more structural than it
is personal, more practical than passionate. Given the limited availability
of divorce, especially as initiated by women, murder emerges as a reliable, if often self-defeating, way to escape a bad marriage.[121]

For Mary Hobry, as a French Catholic woman in late seventeenth-
century London, the options were especially restricted. If Hobry's asess-
ment of her situation, as depicted in various texts about her crime,
corresponds only to the most negative interpretation of her real options, it does concisely express the logic that marriage can only accommodate one full person. While marriage was the subject of intense
scrutiny and redefinition in this period, depictions of marital strife,
whether criminal or comic, reveal the tenacity of the notion that husband and wife are not really partners or yoke fellows, but rather locked
in a deadly struggle for dominance—or existence—which only one of
them can win. Because marriage, so conceived, only allows enough
room for one person, one will, one full life, there is no way out of conflict but to submit or subjugate, die or kill. If only one can have a self
and the husband has an historically and legally privileged claim, then
the wife can only usurp a self from her husband. As we have seen, many
evaluations of battered women today claim that they experience their
options in just this fatally limited way, despite expanding resources and
changing possibilities. Linking this assessment to the history of a legal
fiction suggests that seeing one's choices in this way is not necessarily
the result of mental illness, traumatic experience, or moral failure. I am

not suggesting that all married women experience themselves as erased or think that they can only reassert themselves through violence. I am suggesting, instead, that when they do or when they are presented as doing so, as happens surprisingly often, the idea that husband and wife become one person subtends and limits that depiction of their options.

Coverture—both as the collection of restrictions imposed on married women and as the figurative notion that the wife is "covered" by her husband—is not the source or origin of the idea that the husband subsumes his wife or that marriage can accommodate only one person. That idea long precedes coverture—as the discussion of Genesis in the preceding chapter has shown. But coverture granted this notion prestige, focus, and authority, making it a particularly powerful construction of reality. This conception of the couple long survives coverture, as the earlier discussion of late twentieth-century U.S. films reveals. While coverture no longer defines married women's relation to property or to rights, many researchers argue that it persists precisely as violence. According to Isabel Marcus, "coverture cannot be said to have disappeared when its essential enforcement mechanism [i.e., violence] is available and widely used to maintain power and control in marriage."[122] According to Lenore Walker, Del Martin, Angela Browne, and R. Emerson Dobash and Russell Dobash, wife beating and murder in twentieth-century England and the United States not only defend male dominance but also express some husbands' inability or refusal to imagine their wives as separate and equal. According to Elizabeth Rapaport, men's murder of their wives is not taken seriously enough as capital murder because of the lingering assumption that men's rage at their wives' adultery, independence, or departure is justified.[123]

My own focus is not on whether coverture actually causes violence, but how it shapes our imagination of marriage in ways that make violence *seem* inevitable. At the level of representation, the conception that a marriage can contain only one legal agent enacts violence by concentrating resources and privileges in the husband and erasing the wife. In a subtler way, this conception casts the wife's self-assertion as itself a kind of violence—which, in turn, provokes retaliation. Many historical accounts of murderous wives either lament women's oppression or celebrate their feistiness in killing off their mates. Both lamentation and celebration are too limited and limiting. As Mary Hobry learned, on the pyre if not before, killing is a self-defeating form of self-assertion. Furthermore, celebrating murder as agency compounds the association of women's agency with violence, ignoring while reproducing a history in which married women's agency has often been understood as violently usurped from their husbands.

In debates about battered women who kill, as we've seen, the ghosts of the feme covert and the petty traitor still haunt attempts to understand the extent of a wife's agency and its relation to the violence she both endures and enacts. The fiction of spouses' "unity of person" also retains legal resonance in the practice of a wife surrendering her "maiden" name to take up her husband's last name upon marriage—"a practice that was exclusive to England and England's colonies for nearly 400 years, and a specific reflection of the marital property system"—and in legal privileges protecting confidential communications between husband and wife and protecting a defendant in a criminal trial from the incriminating testimony of his or her spouse on the assumption that the spouses are "a single marital unit rather than . . . individuals with their own interests."[124]

Yet its reach extends beyond the courtroom. As films about marital violence reveal, the zero-sum game of coverture survives as a narrative rather than a legal fiction, as a plot in which each spouse must either die or kill. Because unity of person was always a fiction, perhaps it is not surprising that it endures as one. While a film such as *Enough* can seem to tell a "new" story—since the murderous wife does not end up on the pyre or in prison—it is not new enough because, as I hope I have shown, it still imagines marriage as an economy of scarcity, and the confrontation of two individuals within it as, therefore, inherently violent. Just as feminist political philosophers such as Carole Pateman and Wendy Brown have asked how the "legacy of gender subordination . . . bears on the present," how it "lives" unrecognized in our institutions or terms, I am asking how coverture lives in and structures the very stories we tell about marital conflict and by which we impose shape on experience.[125]

In both the seventeenth century and the twentieth, legal discourse poses a dilemma—the battered woman's agency—that cannot be resolved within it largely because it was created by it. Since a court must determine "who done it," legal discourses dwell on actions; since judges, lawyers, and juries need evidence, they particularly privilege the body and its injuries as proof of a husband's actions and as a gauge of how those actions—battering—have limited a woman's capacity for agency. Less attention is paid to behaviors that do not leave bruises or scars. Considering spouses as individuals, whose ideosyncratic failings lead to or exacerbate violence, prevents us from evaluating the institution that binds them as a couple, defines their roles, and shapes their interactions. Furthermore, concentrating on spectacular and exceptional acts of violence—particularly murder—makes it hard to see the ways in which violence is not an aberration but rather a constitutive part of how marriage has traditionally been defined—and how it continues to be defined long after a supposed reformation of manners or civilizing process occurred. Many histories of women, marriage, and the family separate violence from "normal" marriage: for instance, Olwen Hufton's massive history *The Prospect Before Her* includes a chapter called "Of Difference, of Shame, and of Abuse," which is distinct from her chapter "On Being a Wife." Yet, as Shoshana Felman argues, "violence . . . inhabits marriage as a rule and not as an exception or an accident (although everyone denies it)."[126] This is not to say, of course, that all marriages include acts of physical, verbal, or psychological violence, however these might be defined. It is rather to say that the very process that is marriage, and the changes it requires and transacts, might be understood as violent.

Chapter Three

Fighting for the Breeches, Sharing the Rod: Spouses, Servants, and the Struggle for Equality

Noel Coward's *Private Lives: An Intimate Comedy in Three Acts,* first performed in London in 1930 and then New York in 1931, was immediately recognized as an unprecedented twist on the perennially popular story of the battle of the sexes. The play depicts a divorced couple who honeymoon with their new spouses in the same hotel, rekindle their attraction, and run off together. This is what Stanley Cavell calls a "comedy of remarriage."[1] It assumes that divorce is readily available and socially acceptable, yet it denies that divorce definitively ends marriage. The main characters, Elyot and Amanda, insist to their new spouses that the misery in their marriage was mutually created. When Amanda's second husband, Victor, asks in horrid fascination, Elyot "struck you once, didn't he?" she points out that he struck her "more than once" but that "I struck him too" and that when she broke four gramophone records over his head she found it "very satisfying."[2] In response to such revelations, Victor announces, "I feel rather scared of you at close quarters" (15). In contrast, Elyot is drawn to Amanda's zeal for combat. His second wife, Sibyl, is "a completely feminine little creature" who likes "everything in its place" (7); she assumes that Elyot must need "a little quiet womanliness after Amanda," since, like her, he must hate "these half masculine women who go banging about" (8). But the plot suggests that Elyot finds the "completely feminine" Sibyl less interesting than the "half masculine" Amanda, who can match him round for round.

Violence is not a symptom of marital dysfunction or breakdown in *Private Lives* but rather integral to the very fabric of this marriage; it is part of what Amanda and Elyot miss. They reminisce laughingly about a fight that was a "rouser" in which Elyot first hit Amanda (58). Act 2 ends with a fight in which he slaps her and she "fetch[es] him a welt across the face," and they are found by their new spouses rolling around on the floor (62-64). What makes the play so interesting is that its struggles resemble those in shrew-taming or women-on-top stories, yet it does not resolve the conflict—as do most such stories—by giving one spouse or the other the upper hand. No one is tamed in *Private Lives*. Instead, Sybil and Victor, thrown together by their search for their missing spouses, learn how to fight. As the play ends, Amanda and Elyot go "smilingly out of the door," hand in hand, as Sybil slaps Victor and he "takes her by the shoulders and shakes her like a rat" (90). Can wedding bells be far behind?

Private Lives presents this state of affairs as not quite "normal" but also as the open secret of "private life." As Amanda explains to her second husband, "I think very few people are completely normal really, deep down in their private lives. . . . That was the trouble with Elyot and me, we were like two violent acids bubbling about in a nasty little matrimonial bottle" (16). She says to Elyot, later, "I believe it was just the fact of our being married, and clamped together publicly, that wrecked us before" (43). To be "clamped together publicly" is to be required to perform "normalcy," the simpering devotion, quiet womanliness, and paternal pity represented by the new spouses, Sibyl and Victor. Elyot explains to Amanda that their desire to "bicker and fight" "will fade, along with our passion" (57). In *Private Lives*, conflict and passion are inseparable. Whereas some denunciations of domestic violence—in legal discourses and conduct literature—present it as a consequence of power differentials, a long-standing comic tradition suggests the opposite: that equality leads to violence. *Private Lives*, too, links violence to equality, but it insists that such equality also fuels rather than quells desire. Coward does not suggest that Amanda should abandon her claims to equality so as to achieve domestic peace. It is the fact that she is Elyot's match that excites them both.

Coward's play did not mark the end of stories in which one or the other spouse had to surrender. Although its conclusion distinguishes it, the conflicts that dominate the plot link *Private Lives* to much older stories, including *The Taming of the Shrew* and the wealth of popular and prescriptive texts that participate with it in early modern debates about marriage. Those familiar with these early modern texts will not be surprised by the robust violence in Coward's play. While its early modern precedents help us to understand the violence in Elyot and Amanda's battles as traditional rather than aberrant, Elyot and Amanda, in evening dress or silk pajamas, help us to remember the eroticism that fueled and was fed by those fisticuffs. The texts I will discuss in this chapter all explore the nexus of equality, eroticism, and violence that grants stories about the marital battle of the sexes such enduring appeal.

One feature in the structure of *Private Lives* helps to explain how Elyot and Amanda can maintain their equilibrium as equal combatants rather than resolving their battles in favor of one or the other or retreating from the field (the usual plot resolutions). In Acts 1 and 3, Elyot and Amanda share the stage with their new spouses, with whom they create two intersecting erotic triangles (Elyot, Sybil, Amanda and Amanda, Victor, Elyot). Coward put triangulated desire at the heart of his play *Design for Living* and he plays with the possibilities of these two triangles. But I am interested in a figure who facilitates Elyot and Amanda's desire without participating in it. There is one more character in this tightly constructed play, albeit a minor one. She is a servant. Louise arrives in Amanda's Paris apartment the morning after their night-long battle to "give a little cry of horror" at the wreckage Amanda and Elyot have created, and begins to clean up and to prepare breakfast for the two couples.[3] She does not speak English—in any case she does not say much—and she does little. Why then is she needed at all?

Strapped theater companies must be tempted to cut her part. After all, the battle of the sexes is fiercely dyadic. It concerns conflict that is generated out of—and animates—the couple. At first, Louise seems to be there just to remind us of these characters' affluence. Yet Louise's presence is also a subtle reminder that the dyad is always subsidized by the labors of a third party. Her presence isn't incidental, I will argue, but crucial. Whatever equality has ever been imaginable in marriage has required a supplement, represented in this play by the underdeveloped figure of Louise, who subtly reminds us that someone will have to clean up after Victor and Amanda. Given the nature of the couple's dynamic, Amanda will not be the one.

In this chapter, I will argue that fictions of marital equality depend on servants like Louise. To sustain the erotic tension between equal combatants, the couple must displace some of its resentments and obligations onto a third party, who is usually a servant or slave. The erotic triangle, and its relation to the heterosexual couple, has been much discussed.[4] By downplaying eros to focus on domestic work and discipline, I draw our attention to a less sexy, less studied triangle. At this point, I want to move back to the seventeenth and early eighteenth centuries in order to explore the historical process by which servants become central players in comic resolutions to marital conflicts. The terrain we will skim over here will include jokes and ballads, conduct books and sermons, seventeenth- and eighteenth-century diaries, and Shakespeare's *Taming of the Shrew*. That play, still "highly overinvested real estate," as Barbara Hodgdon describes it, will be our means of moving from the early modern back to the present, a present, I argue, that is deeply indebted to and informed by the past.[5]

The Rod, the Breeches, and the Marital Economy of Scarcity

When Sibyl calls Amanda a "half-masculine" woman who goes "banging about," she tries to dismiss her as a shrew. The shrew has been called the "first native comic role" for women in the English drama; she is a stock character in medieval as well as early modern popular culture, and she persists as a recognizable type into the present.[6] In the early modern period, the identifying features of the shrew became codified.[7] These features include physical violence as well as loquacity and self-assertion. The shrews in folktales and ballads routinely encroach on their husbands' authority by beating them, often with an obviously phallic "faggot sticke," "cudgel's end," or "lusty rod."[8] The rod figures violence as a masculine prerogative that shrews usurp. These texts assume that there should only be one stick or rod per couple and depict the mayhem that results when spouses struggle over who will wield it.[9] When the wife assumes the upper or whip hand, her husband becomes the object of her violence. This too is a zero-sum game in which there can be only one winner; if one has the rod, then the other doesn't. Popular texts about marital conflict never resolve the problem by multiplying weapons.[10] Instead, they depict inversion or its resolution when the henpecked husband regains possession of this phallic emblem of authority. Authority is not synonymous with violence. As I showed with regard to wife beating in Chapters 1 and 2, efforts were underway to define husbandly authority as nonviolent. But as a potent and pervasive symbol, the rod conjoins authority with masculinity, sexuality, violence, and scarcity.

The tradition that Coward draws on and rewrites in *Private Lives* routinely depicts marriage as a battle in which conflict is fueled by the wife's presumption of equality. Marital conflicts arise because, according to Thomas Hobbes, "there is not always that difference of strength or prudence between the man and the woman as that the right can be determined without War."[11] Marriage was widely represented in the early modern period as a struggle for dominance in which violence was, according to Joy Wiltenburg, "the fundamental arbiter."[12] Whereas Coward emphasizes the fun in fighting, most early modern conduct writers condemn marital struggles as fruitless and undignified. William Whately, for instance, laments that "divers houses are none other, but even very Fencing-Schooles, wherein the two sexes seeme to have met together for nothing, but to play their prizes, and to trie masteries."[13]

The problem in early modern conceptualizations of marriage is that husband and wife both are and are not construed as equals. As William Gouge explains, "there is of all unequals the least disparity betwixt husbands and wives." S.B. claims that husband and wife have "a kind of equalitie"; Daniel Cawdrey says that "in regard of" the wife's "place," the husband "must esteeme her (not as a servant, but) as his yoke-fellow and companion, a little lower then himselfe, as nearest to equality." Because husband and wife are construed as spiritual equals and as making separate but equal contributions to the household, as I discussed in

Chapters 1 and 2, "many wives," according to William Gouge, "gather that in all things there ought to be a mutuall equalitie."[14] In other words, wives misread their almost, kind of, nearly equality as complete or actual. This dangerous misunderstanding leads them to contend endlessly with their husbands.

In a frequently reprinted and cited conduct book, Richard Allestree articulates the complexity of these marital power struggles.

The imperiousness of a woman dos often raise those storms, wherein her self is shipwrack'd. How pleasantly might many women have lived if they had not affected dominion. Nay how much of their will might they have had, if they had not strugled for it. For let a man be of never so gentle a temper (unless his head be softer then his heart) such a usurpation will awake him to assert his right. But if he be of a sowre severe nature, if he have as great a desire of rule as she, backt with a much better title, what tempests what Hurricanes must two such opposite winds produce? And at last 'tis commonly the wives lot, after an uncreditable unjust war, to make as disadvantageous a peace; this (like all other ineffective rebellions) serving to straiten her yoke, to turn an ingenuous subjection into a slavish servitude: so that certainly it is not only the vertue, but the wisdom of wives to do that upon duty, which at last they must (with more unsupportable circumstances) do upon necessity.[15]

Allestree acknowledges that dominion is up for grabs and that either husband or wife might "affect" it; he describes spouses who aspire to dominion as "opposite," and apparently equally forceful, winds. But since "commonly" if not invariably the wife will lose such struggles, she should have the wisdom not to raise storms. There must be a leader, Allestree suggests, and there can only be one. Struggle over who it should be is not only fruitless but destructive. Unlike Coward, and, indeed, many early modern jokes and stories, writers like Allestree do not concede that struggling for dominion might have its pleasures.

The fictions of scarcity with which this book is concerned attempt to foreclose spousal combat before it begins by asserting that marriage under God and in law simply cannot accommodate two equal combatants. Marriage is a dominion of one and there should be no question as to who that one is. Yet the most doctrinaire texts waffle as to whether women actually are inferior or should simply act as if they think they are. In fleeting moments, they concede their own status as fictions.

By locating the problem in the wife's imagination, these texts suggest that the solution resides there as well. If a wife believes herself to be her husband's equal then she will contend for mastery rather than submit herself to his authority. The fiction that she is not her husband's equal (despite evidence to the contrary) is thus the founding myth of marriage. Before the wife can commit herself to this fiction, she must abandon what Gouge calls the "fond conceit" that she is her husband's equal.

William Whately, too, argues that the crucial foundation of marital harmony is an act of the wife's imagination. "First then, every good woman must suffer her selfe to be convinced in judgement, that she is not her husbands equall (yea, that her husband is her better by farre), without which it is not possible there should be any contentment, either in her heart, or in her house." "Unlesse the wife learne this lesson perfectly . . . if her very heart does not inwardly and thorowly condescend unto it, there will be nothing betwixt them but wrangling, repining, striving, and a continuall vying to be equall with him, or above him; and so shall their life be nothing else but a very battell, or a trying of masteries, a wofull living."[16] To strive to "be equal with" her husband immediately becomes an attempt to place herself "above him." It is not that the husband inevitably is her superior but that she must agree to act as if he is so that they will not both face the daily task of "trying masteries," "vying to be equall with . . . or above." She must recuse herself from a contest for mastery despite the fact that she might be able to win. Similarly, Cotton Mather writes in 1692: "In every lawful thing she submits her will and sense to his, where she cannot with calm reasons convince him of inexpediences; and instead of grudging or captious contradiction, she *acts as if* there were but one mind in two bodies."[17] Here Mather acknowledges that the one mind of marriage is an illusion, performed by the wife for her husband's benefit.

The wife who would not commit herself to the fiction of her own inferiority was consistently depicted as a battling, belligerent figure, fighting for possession and control of what was in short supply: the rod, as we have seen, as well as the breeches, of which there can only be one pair. The shrewish or insubordinate wife contends for mastery within marriage (figured as the breeches), and in usurping those breeches reduces the gender contrast that, it was presumed, sustains conjugal desire. The resolution is never obtaining another pair of breeches, but rather restoring the breeches to the husband. As Linda Woodbridge points out, breeches are so predominant a figure for marital sovereignty that it is often hard to tell whether literal or figurative breeches are at issue.[18] Female characters in the drama constantly threaten to wear the breeches.[19] This figure so pervaded discussions of spousal relations that it turns up in legal commentary as well as on the stage and in the streets. As Timothy Stretton explains, "it was accepted in the court of Chancery that wives could not appear as witnesses in cases involving their husbands, yet a manuscript commentary which stressed this exclusion also described various cases where wives' testimony was taken," including one from 1576 in which the reason given was that the wife "'wore the Breeches'."[20] One writer tries to link the privilege of the breeches to the kind of "separate but equal" gender specialization I explored in Chapter 1, explaining that just as "the man may not weare womans apparrell, nor the woman mans, how much lesse may the one usurpe the others dignitie, or the other (to wit the husband) resigne or give over his soveraigntie unto his wife?"[21] But the skirt is not associated with anything a husband can be imagined to want.

Women in breeches were both monstrously unnatural and tediously mundane. According to one misogynist satire, when it comes to women in breeches, "such sort of Monsters are now a daies so common, that if they were all to be shewn in Booths for farthings a peece, there would be less spectators, then there was to see the Sheep with five legs, or the great Crocodile."[22]

It is not surprising that a garment should become the symbol of gender differentiation in a culture in which clothing was a crucial marker of identity. Ann Jones and Peter Stallybrass have shown the extent to which clothes made the man or woman in early modern England, although their work directs our attention away from the breeches as the prime signifier of gender difference and toward other "prosthetics" of gender such as the hat, ruff, or beard.[23] In colonial America, too, people's identities were expressed in and created through their apparel. This was so much the case that garments might become part of punishments, formal and informal.[24]

While the particular significance of breeches emerges from the specifics of early modern clothing practices, it has outlasted those practices. "Wearing the pants" is still used to describe a usurpation of marital or domestic mastery, even in late twentieth and early twenty-first century America, where women routinely and unremarkably wear trousers. In Edward Albee's *Who's Afraid of Virginia Woolf?* (1963), Martha responds to George's claim that she's a monster by saying: "I'm loud, and I'm vulgar, and I wear the pants in this house because somebody's got to, but I am *not* a monster. I am *not.*"[25] Albee's terms came to shape responses to Richard Burton and Elizabeth Taylor, who played Martha and George in the 1966 film, Petruchio and Katherina in Zefirelli's film of *Taming of the Shrew* a year later, and, after their divorces, Amanda and Elyot in a notoriously awful stage production of *Private Lives.* A biography of Burton claims that one of the problems in his marriage with Taylor was that "there was no question about who wore the pants," that is, Liz.[26] In her popular advice book, *The Surrendered Wife: A Practical Guide to Finding Intimacy, Passion, and Peace with a Man,* "feminist and former shrew" Laura Doyle advises that, to avoid conflict, spouses need to remember that a marriage contains "one skirt and one pair of pants."[27] Sally Gallagher quotes a twenty-nine-year-old father of one who claims that "feminist groups try to take the pants off the husband."[28] Maureen Dowd claims that "Americans like to see women who wear the pants beaten up and humiliated."[29] Apparently, even today, the skirt is less valued and less contested.[30]

As a figure for the mastery over which husband and wife struggle, the breeches or pants remain so familiar that they would seem to require no explanation. I return to this figure as I do to the biblical figure of one flesh or the legal fiction of marital "unity of person" so as to interrogate it precisely as a figure, to see what it has in common with these other long-lived tropes, and to scrutinize its effects. Why has this figure for marital conflict persisted so long?

In Chapter 1, I explored how Christian marriage advice proposes male headship as the solution to the extreme gender difference that it simultaneously celebrates as the motor for heterosexual desire—the "biblical blueprint for marriage"—and laments as an almost insuperable problem. Coward's play suggests that passion might be fueled not just by high gender contrast but by the very struggles for mastery early moderns associate with wives' claims to equality and figure as their bids for the breeches (that is, for collapsing gender contrast). What gives shrew-taming stories their kick is an assumption that those struggles for mastery created by wives' claims to equality are sexy. The trick to comic resolution, then, becomes retaining just enough parity to keep things interesting while avoiding endless contests over who is the boss. This is where the servant comes in. Once we add the servant to the household then the wife's relation to domestic power changes; she has access to the rod, if not to the breeches. While the wife was prohibited from wearing the breeches or trying masteries with her husband, she was allowed, even enjoined, to wield the rod if she turned it against her subordinates rather than her husband.

Women's Domestic Mastery

When women had authority—over servants and children, for instance—they were empowered to use violence to the same extent that they were construed as inappropriate targets of it. William Gouge's claim, for instance, that "God hath not ranked wives among those in the family who are to be corrected" depends upon the assumption that God *has* ranked others as those who are to be corrected.[31] The distinction made between wife beating and servant beating relied on the assumption that servants (like children, but unlike wives) were unambiguously subordinate to their masters. Even as prescriptive literature censured blows between spouses as disorderly, it defended the corporal punishment of servants as crucial to the maintenance of order. As Dod and Cleaver argue: "God hath put the rod of correction in the hands of the Governours of the family, by punishment to save them [servants and children] from destruction; which if the bridle were let loose unto them, they would runne into."[32] Husband and wife "must joyne in admonishing, incouraging, reproving, and (if need be) correcting their inferiours"; the wife is "like a judge, which is joined in commission with her husband to correct others."[33] The wife asserts and maintains her status as "a joynt governour of the family" by administering "correction," especially corporal punishment.[34] In handling her subordinates, it is acceptable for the wife to "in some measure shew that she had in part the Breeches on."[35] The association of legitimate correction or the rod with the breeches is important here but so is the double qualification in this statement: "in some measure" and "in part."

Advice on running households and governing families often confers on women the right and the responsibility to use force. This is especially clear in instructions on parenting, which assume that mothers will shirk their obligation to discipline their children. As Kathleen Davies argues, this advice pertained across the confessional spectrum: "The rod, if necessary, was the answer, whatever the theology."[36] One particularly extreme statement describes how the good mother "holds not [the father's] hand from due strokes, but bares their [the children's] skins with delight, to his fatherly stripes."[37] At the very least, "if he will correct the children, she must not grow angry and save them (as if she thought it much they should be kept under nurture) neither must he save them out of her hands, when she seeth cause to give chasticement." If husband and wife disagree about punishment, they must debate this in private, not in front of inferiors; "for if hee doe and she undoe, if he correct and shee cocker, or if she chide and he defend: (besides the distempers and heartburnings which will grow betwixt themselves) they shall also so lighten and lessen each others power in the family, that both at last shall grow into contempt, because of their indiscretion."[38] In these last two quotations from William Whately's *A Bride Bush*, he assumes that the mother and mistress might be the one who chastises, corrects, and chides, and not invariably the one who saves, cockers, and defends. Whately's warning suggests that discipline might often become a bone of contention between spouses, precisely because women were empowered to administer it and therefore might resent attempts to curb their exercise of their authority to either correct or cocker as they deemed appropriate.

Corporal punishment remained a crucial part of women's work in colonial America. Cotton Mather, for instance, advises that a mother will not "spare *Corrections* where their Miscarriages do call for the *Rod*; and she will not *overlay* them with her sinful Fondness, lest God make them *Crosses* to her, for her being afraid of *crossing* them in their Exorbitances."[39] Mary Beth Norton asserts that "in the seventeenth-century colonies beating one's children seems to have been taken for granted."

While all mothers were supposed to beat their children, only higher-status women would have had subordinates to discipline. Norton argues that in colonial America as in early modern England, "in effect, one's ability to strike a person determined one's standing as that individual's proper superior."[40] The assumption in early modern England and colonial America that wives, mothers, and mistresses should wield authority over their subordinates reminds us of the complexity of women's status in households. Women allied with their husbands as governors, or standing alone as heads of their own households, were expected to govern authoritatively. Yet the fact that their power is so explicitly understood as the power to beat others serves as a grim reminder not to celebrate authority uncritically. One woman's power might be someone else's bruise.

Although household chastisement was an obligation, it was not a license to lash out in anger. Instead, domestic discipline was expected to operate within carefully delineated rules.[41] Conduct books even describe a gendered decorum of domestic violence. As early as 1543, Heinrich Bullinger confers on mistresses the dominion over female servants and advises that

menne behave themselves unto theyr maydens in the house, and commyt all the rule and punyshment of them unto theyr wyves, and not to meddle wythe the servauntes agaynste them, excepte the wyfe wolde deale unreasonably wyth theyr poore servauntes. Contrary wyse, the wyfe must not take upon her the rule or punyshment of the men servauntes. For hereof commeth great unite: Lyke as whan the husband medleth to muche with the women servauntes, and the wyfe wyth the menservauntes, there ryseth great suspicion and discension amonge marryed folks.[42]

The gendered etiquette for household beatings licenses women to inflict corporal punishment, yet assumes that they, like men, should follow a complex set of rules so that this violence will support gender and class hierarchies, rather than upset them.[43] The assumption here is that discipline can only become unseemly when the dominant and submissive roles are played by people of different genders. Such formulations ignore the possibility that same-sex beatings might also be erotic and therefore "unseemly," a possibility that is everywhere acknowledged in discussions of the pedagogical floggings schoolmasters administer to boys.[44] Although Bullinger first advises men against meddling with the maids, he also concedes that the husband might need to intervene if his wife deals unreasonably with the servants but not that she might make a similar intervention.[45] His warning about the suspicion and dissension that can arise from cross-sex "meddling" or chastisement becomes a theme with later conduct writers. Dod and Cleaver, for instance, advise: "And as it is not comely or beseeming, that the wife should take upon her to rule and correct the men-servants; so likewise, it is not comely or meet, that the husband should meddle with the punishing or chastising of the maid-servants"; "for a mans nature scorneth and disdaineth to be beaten of a woman, and a maids nature is corrupted with the stripes of a man."[46] Like Bullinger, Dod and Cleaver use the verb "meddle" to describe a husband's incursions on his wife's domestic authority over her female subordinates.

The assumption that same-sex beatings are more seemly helps to grant women some authority over their maids and to position their husbands' attempts to hire, fire, direct, and correct maids as "meddling." Many early modern women also use this word in similar contexts. As we will see, for instance, Lady Sarah Cowper describes her husband as "meddling with" her maids. While in all of these instances the word seems to refer specifically to the domestic management of maids it also has sexual connotations. Tim Meldrum cites a case from 1684 in which the wife of a husband who molested his female servants advises him "that if he must have a whore he should go abroad for one and not meddle with her maids, for as they came honest into her house she desired they might go away so."[47] Emphasizing these sexual connotations, Laura Gowing scrutinizes the praise many conduct book writers (including Dod and Cleaver and Gouge) confer on Abraham's promise to Sarah (in Genesis) that he "would not meddle with his maid" Hagar, instead handing her over to his wife to discipline. As Gowing reminds us, the reason Sarah was mad in the first place was that Abraham had meddled with Hagar to the extent of impregnating her.[48]

The gendered decorum of household chastisement was proposed so as to divide the labor of correction, limit turf battles between husbands and wives, and restrict the eroticism of the master-servant relation. But, as we will see, it was impossible to maintain a sharp boundary between conjugal eroticism and the eroticized master-servant relations that surrounded, rivaled, and supported it. Furthermore, etiquette could not prevent constant squabbles between husbands and wives regarding the management and discipline of servants. Such squabbles figure significantly in the diaries of William Byrd and Samuel Pepys. Because these diaries are remarkably detailed, Byrd's and Pepys's depictions of these conflicts have earned an important place in the histories of Anglo-American marriage.

Diaries of Discipline: William Byrd and Samuel Pepys

William Byrd (1674–1744) was born in 1674 in Westover, Virginia, to a wealthy family.[49] Byrd was educated in England and held various political posts during his life. After his first wife's death, he returned to London for several years. He was a man of fascinating contradictions: a plantation owner and a London man-about-town; a slave owner who ultimately argued against the slave trade but never freed his own slaves; a gentleman and patriarch who struggled to define and maintain both identities in two very different worlds. He serves as an important example in histories of the family, sex, and marriage in early modern England, of "anxious patriarchs" in colonial Virginia, and of American identity. He is so much discussed in part because he kept a series of diaries written in shorthand; segments survive for 1709–12, 1717–21, and 1739–41.[50] I will focus on the earliest diary, covering 1709 to 1712, years when he was living on his Virginia plantation with his first wife, Lucy.

Byrd describes Lucy as "unkind," "indisposed" (especially because of pregnancy), and "out of humor."[51] He quarrels with her about plucking her eyebrows before a ball, her eavesdropping on him, and her care of her body: "I had a small quarrel with my wife because she would not be bled [as a treatment to prevent miscarriage] but neither good words nor bad could prevail against her fear which is very uncontrollable" (364). Mostly the couple quarrel about how to care for their children and discipline their slaves.[52]

By the seventeenth century, many Anglo-American households included both servants and slaves. Carole Shammas claims that the most remarkable feature in the history of American households is the "large number of unrelated dependents they contained prior to the Civil War."[53] While the presence of slaves may have left all servants more vulnerable to abuse, "as the difference between rights to an individual's labor and rights to an individual's person became less distinct," by the eighteenth century, certain penalties, such as being whipped naked, were forbidden for servants and reserved for slaves as part of the process of dividing the two groups against one another.[54] Thus if the presence of slaves in colonial households led to increased violence, that brutality was steadily directed toward slaves themselves, as they were gradually defined as those without legal redress.[55] The presence of slaves and servants complicated the position of the wife and mistress in the household, as has been much discussed. Weaving a narrative of decline, Susan Cahn argues that in the seventeenth century wives lost their power and authority in the household, sidelined from productive labor into consumption and idleness, their labor assigned to servants (or slaves) and their power reduced.[56] While bringing servants and slaves into households probably diminished women's power in some ways, it must have extended it in others. It also, I will suggest, produced certain marital tensions and deflected others away from the couple.

Discussions of Byrd's diaries tend to single out Lucy's conduct as somehow distinct from and less appropriate than William's. Disregarding the gendered decorum of domestic violence prescribed in English conduct books, both Byrds beat male and female slaves alike. According to the diary, sometimes they do this themselves, sometimes they "have" them whipped (by an overseer presumably), and sometimes Byrd obscures responsibility by recording that a slave "was whipped." Most of their servants appear to be slaves although Byrd does not consistently identify them as such.[57] William holds Lucy accountable for her servants' conduct, complaining on one occasion that they are lazy and that, apparently, she is not a sufficiently strict taskmaster. Often William presents Lucy's violence as unremarkable: on May 13, 1709, for instance, Nurse (a white servant), upon being reprimanded by William "gave me as good as I brought and she was so impudent to her mistress that she could not forbear beating her." On this occasion, William and Lucy share their distress—he, too, is "out of humor with Nurse" and regrets that he "was in too great a passion with her"—Lucy does the beating, and William seems to accept this as a reasonable response to Nurse's conduct (34–35). William can construe Lucy's robust violence as an indicator of health, as when, on September 3, 1712, he remarks "my wife was pretty well and gave Prue a great whipping for several misdemeanors" (579). He might also approve unambiguously, as on September 12, 1712, when "my wife had . . . a great quarrel with her maid Prue and with good reason; she is growing a most notable girl for stealing and laziness and lying and everything that is bad" (583).

Yet William several times remarks unfavorably upon Lucy's treatment of slaves; since the account is his, his perspective informs subsequent interpretations. For instance, in the introduction to his edition of the earliest portion of the secret diary, Louis B. Wright points out that Byrd "occasionally . . . lost his temper," of which there are abundant examples, and "sometimes forgot himself so far as to quarrel undignifiedly with the servants." Yet Wright also claims that "Mrs. Byrd, who had a violent and uncontrollable temper, shocked her husband by the severity of her punishments." Wright immediately acknowledges that "Byrd himself in a few instances meted out what seems to have been cruel punishment," which would include putting a bit in a slave's mouth.[58] In *The Family, Sex, and Marriage in England, 1500–1800*, Lawrence Stone claims that Lucy Byrd "had clear sadistic tendencies," but does not similarly diagnose William. Pierre Marambaud describes Lucy Byrd as "moody, high-strung, and easily wrought up." He attributes her "violent temper" to her "rakish and violent" father and announces that Byrd's "household was often in an uproar because of his quarrels with his spoiled and temperamental wife" with whom he also shared "mutual affection." Kenneth Lockridge describes Lucy as requiring her husband to fight "a daily struggle for the upper hand" because she was "plainly willful and violent."[59]

Rather than dwell on how brutal both the Byrds are, which is of course the case, I want to turn a cold eye on what if anything makes Lucy Byrd's treatment of servants and slaves remarkable. Given what William routinely does, what is the basis for Lucy's reputation as having a violent and uncontrollable temper and behaving shockingly? What were the standards by which her husband sometimes found Lucy Byrd's administration of corporal punishment unseemly?

Scholarly attention focuses on conflicts Lucy Byrd had with what might be two different female slaves, one called Jenny and the other, confusingly, little Jenny. Most commentators conflate the two and they do not seem to appear simultaneously in any entry; Wright and Tinling's edition of the diary offers separate entries in the index for each. It is impossible to tell from the entries if they refer to two different slaves or just one. Let me consider references to little Jenny first, all of which record occasions on which she was beaten. On July, 15, 1710, "my wife against my will caused little Jenny to be burned with a hot iron, for which I quarreled with her" (205). But on August 22, 1710, William himself confesses, "in the evening I had a severe quarrel with little Jenny and beat her too much for which I was sorry," revealing that he did sometimes regret his own conduct (221).

An incident that fascinates scholars but about which William refrains from judgment occurs on February 27, 1711: "In the evening my wife and little Jenny had a great quarrel in which my wife got the worst but at last by the help of the family Jenny was overcome and soundly whipped" (307). This incident suggests that little Jenny fights back, as she does not appear to do when William beats her. William Byrd never describes a male or female slave who forcefully resists the discipline he imposes on him or her. Byrd's use of the word "quarrel" to describe his and Lucy's altercations with little Jenny confers on her the status of an equal combatant more than a subordinate although their recourse to beating reasserts their power over her.

Based on court cases in York County in Virginia from 1646 to 1720, Terri L. Snyder argues that servants (as opposed to slaves) were more likely to resist disciplinary violence imposed on them by women, especially when those women headed households and did not have the support of a husband or "family" (which in Byrd's use of this term seems to include other slaves) as Lucy Byrd did in order to regain the upper hand in her "quarrel" with little Jenny. [60] "In York County," according to Snyder, "ten cases of servant-on-master violence were brought before the court between 1646 and 1720. Six involved attacks on women—five wives whose husbands were absent"; "four female and two male servants struck female masters, while no court records note female servants who struck male masters."[61] Similarly, Bernard Capp finds that, in early modern English assize court records, "allegations of physical cruelty were levelled mainly at female employers."[62]

Because of such distrust of mistresses' authority, Snyder concludes that servants were more likely to resist mistresses who disciplined them, grabbing a stick out of their hands and turning it on them. When servants struck male masters, these assaults did not occur in the midst of beatings. For Snyder this suggests that, while "in theory mistresses as well as masters were entitled to correct their servants and slaves," in practice subordinates resented and resisted mistresses' use of physical discipline.[63] This in turn suggests that it was not just that women's abuses of authority were demonized but that women's authority was resented in itself.[64]

Fights between master and mistress over disciplining servants or slaves reveal that the rod, like the breeches, was a symbol of privilege and power in scarce and thus contested supply. On the one hand, women could make a legitimate claim to the rod, as they could not to the breeches. On the other hand, it might be denied them not only when they wielded it against husband instead of child, servant, or slave, but when a servant challenged his or her mistress's right to wield it, or a master intervened to countermand his wife's authority. As we saw above, William Whately predicts that a master might need to intervene in his wife's administration of punishment but not vice versa. In the Byrd household, William describes himself as having just such a prerogative but does not suffer his wife to criticize his own actions as a disciplinarian.

We might contrast the Byrds' household to that of Lady Sarah Cowper in London, where servants rather than slaves are at issue but where the conflicts between husband and wife are similar if less violent. Anne Kugler uses Lady Sarah Cowper's extensive and fascinating daily diaries, kept from 1700 to 1716, to show that "the main bone of contention" in Sir William and Lady Sarah Cowper's miserable forty-two-year marriage "was power in the household, especially, though not exclusively, authority over the servants." They appear to have had five servants, including two maids. From Lady Sarah's perspective, her husband neither governed the servants nor allowed her to do so; in particular, he "overruled or undermined" her attempts to discipline servants. She turned to prescriptive literature, including William Gouge's *Of Domesticall Duties*, not to remind herself of her chief duty to obey but to assure herself of the authority prescription allotted but her husband denied. "Lady Sarah . . . did not so much feel repressed by patriarchy as she was outraged that its prescriptions, as she understood them, were not being fulfilled." Lady Sarah was so frustrated at being denied "the Common power of all housekeepers . . . to dispose of the women Servants" that in December of 1701 she went on strike, refusing to run the household and resigning that duty to her husband. At this point, she had been married for thirty-seven years and was fifty-seven years old. Although she consciously chose this as a strategy, she did not want people outside the household to know that her husband "is turned House:keeper and Misrules the Maids." After he eventually asked her to return as housekeeper, she was able to confide to her diary in 1702 that "Sir Wm having left off to Meddle with the Maids I dispose of them as is fitt."[65]

Like William Byrd and Lady Sarah Cowper, other diarists in seventeenth- and eighteenth-century England report conflicts over managing households and disciplining servants. Ralph Josselin describes the various ways in which his wife tries his patience and does not quite live up to her role as his comfort, including the fact that she "fayles somewhat in her household diligence."[66] Alice Thornton, whose expressions of resentment are always oblique, records one episode when maids take her daughter with them to a celebration of Charles II's coronation, "against my mind, having Mr. Thornton's consent."[67] Ralph Baxter complains that his wife has wasted servants' time with "much ado about cleanliness and trifles," and that "when her servants did any fault unwillingly, she scarce ever told them of it."[68] The wife might be too slatternly or too scrupulous. While a husband, like the writers of conduct literature, might hold his wife accountable for her house and servants, he might also scrutinize, criticize, and interfere in her exercise of this legitimate authority. His wife might, in turn, resent his interference. In her study of marital breakdown, Joanne Bailey argues that wives felt acutely any abrogation of their domestic authority. In separation proceedings, women whose main grievance is their husbands' cruelty often also complain that their husbands "denied them their right to manage their households."[69] Thus in widely different households, husband and wife might disagree about the extent of the wife's authority over servants.

The conflicts over domestic authority recorded in early modern diaries and depositions, and the court cases Snyder studies, provide a context for the "quarrel" between Lucy Byrd and little Jenny. Little Jenny approaches her disciplining as if it is a fight in which her mistress might get the "worst." At this moment, the diary opens up the possibility of imagining little Jenny's own perspective. Perhaps she pictured this occasion as an opportunity to resist and even shame Lucy, or to play one spouse against the other.[70] In some households, female slaves might have been more likely to resist mistresses because they knew them better. While overseers rather than male masters usually supervised male workers in the fields, mistresses worked with female slaves in the household. This seems to have led to greater intimacy and more heated conflicts.[71] In the Byrd household, both husband and wife lived on intimate terms with their slaves. At least in William Byrd's account of his household, intimacy seems to breed violence; violence in turn facilitates certain kinds of intimacy.

The second encounter that elicits William Byrd's and subsequent historians' particular comment occurs between Lucy and Jenny. If one traces Jenny through the diary, one finds that she figures almost exclusively as the object of vomits, purges, and chastisement, mostly administered not by Lucy but by William.[72] She is beaten for throwing water on the couch, "abundance of faults," concealing another slave's bedwetting, being the whore of a fellow slave, and often for no apparent reason. While William routinely beats Jenny, Lucy's treatment of Jenny on March 2, 1712, almost leads to violence between husband and wife.

I had a terrible quarrel with my wife concerning Jenny that I took away from her when she was beating her with the tongs. She lifted up her hands to strike me but forbore to do it. She gave me abundance of bad words and endeavored to strangle herself, but I believe in jest only. However after acting a mad woman a long time she was passive again. I ate some roast beef for dinner. . . . At night we drank some cider by way of reconciliation and I read nothing. (494)

There are several layers to this remarkable episode. First, Lucy's use of tongs against Jenny sparks William's intervention. Perhaps the tongs are more likely to injure or damage Jenny than the whip William himself routinely uses. Perhaps grabbing whatever comes to hand, in this case the tongs, smacks more of rage than of discipline and therefore undermines William's sense of his own dignity and the righteousness of his impositions of discipline.[73] But William's intervention also threatens to place him as the object of Lucy's rage: she lifts up her hands to strike him but, realizing she should not, then turns them on herself. When Lucy Byrd turns her violence from Jenny, toward William, and then to herself, we can see the consequences when a circuit of displacement is interrupted. After William "took [Jenny] away from" Lucy, she is not sure what to do with her rage. She threatens to strike William; "forebears," since this is the one kind of violence good wives are not supposed to resort to; and finally begins to choke herself, a gesture so confused that William tries to take it as "in jest."

It is impossible to know what first enflamed Lucy Byrd's anger against Jenny. But in Lucy's quarrels with her husband, what seems to be at issue is Lucy's right to assert her authority over slaves without being countermanded. My point here is not that Lucy Byrd has a right to beat Jenny with tongs. It is, rather, that even William Byrd's diary presents Lucy as thinking that she has such a right and being incensed when it is denied. Violence toward slaves, and indeed servants and children, is assumed in this household. Yet Lucy's use of violence is simultaneously licensed and questioned. Recent work in women's history tends to

emphasize that women had more authority in practice than they were allotted in theory. This is one arena in which the opposite seems to have
been true: women's domestic authority was legitimate in theory but
often not treated as such in practice.

That the issue for Lucy Byrd is her own domestic authority becomes
especially clear on December 31, 1711, when Lucy has a male slave
beaten while company is in the house.

> My wife and I had a terrible quarrel about whipping Eugene while Mr. Mumford
> was there but she had a mind to show her authority before company but I would
> not suffer it, which she took very ill; however for peace sake I made the first ad-
> vance towards a reconciliation which I obtained with some difficulty and after
> abundance of crying. However it spoiled the mirth of the evening, but I was not
> conscious that I was to blame in that quarrel. (462)

In this incident, Lucy Byrd wants not only to exercise her authority but to
"show" it. Such display of her authority over the body of a male slave
seems to be what provokes the "terrible quarrel" with her husband. It is
not clear whether Lucy provokes William's sense of unseemliness by exposing the tawdry details of household conflict, performing her authority
over a male slave, disrupting the evening's mirth, or by some combination
of the three. Although Lucy Byrd insists on her prescribed authority to
discipline this slave, her attempted exercise of discipline promotes disorder rather than order, in her husband's view, because it challenges rather
than upholds his domestic and social authority. In this quarrel, more than
in the others, Lucy Byrd's insistence on wielding the rod seems to
threaten to usurp the breeches.

On one occasion, husband and wife use their female slaves as proxies
in a contest for marital and domestic mastery.[74] On May 22, 1712,

> My wife caused Prue to be whipped violently notwithstanding I desired it not,
> which provoked me to have Anaka whipped likewise who had deserved it much
> more, on which my wife flew into such a passion that she hoped she would be re-
> venged of me. I was moved very much at this but only thanked her for the pres-
> ent lest I should say things foolish in my passion. . . . My wife was sorry for what
> she had said and came to ask my pardon and I forgave her in my heart but
> seemed to resent, that she might be the more sorry for her folly. She ate no din-
> ner nor appeared the whole day. I ate some bacon for dinner. (533)

These spousal quarrels over the disciplining of slaves, and the fact that,
for William at least, they are always resolved by dinnertime, draw our attention to the interrelationship between the Byrds' treatment of their
slaves and their treatment of one another. Byrd's diary never records
any physical violence between husband and wife. Byrd describes moments when his wife is on the brink of hitting him but never an episode

in which she actually does; he describes his routine physical chastisement of his slaves, but never records or justifies a similar punishment of his wife. The rage each spouse seems to feel toward the other is vented particularly on female slaves, who serve at least in this household as outlets for anger and brutality. Byrd's diary does not tell us whether he also exploited his female slaves as sexual supplements to his wife, as was so often the case. He does seem to have taken a white English servant as his mistress after Lucy's death.[75] When masters developed sustained relationships to favored slaves, as Lauren Berlant and others have argued, these relationships might work to mask and thereby sustain the domination inherent in both slavery and marriage.[76] Whether Byrd exploited his slaves sexually or not, his relationship to his wife, which includes "flourishing" and "rogering" her, seems to be rendered nonviolent by having these available surrogates for both spouses' rage.[77] The Byrds' freedom to beat their slaves—brutally, arbitrarily, and with no one to answer to except one another—fostered a marriage—or at least a fragmented and quotidian account of a marriage—that is animated by struggles for mastery yet remains largely nonviolent. Lucy's sense of her own right to inflict violence on slaves, but not on her husband, leads to "quarrels" with him about when and how she exercises this prerogative, compensates her for the other ways in which she is subordinated to William, and protects her from William's potential violence, since she is allied with him as a domestic governor and not positioned with the slaves as subject to his physical punishment.

The Byrd marriage has been variously assessed—as fraught with conflict because of Lucy's willful temper, as I've discussed above, and as sexually lukewarm. Taking the diary as an accurate record, Lawrence Stone diagnoses what he terms a "low level of marital intercourse"—twenty-five times per year. Pointing out that sex sometimes follows "a whipping given to one of the female domestic slaves, usually by his wife," Stone suggests that Byrd was aroused by his wife's violence toward female slaves, but that otherwise he maintained "placid, almost sexless domesticity" in Virginia. After he is widowed, Byrd engages in a much higher level of sexual activity with prostitutes in London, or so his later diary claims. For Stone, this disparity between his sexual activity as a husband and as a widower suggests that he had needs that were unmet back in Virginia.[78] One might also surmise that his slaves and his wife fulfilled his desires in ways other than those itemized in his later diary. The prostitutes in London were, like his slaves, women of whom he could make any request. As a wife, Lucy Byrd's status is considerably more vexed than that of the other women in William's diaries.

In his meticulous statistical analysis of the diary, Michael Zuckerman documents even less intimacy between William and Lucy Byrd. He counts the couple's frequent separations, William's infrequent expressions of affection for Lucy, and "not much more than one mating a month." Like Stone, Zuckerman assumes that Byrd's records are accurate. For Zuckerman, however, the Byrds' quarrels are not foreplay but rather the predominant way husband and wife interact. Lucy *impinges* on William's consciousness, and earns her place in the diary, largely when she fights with him: "Of her impingements upon him, almost half again as many revolved around their battles as around their fondlings and fondnesses." Zuckerman views Lucy more positively than most but largely in the service of his critique of William as "no doting husband to his fiery and free-spirited spouse." For Zuckerman, the Byrd marriage only seems modern because "the battle of the sexes has remained a Western perennial"; it is more premodern than modern, he argues, because it is not companionable or intimate. My contention is that quarreling and companionship are coordinates rather than contraries. If, as Zuckerman contends, Lucy Byrd "impinges" on William when they fight, then those are also the moments in which she asserts equal domestic authority, claiming her place as partner, if not as object of devotion, in William's diary and thereby in the history of marriage.[79] Long on lists and short on reflection, Byrd's diary is an inadequate gauge of the relationship between husband and wife; it does not explain the relationship between quarreling and "flourishes" on the couch and the billiard table, leaving that connection to speculation. But it is certainly the case that Lucy figures in the diary largely as her husband's partner in those two activities.

Stone's depiction of violence as foreplay for the Byrds seems a more accurate description of the dynamics between Samuel Pepys, another assiduous and promiscuous diarist, and his wife, Elizabeth. Although the Pepyses did not have children or slaves, their London household included at least three servants, with and about whom Samuel and Elizabeth fought. Samuel fondles female servants, but generally seems to stop short of having intercourse with them.[80] While Pepys's sexual exploits have been much discussed, the daily violence of his household, and Mrs. Pepys's participation in it, has been less remembered. Both husband and wife sometimes beat servants, especially young boys.[81] Mrs. Pepys once boxes the ear of a live-in companion (and therefore a woman of roughly her own class) who strikes her back.[82] This episode worries Samuel because he takes it as evidence not of the companion's insubordination but of his wife's jealousy (which he concedes is justified) and his "own folly in giving her too much head heretofore." He anticipates the trouble he'll have "to get down her head again," to "keep my wife within bounds."[83] The couple's most famous and protracted fight involving a servant is over Samuel's sexual attentions to their maid, Deb Willet. Although Samuel confesses interest in and attraction to Deb from the start, he suggests that his relationship with her begins as he is drawn into her conflicts with his wife. Shortly after Elizabeth hires Deb (at the age of seventeen in 1667), Pepys finds her crying one evening "that her mistress had been angry with her, but I would take no notice of it." He cannot refrain from intervening for long. Their first sexual encounter follows an episode in which Deb cries because she cannot write well, Mrs. Pepys angrily acuses her of sullenness, and Pepys "seemed angry with her too" so as to placate his wife but later advises Deb and consoles her with caresses. Months later, his wife finds him fondling Deb as she combs his hair; Mrs. Pepys "was struck mute and grew angry, and as her voice came to her, grew quite out of order." Elizabeth threatens to fire Deb, badgers her husband and the girl about what exactly they were up to, and threatens to "publish [his] shame." Pepys concedes that his wife has good reason for her jealousy and that she would be within her rights to fire Deb. Finally, about three weeks after the fondling incident and many fights, Pepys himself "discharges" Deb. But the story doesn't end here; months of suspicion, recrimination, subterfuge, and infidelity follow.[84]

In many ways, the vexed triangle of husband-wife-servant produces a very different plot in the Pepyses' household than it does in the Byrds'. This may be, in part, a consequence of Pepys's narration; his diary is more richly detailed, more introspective, and more narrative than Byrd's. It is also important that Deb is a servant, who can be fired and can then find other employment, rather than a slave. She is also Elizabeth Pepys's sexual rival; William Byrd never presents any of his slaves in this way nor does he suggest that jealousy played any role in his conflicts with his wife over their slaves. Pepys even links his diary-keeping with his need to document his affair with Deb and to keep that record secret from his wife; in May, 1669, he ends the diary because his eyesight is failing and "my amours to Deb are past" (9:564).[85] But, like William Byrd, Samuel Pepys presents his wife as violently out of control and himself as admirably restrained. Pepys reports that his wife "could not refrain to strike me and pull my hair; which I resolved to bear with, and had good reason to bear it" (9: 369). She twice threatens to slit the servant's nose but mostly directs her violence toward her husband. On January 12, 1669, about three months after she first finds Samuel fondling Deb and two months after Deb has left their household, Elizabeth refuses to join Samuel in bed, and "at last, about one a-clock, she came by my side of the bed and drew my curtaine open, and with the tongs, red hot at the ends, made as if she did design to pinch me with them" (9: 414).[86] While Elizabeth Pepys resembles Lucy Byrd in reaching for the tongs, she turns them on her husband not a slave or servant.

Pepys fears that, by being caught in infidelity, he has given his wife the upper hand. He confesses himself "troubled to see how my wife is by this means [the conflict over Willet] likely for ever to have her hand over me, that I shall for ever be a slave to her; that is to say, only in matters of pleasure, but in other things she will make her business, I know, to please me and to keep me right to her" (9: 363). What gives Mrs. Pepys the upper hand is her knowledge that she cannot trust her husband. Yet, as Pepys confides in this same passage, the resulting conflict, sleep-lessness, and role reversal have also intensified the couple's sexual con-nection. "I must here remember that I have lain with my moher [*mujer*, woman or wife] as a husband more times since this falling-out then in I believe twelve months before—and with more pleasure to her then I think in all the time of our marriage before."[87] Elizabeth Pepys, appar-ently, is aroused by her own anger and violence and, perhaps, by "having her hand over" her "slave." In the Pepys household, female servants compete with but also animate and support the passionate bond be-tween husband and wife, a bond that includes, in these eventful months, pleasant conversations and "very great joy" in bed at night and in the morning, as well as wrenching fights. Although Stone diagnoses the Pepyses, like the Byrds, as having insufficiently frequent sex, the mar-riage Samuel describes is passionate in every way, even if he generously supplements it with a wide range of women over whom he could exert power—from servants, to the wives and daughters of men seeking pro-fessional advancement and favors from him, to tavern girls.

The diary as a form of evidence is skewed toward those privileged enough to have the leisure, skills, and self-importance to record and preserve their thoughts and activities. In looking at diaries, I might seem to suggest a top-down model of social change, by which a particu-lar ideal of marriage, as a partnership between equals, emerges among the privileged and then trickles down to their social inferiors. My atten-tion to the relationship between spouses and servants, however, should demonstrate that the appearance of mutuality between those on top is made possible by the presence and work of those at the bottom. Fur-thermore, especially since diarists are always more exceptional than rep-resentative, texts such as those by Byrd and Pepys serve as evidence not of actual changes in marital relations but of the terms and forms through which we have constructed modern marriage and written its history. Those terms and forms are based on skewed sources like these diaries. Yet, as I emphasize here, these diaries themselves record traces of how servants' and slaves' obscured labor helped to shape and enable a version of marriage that appears at first to be privileged and exclusive. They also provide glimpses of other histories altogether, such as the his-tory of slaves' "family, sex, and marriage," in which white masters and mistresses, if they appear at all, serve as obstacles and intruders, but also as subjects of dispute, targets for rage, and supplements.

William Byrd's and Samuel Pepys's diaries offer us remarkable access to a past that can seem alien and disturbing in its detailed accounts of how intimacy and violence intertwine. I contend that the Byrd and Pepys households are not shocking aberrations but rather revealing episodes in a history of marriage that informs our own experience. This argument might seem to underestimate the crucial otherness of the past and to fall into what is dismissed as "presentism"—that is, projecting our assumptions about modern marriage and households back onto the early modern and colonial periods.[88] In the Introduction, I discussed my commitment to a "presentist historicism." I am certainly mindful of E. P. Thompson's scathing put-down of Stone's *Family, Sex, and Marriage in England*: "The prospective purchaser is supposed to squeal excitedly: 'Darling, look, the history of *us*!'"[89] The colonial context is especially helpful in opening up to question who that "us" would be anyway; the violence on which I dwell might discourage identification. The elite Anglo-American tradition I am discussing always depended on exploitation; if it is our legacy it is one we might prefer not to acknowledge. But that is my point. Whereas presentism might err in the direction of neglecting important ruptures, shocked (or delighted) "discoveries" of the weirdness of past domestic arrangements and practices can also protect us from exploring disturbing continuities. The specifics of daily life in the Byrd and Pepys households, in which spouses live so intimately and so violently with their slaves and servants, expose one of the conditions under which a highly sentimentalized modern idea of marriage becomes possible. If little Jenny and Deb belong in a history of marriage, they do not go in the "dark ages" chapter. They are part of the history by which wives like Lucy Byrd and Elizabeth Pepys emerge as problems, combatants, and companions in their husbands' narratives. In attempting to explain her loneliness and need for a companion to her husband, Elizabeth Pepys presented him with her own account of her domestic and marital experience. But it "being writ in English [rather than his own cipher] and so in danger of being met with and read by others" and being "of so much disgrace to" Samuel, he "forced it from her and tore it."[90] As a consequence, Elizabeth, like Lucy, survives as a character in Samuel's account rather than the central figure in her own narrative of this famous, well-documented marriage.

The Byrd and Pepys diaries are not "stories" in the way that *Private Lives* or *Taming of the Shrew* is. But each has become a story in the hands of historians, who read it and represent it as one. As each husband's writings congeal into a story about marriage, the wife is cast into a role that is made possible by the servant's presence. By relieving the wife of some responsibilities, granting her authority, and deflecting some of her aggression away from her husband, the servant or slave actually makes room for the wife to expand into a more fully developed character in her husband's text. The servant's presence (and work) make it more practically and affectively possible to begin to imagine the wife as her husband's "companion."

The Taming of the Shrew

We have traveled from *Private Lives* on the London and New York stages in 1930, to conduct books published in the sixteenth and seventeenth centuries in England and circulated in both England and its colonies, to the Byrd plantation in Virginia in the early eighteenth century and the Pepys household in late seventeenth-century London. I land now on Shakespeare's play *The Taming of the Shrew*, first performed in 1594. As in earlier chapters, I have moved from the present backward on the assumption that the past is not just prologue. The past lives on in the present, often in unacknowledged ways that my methodology seeks to unmask. Like Genesis or the common law, Shakespeare's play is not safely confined to its moment of origin, unambiguously prior to the twentieth century.

The Taming of the Shrew, especially Katherina's final speech, commands a curious centrality in histories of marriage. In front of the assembled cast, but directing her remarks particularly at other wives, Katherina delivers what amounts to a sermon on marriage:

> Thy husband is thy lord, thy life, thy keeper,
> Thy head, thy sovereign; one that cares for thee
> And for thy maintenance; commits his body
> To painful labour both by sea and land,
> To watch the night in storms, the day in cold,
> Whilst thou li'st warm at home, secure and safe,
> And craves no other tribute at thy hands
> But love, fair looks, and true obedience—
> Too little payment for so great a debt.
> Such duty as the subject owes the prince,
> Even such a woman oweth to her husband.
> And when she is froward, peevish, sullen, sour,
> And not obedient to his honest will,
> What is she but a foul contending rebel
> And graceless traitor to her loving lord? (5.2.146–60)[91]

Critics debate Katherina's tone and purpose in making this speech. Does she earnestly describe a conversion experience, brokenly submit to taming, or exuberantly parody convention? The values she articulates have been described as obviously obsolete or strikingly new in the late sixteenth century.[92] But historians who enlist the play as evidence ignore questions of tone and posit a fairly simple correspondence between the central marriage the comedy depicts and mainstream attitudes toward marriage. Writing of early modern England, David Underdown claims that "although it's tempting for a modern audience to take Katherina's final speech ironically . . . the fact is that it expresses fairly accurately the ideal of husband-wife relations propounded by countless Elizabethan sermons and conduct books."[93] More surprisingly, historians of marriage in nineteenth- and twentieth-century America also cite Katherina's speech. In a section on "Husband's Duties" in *Man and Wife in America: A History*, Hendrik Hartog reads the passage for its "evocations of central themes of early modern political theory, themes of continuing significance in the nineteenth-century law of marriage. At the heart of Kate's language lay a conception of the reciprocity that ought to exist between rulers and ruled. . . . A wife ought not rebel against a loving lord. But nothing in the discourse required a wife to submit to cruelty or to tyranny."[94] In *Public Vows: A History of Marriage and the Nation*, Nancy Cott similarly emphasizes that "Kate justified wifely obedience by reciting the many benefits and protections a husband was obliged to give to his wife, including laboring to support her. Marriage governed the wife, but it also governed the husband. Like a good prince, a husband had to behave in certain ways to deserve his name and was not an unconstrained wielder of power."[95] Both historians use the speech to emphasize the analogy between public and private, and the reciprocity that structures ideals for marriage. Both readings, however, isolate the speech from its context. How does this vision of reciprocity relate to the taming process that precedes it and to the actual roles we have seen Petruchio and Katherina play? What has Petruchio done to earn obedience? Given the controversy that animates criticism of the play, and particularly of this speech, Katherina, the supposedly tamed shrew, would seem an unreliable spokeswoman for marital ideals. Yet, as Hartog's and Cott's two histories make clear, *The Taming of the Shrew* counts as evidence of attitudes toward marriage in nineteenth-century America as well as sixteenth-century England.

My point is not just that we miss the tone and the uneasy fit between the plot and this concluding speech when we read the speech out of context. We also miss layers of the household and community, the many characters in addition to husband and wife who affect and are affected by this rapprochement between them. Hartog and Cott do not remind us of the other men who wager with Petruchio about his wife's behavior and bear witness to his apparent victory, the other women over whom Katherina triumphs, or the servants over whom she will now be mistress. Historians ignore this context because in her final speech Katherina does.

The ideal as Katherina articulates it, whatever her tone, excludes any reference to the other members of the household who make that reciprocity possible. Whatever mutuality there might be in this sermon runs only between husband and wife in a closed circuit. Petruchio does not labor at land and sea; he stays home to tame his wife. Katherina does not lie warm at home, secure and safe, precisely because Petruchio is there disordering the bed clothes and keeping her awake. Natasha Korda points out that in her final speech Katherina erases her own work so as to position herself as a kept woman and indebted consumer rather than active domestic manager; I would add that, as part of this process, she also erases servants' work. Korda argues that the play recasts the shrew tradition in strikingly new terms, by showing that the housewife's subjectivity was constructed in relation to status objects.[96] Like Korda, I am interested in how a third term helps to maintain the relationship between husband and wife; in my analysis, domestic servants, those people who function in part as status objects in the household, occupy that position. In Petruchio's household, a large cast of servants, including four named male servants and several others unnamed, maintains domestic order. The ideal that Katherina articulates requires but erases their presence not only from the end of the play but, because of the appropriation of this moment, from the history of marriage.

Many scholars have emphasized that the presence of servants should remind us that the early modern home was not necessarily focused on the married couple and their children. Wendy Wall, for instance, advocates shifting our "focus away from the marital dyad" so as to reveal "the queer nature of the early modern household, not only the homoeroticism that pervades its turf, but also the unstable passions and irregular desires subtending its relationships."[97] I participate in the project of widening our focus from the married couple to the many people who populated early modern households. But I use that wider angle of vision in order to queer marriage itself. Where, if anywhere, are the "stable passions" and "regular desires" in the early modern home? When households do include married couples, as they did not inevitably do, how is that coupling supported and compromised by its interdependencies? Is marriage rendered "stable" and "regular" on the backs of servants?

As part of Petruchio's "politic" regime for taming Katherina, he relies on physical violence directed at those near her and enacted before her eyes. The first instance of violence we see in the play occurs when Petruchio "wrings" Grumio "by the ears" (1.2.17, stage directions). At the wedding, we're told, Petruchio cuffs the priest and throws winesops in the sexton's face (3.2). Grumio claims that on their way home from the wedding, Petruchio beats him because Katherina's horse stumbled (4.1); once at home, Petruchio berates and threatens his servants (4.1). The text implies that he may strike them, giving him lines such as "take that!" But, as Barbara Hodgdon shows, performance and editorial tradition have exaggerated Petruchio's violence, adding actions that are not made explicit in the Folio text, which leaves a production room to interpret the extent and meaning of Petruchio's violence.[98] We might imagine a Petruchio who is routinely violent or one who, in collusion with his servants, stages his own volatility to taming effect. But there is no question that the violence the text describes and implies is directed largely at Petruchio's subordinates. While it is "not aimed at Kate," she responds as if she is under threat.[99] At the wedding, we are told that Katherina "trembled and shook" (3.2.157); when Petruchio abuses his servants, she intervenes to stop or reprimand him (4.1).

Katherina does not learn to be violent from Petruchio. Before the taming process begins, she threatens to hit Hortensio on the head with a three-legged stool (1.1.64–65); she ties up Bianca and "strikes" her (2.1.21, stage directions); she breaks Hortensio's/Litio's head with the lute; and she "strikes" Petruchio (2.1.213, stage directions). Petruchio's servants assume that, after the marriage, Katherina will be violent toward them. Grumio warns Curtis that he will "soon feel" their new mistress's hand, "she being now at hand" (4.1.22–23). Indeed, later at Petruchio's house, Katherina "beats" Grumio for refusing to feed her (4.3.31, stage directions).

Katherina's violence toward characters other than Petruchio is not necessarily, or not only, "shrewish." That is, it is not invariably depicted as something she must learn not to do. For if the blow she strikes at Petruchio allies her to the shrew tradition, some of her other outbursts place her in the tradition of spirited English lasses or, as Petruchio says admiringly, "lusty wench[es]" (2.1.156). In this tradition, in which women's violence is celebrated as helpful and fun, women assault others (usually men) in the interests of English nationalism, sexual probity, and social order.[100] Long Meg of Westminster, and Moll Frith, the Roaring Girl, dress as men and use violence to defend themselves and other "good women" and to triumph over and humiliate men by being better fighters. But Moll Frith never marries, and Long Meg refuses to hit her husband, even in self-defense. After her husband decides to "try her manhood" by arming her with a staff and cudgeling her, she simply bows her head, drops to her knees, and submits to the beating. When her husband asks why she doesn't fight back, she replies: "Husband . . . whatsoever I have done to others, it behoveth me to be obedient towards you; and never shall it be said, though I can swinge a knave that wrongs me, that Long *Meg* shall be her husband's master: and therefore use me as you please."[101] Long Meg expressly distinguishes herself from shrews here, both by assuming that her husband is not "a knave that wrongs her," despite his cudgel, and in asserting that she does not want to master him. In all of these cases, women vent their spleen only against those who have no authority over them, and who are stout antagonists rather than dependents or superiors; the spectacle is therefore entertaining rather than threatening.

In the last scene of *The Taming of the Shrew*, Petruchio urges Katherina to play the role of lusty wench in her verbal sparring match with the widow: "To her, Kate!" (5.2.33). Even he, then, can applaud his wife's verbal wit and aggression, as long as it is not directed at him. Pamela Brown delineates a rich popular tradition in which women are the jesters and not inevitably the butts of jokes. As Brown shows, many popular texts, although not Shakespeare's *Taming of the Shrew*, value the shrew's lustiness and cleverness, and disdain meekness. For Brown, this set of popular values is summed up in the proverb "better a shrew than a sheep."[102] For Anthony Fletcher, both comic and serious depictions of violent marital conflict should remind us "of a huge untold story of the contestedness of English patriarchy within the early modern home." Bernard Capp proposes "to tell something of that story" especially focusing on women and how "without challenging the general principles of patriarchy, women frequently sought to negotiate the terms on which it operated within the home and neighbourhood, seeking an acceptable personal accommodation that would afford them some measure of autonomy and space, and a limited degree of authority."[103] *The Taming of the Shrew* can certainly offer some evidence toward the story of marital give and take. For my purposes, the issue is not whether or not Katherina is really tamed but rather how the play depicts what other members of the household and community contribute to and suffer for whatever rapprochement husband and wife finally achieve.

In *The Taming of the Shrew*, we begin with the familiar spectacle of a woman who abuses authority—Katherina binding and striking her younger sister—and then watch the process by which she learns the complex etiquette for domestic violence. Obviously, Petruchio teaches other husbands how to tame their unruly wives. Under his instruction, Katherina also learns not only how to be an obedient wife but how to assert dominance in more socially acceptable ways. (Like Lucy Byrd and Elizabeth Pepys, she never quite gets this right, since it is impossible to do so.) Although many critics argue that, as actress Fiona Shaw puts it, "Petruchio abuses a servant to teach her that the abuse of servants isn't right," I would argue that Petruchio inducts Katherina into a moral universe and network of power relations more complex than this.[104] This is especially clear in *The Taming of a Shrew*, in which the violence progresses differently. In this "alternate version" of the play, printed in 1594, the first violent act we witness is Ferando (the husband and master, or Petruchio figure) beating his servants in front of Katherina; as a stage direction explains, "He beates them all."[105] Here, Katherina's first act of violence is not to beat her tutor, her suitor, or her sister (none of whom she ever hits in this version), but to beat her husband's servant *after* she has watched him do so repeatedly.

While it is true in *The Shrew* that Katherina often resorts to violence "because of provocation or intimidation resulting from her status as a woman," as Coppélia Kahn has argued, she also acts out of an empowerment resulting from her status as a *gentle*woman.[106] She acts simultaneously out of gender subordination and class (or age) privilege. It is not just that class gets displaced onto gender, as Lynda Boose has brilliantly argued, but also that attention to gender alone can obscure conflicts of class in which Katherina is a privileged participant. Richard Burt argues that "Petruchio and Kate become emotionally closer whenever Petruchio enables Katherina to redirect the aggression he directs at her at another victim"; Burt identifies other women as the "socially acceptable target of aggression" for Katherina.[107] As Northrop Frye points out: "When we first see Katharina, she is bullying Bianca, and when we take our leave of her she is still bullying Bianca, but has learned how to do it with social approval on her side."[108] What Katherina learns is not to be less aggressive, but to redirect her aggression toward more appropriate targets. When Katherina dominates servants and other women rather than resisting her father and husband, her conduct is presented as acceptable, even admirable. That Bianca becomes an acceptable target by the end of the play—a "breeching scholar"—suggests how the balance of power has shifted between the sisters. In her violent outbursts, then, Katherina exhibits "the simultaneous recognition of [her] own oppression and a will-to-power" that Kim Hall identifies in some women's writings; she also participates in the dramatic representation of "aggressive female characters [who] manipulate and coerce other female characters" to which Douglas Bruster has drawn attention.[109] As Hall's and Bruster's work makes clear, women become acceptable targets of violence especially when they are marked as inferior to or weaker than the women who dominate them.

In the taming process, however, Petruchio does not simply teach Katherina to look for female scapegoats; instead, he instructs her to look down the social scale. In her first bout with Petruchio, she imperiously advises him that she is not one of his subordinates: "Go, fool, and whom thou keep'st command" (2.1.247). Marriage transforms her into one whom he keeps and therefore can command. But it also confers on her more authority than she exercised before. After the wedding, at the same time that Petruchio demonstrates that Katherina cannot do as she pleases, and that she cannot command him, he also suggests that she look elsewhere for the pleasures of domination, to those who should "attend" on her: "*They* shall go forward, Kate, at thy command. / Obey the bride, you that attend on her" (3.2.211–12; my emphasis).

The turning point in Katherina's assumption of command precedes her submission to Petruchio in the famous Sun and Moon scene (4.5). It occurs in the course of the scene in which she "beats" Grumio because he refuses her request for food, teases her, and "triumph[s] upon . . . [her] misery" (4.3.34). At this moment in Petruchio's household, Katherina's relation both to him and to the servants is uncertain. Grumio acts as if he is Petruchio's ally here, empowered to thwart and discipline Katherina. But Katherina tests out domestic authority (on Petruchio's model). As she learns, she can domineer over anyone except Petruchio. Indeed, Grumio, who has violated class hierarchy throughout the play, "knocking" Petruchio, tormenting Katherina, and hitting a fellow servant, becomes a more obedient and less raucous servant, and therefore less visible, as Katherina submits to taming. This slap does, then, seem to discipline him.

Katherina not only shifts the targets of her aggression, she also shifts her tactics; this exchange with Grumio is also pivotal in that process. Throughout *The Taming of the Shrew*, physical and verbal violence are complexly interconnected. Katherina's speech is presented as abusive, disorderly, and wounding; when Hortensio enters pilloried in the lute, he conflates Katherina's verbal and physical assaults: "And with that word she struck me on the head" (2.1.149). This commingling of physical injury and discursive harm is not unique to the shrew. Grumio warns that Petruchio can use rhetorical figures to "disfigure" Katherina (1.2.108–9). Grumio himself uses violence to command attention. Asking Curtis to lend him his ear, he then cuffs him: "This cuff was but to knock at your ear and beseech listening" (4.1.47–48). Even in the play's last scene, words can wound: Katherina complains of the Widow's "mean meaning," and Petruchio remarks that jests about shrewish wives can "glance away from" him and "maim" the other two husbands "outright" (5.2.61–62). The text does not make clear precisely how Katherina complies with Petruchio's directive that she "swinge" Bianca and the widow "soundly forth unto their husbands" (104), or by what means she "brings" these "froward wives / As prisoners to her womanly persuasion" (119–20). Here, as elsewhere in the play, the relationship between persuasion and coercion is not clear. The focus has shifted from overt physical violence (striking, and beating, to use the play's own vocabulary) to discursive domination (the longest speech in the play, as many critics have remarked). In relation to more acceptable targets and by means of more acceptable tactics, Katherina still dominates others.

I am *not* arguing here that Katherina and Petruchio are "equals" in the culture of domestic violence.[110] He clearly has the upper hand because he controls Katherina's access to material resources (like food), he is stronger, he has more lines, he addresses the audience directly and when he is alone (we never see Katherina alone), and, as the husband, he is assumed to be the one who should be "on top." Indeed, he rewards

Katherina's submission to him by authorizing her to domineer over others. But rather than condemning Katherina's violence or self-assertion entirely, Petruchio redirects her claims to mastery away from him. The two remain equals with regard to their desire to domineer over their own servants and the outside world. Katherina recognizes only Petruchio as her superior. In a fairytale logic, then, Petruchio seems to get a wife who is a sheep with him and a shrew to servants and other women.

Attending to women's authority in the household enables us to consider the ways in which the couple is embedded in a web of relations, a web in which the wife is often a powerfully authoritative rather than subordinate figure, in which she wields the rod rather than being subject to it. *The Taming of the Shrew* resolves the problem of the battle for the breeches by allowing the wife to wield the rod instead: to be both subordinate and authoritative, her husband's equal in some registers and his subordinate in others. It thus shows, in a way distinct from yet related to *Private Lives*, that violence is not only the problem but part of the solution. *The Taming of the Shrew* also suggests a clever answer to the conundrum of desire and violence. A wife can remain a desirably "lusty wench" by being only partially tamed. Thus *Private Lives* and *The Taming of the Shrew*, like Byrd's and Pepys's diaries, suggest that marital harmony depends upon rather than standing distinct from carefully managed domestic violence.

What has been gained in grouping these generically and chronologically disparate texts? All participate in a long-standing, unfinished Anglo-American inquiry into the volatile combination of equality, desire, and violence in marriage. Equality and its attendant violence can be relished (as in *Private Lives*), or displaced from spouses onto more suitable, that is subordinate, targets, such as slaves (as in the Byrd and Pepys diaries). In *The Taming of the Shrew* antagonism between spouses is both relished and displaced. *Private Lives* draws our attention to the sexual charge granted to both equality and its correlary, combat; the Byrd and Pepys diaries direct our attention to the margins, to the figures who support the marital dyad by doing the work and taking the beatings. *The Taming of the Shrew* conjoins these two narratives—the account of chastisements and the stylish comedy of marital conflict—and resolves the conflicts and contradictions I have used those texts to highlight. In its conclusion, it puts an end to the combat between the spouses, as Coward's comedy refuses to do; it also suppresses the role of the servants in its own resolution. Perhaps *The Taming of the Shrew* has won its place in histories of marriage precisely because it indulges the pleasures of combat and the violence written into ideals of marriage and then protects us from that insight with a celebration of "peace . . . , and love, and quiet life" (*Taming of the Shrew* 5.2.108).

Home Discomforts

The Byrds and the Pepyses may seem historically remote; Amanda and Elyot, Katherina and Petruchio seem too stylized to be real and therefore are detached from daily life. But in the early twenty-first century as in the early eighteenth or late sixteenth, in actual households as on the stage, marriage is still married to domestic service—to an intimate and exploitative relation to housework. Although slavery was abolished in the United States in 1866, and servants began to disappear from American households in the early twentieth century, they reentered in one form or the other in the 1970s, when women began joining the paid work force in greater numbers.[111] Having two paychecks can equalize spouses' involvement in family decisions and control over resources, but that apparent equality is often subsidized through the work of other people, who enter the home to clean it or care for children, or who operate at sites outside the home to support it. Depending on anonymous "services" rather than intimately known servants, and sending domestic work (such as child care and laundry) outside the home, can obscure this fact. "Servants" are still there but we might not see them or know their names. Barbara Ehrenreich points to the booming business in cleaning services and the ways in which such services protect customers from having to deal directly with those who clean their houses. According to Ehrenreich, "managers of the new corporate cleaning services . . . attribute their success not only to the influx of women into the workforce but to the tensions over housework that arose in its wake." As a result, some corporate cleaning services even credit themselves with saving marriages.[112]

Critics of the solution of outsourcing housework point to four main problems with this reliance on paid domestic help. First, domestic workers are often exploited—ill paid and without benefits. Exposing this exploitation is Ehrenreich's project in her chapter on cleaning services in the best-selling and influential *Nickel and Dimed*. This problem could be addressed by offering domestic workers better pay and benefits, unless, of course, there is something inherently wrong with depending on someone else in this way.

Second, this solution deflects demand away from men without requiring them to do what many women perceive as their fair share. As Arlie Hochschild has documented, women who work outside the home continue to work a second shift at home, and to bear more of the responsibility for child care, food preparation, laundry, and cleaning. Hochschild documents women's disappointment when men hire help rather than sharing housework and child care with their partners. For such women, "money could not buy a complete solution." While couples at different income levels experience conflicts differently, according to Hochschild "the tug between traditional and egalitarian models of marriage runs from top to bottom of the class ladder."[113]

Third, as a result of the fact that many women remain largely responsible for all the kinds of work the "second shift" includes, they also get the blame for exploiting domestic workers, who are often other women.[114] Such critiques suggest that some privileged women achieve equality with men in the workplace on the backs of other women.[115] This pattern of blame helps to reinforce the assumption that women are, after all, the ones responsible for running and cleaning a house. If they cannot or will not do it, then they are responsible, practically and morally, for hiring others to do it. It is often calculated that the cost of prepared foods, housecleaning, and child care come directly out of the wife's wage alone, thus nullifying it.[116] Also, as Delphy and Leonard remind us, "having servants in itself involves work for women. Servants have to be hired, trained and managed."[117] Critiques of women's exploitation of other women also ignore the fact that men's engagement in work outside the home has always been subsidized by women's work; those women were usually their wives.

The final objection to hired domestic help seems at odds with the others, especially the concern about exploiting workers. This is the claim that hired domestic workers do not do a very good job. Ehrenreich's description of the cleaning protocols of the Merry Maids, the national service for which she worked, emphasizes that they value appearance over sanitation, and stresses both the repulsiveness of cleaning someone else's toilet and the creepiness of having a cleaning service bring other clients' germs into your home. While Ehrenreich censures clients' apparent disdain for their cleaners, her vivid descriptions of unsanitary practices suggest that it is unadvisable to hire a cleaning service because they are sloppy. You're really better off cleaning your house yourself; it will be cleaner and you will feel better. On this point, Ehrenreich is strangely aligned with a writer like Cheryl Mendelson, whose rapturous and rigorous celebration of housecleaning in her book *Home Comforts: The Art and Science of Keeping House* attracted feminist bewilderment and indignation. Mendelson insists that "housework in itself is physically and emotionally pleasant and restorative. . . . Your own housework can be a joy to you because of the way it is integrated into your life and because of your intense identification with your home and its contents. It does not feel the same to the hired worker."[118] While I do not doubt that last statement, I do question whether joy and intense identification necessarily attend cleaning one's own house and things. Mendelson seems to suggest that, after all, one cannot hire a wife, because of the ways that job description requires a heady combination of pleasure, entitlement, and unshared work. The dissatisfaction dogging evaluations of hired domestic workers reveals that these household tasks are still weighted with expectations workers cannot really meet.

The morality invested in cleaning one's own house is thus a complicated one. It is not just a matter of not exploiting someone else. If it were, then one could simply pay better. Ehrenreich allows herself a moment of boastfulness:

> But I will say this for myself: I have never employed a cleaning person or service . . . even though various partners and husbands have badgered me over the years to do so. . . . Partly this comes from having a mother who believed that a self-cleaned house was the hallmark of womanly virtue. . . . But mostly I rejected the idea, even after all my upper-middle-class friends had, guiltily and as covertly as possible, hired help for themselves, because this is just not the kind of relationship I want to have with another human being.[119]

Ehrenreich mentions partners and husbands who badgered her to get help but not the division of labor in those relationships. Her presumably female friends, not their male partners, give in and hire help "for themselves." The good wife and mother cleans her own house; male partners and husbands badger her to get help but they don't do their share. It is hers to manage well or to dump on others. The self-reliance of which she boasts—instilled by her mother, upheld despite the hectoring of male cohabitants—is a distinctly feminine one, although Ehrenreich does not acknowledge this. The assumption is that it is women who hire cleaners, because it remains women who are responsible for housework, women who feel guilt.[120] I risk exacerbating that guilt by pointing out that the nameless teams who work for Merry Maids are more like little Jenny than we might hope. But my point is that their labors don't just enable women to work. They underwrite the fiction of spouses as equals and companions.

Although Ehrenreich connects her self-righteous housecleaning to her mother's sense of "womanly virtue," she does not connect the relationship she does not want to have to hired help to those relationships she did want (with her partners and husbands). As she boasts about the servants who have never been in her house, those serial partners and husbands fade into anonymity. My argument in this chapter has been that the "unwanted," covertly conducted, sometimes violently exploitative relationship with the supplemental servant underwrites the marriage of apparently equal partners. Ehrenreich's book is about wage labor and not about marriage. But as this eruption in her text reveals, the two histories intertwine. Household help does not just subsidize domestic comfort; it subsidizes middle-class marital harmony. As one of my own mentors once advised, "don't fight about housework. Hire help." In all of the texts that I've discussed in this chapter, the servants, those apparently minor characters, have turned out to be central to the precarious equilibrium spouses can achieve. At the simplest level, I want us to notice them and the complexities of interdependence they represent. While I cannot fix this particular model of marriage, since that would involve a radical reorganization of society, I seek as a first step to excavate the tangled histories that link companionship and subjection in marriage and to raise the question of what it would mean to conceive an equality that is not underwritten by someone else's subordination.

Chapter Four

How a Maiden Keeps Her Head: Anne Boleyn, Elizabeth I, and the Perils of Marriage

Historical novels offer an escape from the daily grind of domestic conflict about who washes the dishes or who does the laundry. Novels about Renaissance queens are consistently popular, in part because, while they describe the arduous work of preparing food and medicine, emptying slopjars, or making and cleaning clothes in early modern England, they also make it clear that our heroines do not do this work. They do not even directly supervise those who do. Yet the novels do not use these apparently exceptional characters and their remarkable stories to evade the conflicts of modern marriage. Instead, they use them to explore lingering unease about whether marriage constitutes a sufficiently or reliably happy ending for women. While there are historical novels set in many different periods, those set in the Tudor period are especially focused on marriage. Indeed, the Tudor court is almost a "brand"; no matter the decade or the author, readers can expect to find negative attitudes toward marriage in novels about Tudor queens. These novels are usually written by women and their readers are largely but not exclusively female.[1] Placing their narratives in the Tudor court, the novelists are free to be critical of marriage because they can suggest that marriage was too restrictive *then*, for *those* privileged women. Yet the novels consistently suggest that the problem the heroines face is a definition of marriage that is both particular to the Tudor period and still recognizable to readers.

While popular biographers and novelists share somewhat reductive assumptions about what marriage meant for women in the Tudor period, popular biographers articulate those assumptions most directly and authoritatively. Marriage, they explain, offered women a route to social advancement and security, yet it also required their "subjection," "subjugation," or "self-abnegation." According to Alison Weir, "for women, even queens, marriage often brought with it total subjection to and domination by a domestic tyrant." Although a clever royal bride might achieve some power and influence, "such status and power emanated solely from her husband. She enjoyed no freedoms but those he permitted her. Without him, she was nothing." As Weir stresses in her biography of Henry VIII's wives, his third wife, Jane Seymour, "took as her motto the legend 'Bound to obey and serve,'" while Catherine Howard, his fifth wife, took the motto "'No other will than his.' They, like the King's other wives, accepted their subjugation; it was the price of their queenship and of marriage."[2]

Similarly, Antonia Fraser reminds the readers of *her* biography of Henry's wives that "marriage was the triumphal arch through which women, almost without exception, had to pass in order to reach the public eye. And after marriage followed, in theory, the total self-abnegation of the woman." But she also emphasizes that "rich, feisty characters flourished in this atmosphere of theoretical subjection." For Fraser, Henry's wives were such characters. They were more subjected than most: if a wife's subjection "were held to be true of ordinary wives bowing before ordinary husbands, how much more awe-inspiring must the power of a royal husband have been!" But this just makes their feistiness all the more "exhilarating."[3] The perceived conjunction of a constraining institution and exhilaratingly feisty women helps to explain why biographers and novelists keep revisiting the history of Henry VIII's marriages. His wives' stories make it possible to explore the fear that marriage is repressive, even deadly, for women and to reassure readers that some can outwit "theoretical subjection."

In historical fiction set in England, the most popular queens are a mother and daughter famous for their extreme experiences of marriage: Anne Boleyn and Elizabeth I. Henry VIII infamously divorced Catherine of Aragon, his wife of almost twenty-four years (1509–33), to marry Anne. Divorced in favor of a younger woman, Catherine might seem a logical protagonist for a novel that scrutinizes the costs and benefits of marriage for women. While there have been several novels about her, she does not command the level of attention that has been devoted to Anne or Elizabeth. Considerable evidence survives about her marriage to Henry, since it was so long, yet she is a shadowy figure even in television series about Henry's wives, as if the story doesn't really begin until she is out of the way and Henry undertakes the urgent, bloody process of securing her replacement. Readers might be expected to identify with what happened to Catherine—a contested divorce—more than the brutal end met by her successor.[4] But it is Anne who dominates representations, in part because, in the end, she becomes the object of an excessive show of husbandly and kingly force. Three years after Henry married Anne, she was tried on trumped-up charges of adultery with five different men including her brother (all of whom were executed), as well as "treasonable conspiracy to procure the king's death," and was convicted and beheaded.[5] This is both a spectacular punishment of the other woman, if one imagines the first wife's point of view, and a reminder of what husbands and kings can do. Henry and Anne's daughter, Elizabeth, never married. Popular representations of Anne and Elizabeth, taken together, suggest that the conflict between the self-possessed woman and marriage ends in stalemate: one either marries and dies or avoids marriage altogether.

Anne Boleyn and Elizabeth are especially useful for my purposes because each was always at the center of what Susan Frye has called a "competition for representation."[6] That is, rumors and stories always circulated about them and shaped their options. As a consequence, I will not contrast the historical truth about these queens with how novels depict them. Instead, I will examine how, why, and to what effect particular stories have been told about them from the start. Here again, I examine "fantasies of past fantasies."[7] Although it is certainly possible to dwell on the inaccuracies, inventions, and distortions in recent historical novels, that is not the most useful approach. It is more interesting to think in terms of the continuities between present and past that the novelists reveal rather than the nuances of historical difference they ignore. As I will show, when characters in these novels explain their reservations about marriage, they do so in terms strikingly familiar from my preceding chapters. Whether the novelists know the complexities of this history or not, they know that a particular way of thinking about marriage is associated with the early modern period and that the risks of marriage might be vividly depicted through the stories of these two queens. These novels are "historical," then, not just because they choose to situate their stories in the sixteenth century, but also because the terms available for imagining marriage are not projected onto the past as much as inherited from it. We should view these popular novels not as anachronistic but as intuitive; they identify insights into marriage that readers have inherited, as Elizabeth is supposed to have inherited them from her mother.[8]

Critics suggest that popular re-creations of the Renaissance, whether at tourism sites or in mass media fictions, serve a double purpose: in Stratford, England, for instance, Barbara Hodgdon identifies a "double story" that "insists on fixing the space in past time while simultaneously denying time altogether" and creating the "illusion of time past as time present."[9] In the particular case of representations of Tudor marriage, we find a similar doubleness. The novels claim both that daring, path-breaking heroines demand love and sexual fulfillment from marriage (thus connecting them to readers in the present) and that they fear marriage as restrictive, even dangerous (because of the repressive constraints attendant on marriage, depicted as both "historical" and as recognizable).

By emphasizing this doubleness, I want to draw attention to the critique of heterosexual marriage that accompanies the novels' presumptive heterosexuality. Historians of sexuality have shown that neither the terms nor the categories of "heterosexual" and "homosexual" existed in the early modern period; sexual practices did not necessarily translate into identities; and sexual identities were therefore less rigidly defined, less legible, than they are today. This complexity does not generally inform popular novels set in the period. Most novels about Anne and Elizabeth assume the heroines to be heterosexual; they assume what "heterosexual" would mean; and they assume that intercourse and marriage should be the shape of a happy heterosexual ending. As Hodgdon has argued, popular representations of Queen Elizabeth "work to erase . . . contradictions and to reinscribe her within the binaries of dominant heterosexuality."[10] In many ways, Hodgdon's analysis extends to the novels I discuss here. Yet such an analysis belies the strikingly negative attitudes toward heterosexual marriage that these novels consistently assign to their protagonists, who despair as to whether women can combine erotic fulfillment, independence, and marriage. In short, the presumptively heterosexual queens in these novels feel rather queer about marriage. Whatever Anne's and Elizabeth's own desires might have been, their stories invite readers to look askance at marriage, questioning how successfully it fulfills women's needs, whether or not they are queens. These queens confront an extreme version of a problem all wives face when marriage is construed as a zero-sum game—how to enter into marriage and gain more than lose? The message they convey about heterosexual marriage is thus mixed: marriage is desirable; it is optional; and it is a potentially fatal conflict in which one must either kill in self-defense or risk erasure or annihilation.

I will consider first how popular biographers and novelists depict Elizabeth's fear of men and marriage as her "legacy" from her disgraced, beheaded mother. I next show how Elizabeth and her contemporaries represent her marriage as a no-win proposition. Thus the depictions of marriage as a zero-sum game in popular biographies and novels have their roots in Elizabeth's own reign and its seventeenth-century afterlife. Finally, I consider novels by best-selling author Philippa Gregory about early modern women who are not queens but rather their sisters or servants. Gregory's heroines boldly assert their fear and resentment of marriage; ultimately, however, they find in marriage and motherhood greater happiness than is possible in the corridors of power, or so we're told.

A Dreadful Whirlpool from the Past: Anne Boleyn's Legacy

The Anne Boleyn one encounters in novels is a somewhat freakish character. While early mythmakers, such as John Foxe, emphasized Anne's erudition and her commitment to reform, novels instead emphasize her smoldering attractiveness and ruthless cunning.[11] They thus take up the position of those detractors who contributed to her spectacular downfall. They also dwell on her supposed physical deformities—a sixth finger and a large wen under her chin, which she disguised with the long sleeved, high necked gowns she made fashionable. While the image of a deformed temptress is captivating, our only evidence of these deformities is a description published almost fifty years after Anne's death by Nicholas Sander, who sought to discredit both the Reformation and Anne's daughter Elizabeth by inventing Anne as a moral and corporal monster.[12] Whereas scholarly biographers raise questions about which stories about Anne are true, novels privilege the sensational stories, whatever their provenance. Who can resist a six-fingered Anne who bewitches her lover, poisons his wife and daughter, and has sex with her brother? These lurid details work to suggest that Anne isn't like other women; perhaps that's why she ended so badly.

Why were Anne's contemporaries willing to believe the charge that she was guilty of extraordinary, murderous, treasonous sexual excess and imprudence? One biographer, David Starkey, suggests that the monstrous caricatures of Anne—in her husband's charges, in the libels spread about her by her detractors, and in the gossip that now animates biographies and novels alike—built on an assumption that Anne's ambition and self-assertion were monstrous in themselves. A woman like Anne, the assumption goes, could not really be a wife, and certainly not a good one. "For such a woman marriage was a restriction and a husband a nuisance. Hence the culminating charge that she had conspired Henry's death; had promised to marry one or other of her lovers when he was gone; and, in a sort of travesty of the marriage vows, had affirmed 'that she would never love the King in her heart'."[13] Starkey here exposes the assumption that an ambitious woman is inevitably adulterous and murderous. Everything contemporaries knew about Anne prepared them to believe even the most outrageous charges against her because these seemed logical extensions of what they already accepted as true. She had achieved her status as wife by disregarding all of the expectations about what wives should be like.

Yet novels about Anne also appeal to readers by saying that even Anne is more like most women than unlike them. In venturing some sympathy for Anne, novels simultaneously associate the constraints of marriage with the past, and with the unusual circumstances of marrying a king, and associate self-assertion with the woman of the future. Thus Anne becomes a modern woman, demanding power, as well as love and respect from her husband—but before her time. The very qualities that can degenerate into the "monstrous caricature" of the adulterous traitor also link her to readers. The novels suggest that her needs, so recognizable *now*, simply could not be asserted, let alone satisfied, *then*. They also associate those needs, as did Anne's contemporaries, with violence.

Whereas Jean Plaidy's novel *The Lady in the Tower* (1986) depicts an Anne who thinks she would have found "greater happiness" in a love match and "looked upon my brilliant future as a kind of consolation prize,"[14] Suzannah Dunn's novel, *The Queen of Subtleties*, published almost twenty years later, presents Anne as more openly ambitious. Dunn assigns Anne strikingly anachronistic language to express her goals:

Imagine having found your soulmate—the luck of it, the joy of it—and, against gargantuan odds, having married him. Then comes a stunning baby, plus a second on the way. Imagine being at the same time at the very top, doing the job you always knew you'd do better than anyone else. Now imagine a mad old woman claiming that none of it was ever yours to have: it's all hers. And, unbelievably, she has the ear of the people, and their hearts; she has them under a spell that you, for all of your cleverness, can't break.

Dunn's Anne has it all: a "soulmate," a "stunning baby," and a "job." Yet Dunn also associates this anachronistic vision of female happiness with murder. Since Henry's first wife, Catherine, and his daughter, Mary, stand in her way, Anne reassures herself that "if the worst came to the worst, two bodies wouldn't be so hard to get out of the way."[15] Just as Starkey argues that, for Anne's least sympathetic contemporaries, her ambition made her monstrous, so in Dunn's novel the desire to "have it all" slides inexorably into the willingness to kill for it. To be a wife who has a soulmate, children, and the job she knows she can do better than anyone is to be, inevitably (as this logic goes), a killer.

While most popular accounts of Anne tend to agree on her ruthless ambition, most do not go quite this far in depicting her as willing to resort to violence, emphasizing instead her calculating manipulation of sex. Anne's sister, Mary, might have been willing to be Henry's mistress, but Anne "would be Queen or nothing."[16] Most accounts agree that, to achieve this goal, Anne had to withhold sex from Henry for as long as possible without discouraging his sexual interest altogether. The irony that Anne strategized to be wife and queen, rather than royal mistress, and thereby ensured that she would be executed rather than pensioned off, underpins the plotting of these novels. They build slowly toward the marriage and then draw to a conclusion rapidly thereafter. The time scheme of Henry and Anne's relationship did follow this pattern of protracted delay, consummation, and rapid dissolution. Five or six years elapsed between Henry's first indications of interest in Anne (in 1525-26) and when the couple began cohabiting (in 1532). They transacted a secret marriage in January 1533, and their daughter Elizabeth was born September 7, 1533. Then the marriage began to disintegrate. In May 1536 Anne was convicted on charges of adultery, incest, and treason; she was beheaded on May 19. Henry was betrothed to Jane Seymour the next day; she gave birth to their son Edward on October 12 and died twelve days later.[17]

In response to this timeline, offered in its barest outlines here, novelists tend to stress that Anne had power over Henry only as long as she sustained but did not satiate his sexual interest. The novels' plots collude in this ruthless courtship logic. Anne is most interesting as a protagonist before she is a wife. Before consummation and then marriage, she has will, desire, and cunning. Afterward, she is consistently outmaneuvered. In Plaidy's *Lady in the Tower*, Anne comments that it was probably her indifference "which had enslaved the King. He had been used to surrenders . . . and he had come to suspect that in his case the hunt was over almost before it began. That I was not ready to give way, set me apart and made the chase more exciting." In this novel and in others, once Anne gives in to Henry, their sexual encounters quickly lose excitement; when Henry makes Anne his queen, he reminds her that he is the king and she his subject and that he can lower her just as he has raised her up.[18] As it is told and retold, Anne's story becomes a prescription for female sexuality: hold out! Weirdly, even a version of the story written for girls—Carolyn Meyer's *Doomed Queen Anne*—dwells on this narrative of strategic sexual deferral.[19]

If Anne's story is presented as a cautionary tale about courtship, sex, and marriage, then the person who is most instructed by its lesson is usually taken to be Elizabeth. In Robin Maxwell's *The Secret Diary of Anne Boleyn*, Elizabeth reads the diary her mother has left for her and realizes that

> Henry had fought at Anne's side for as long as she was strong, as long as she withheld from him that which he desired above all. Her sex. The moment she had succumbed to his advances and, thought Elizabeth bitterly, to the holy estate of matrimony, he had turned on her. Viciously. Suddenly. Sickeningly. He'd punctured the steely armor, impaled the woman he had once loved in the vulnerable place between her thighs.[20]

Attributing to Elizabeth a vision of sex as an impalement, a wounding, a defeat in battle, the novel helps to explain why Elizabeth did not marry and how Anne's fate and Elizabeth's own choices might have been connected. In her secret diary, Maxwell's Anne concludes: "Tomorrow I die because I lusted not for flesh, but to command my own destiny. This is not a womanly act, I know, but I have oft thought that in this way my spirit is much the same as a man's." She insists that she feels no regret. "So, daughter, tho I have suffered and shall soon die for this selfish need to rule my fate, I beg of you to do the same. Let no man be your master. Love, lust, marry if you will, but hold apart from all men a piece of your spirit."[21] Although Maxwell's Anne suggests that Elizabeth can "marry if she will," Anne's own story also suggests that avoiding marriage is the best way to "hold apart . . . a piece of your spirit." In the novels about Anne Boleyn and Elizabeth, a wife cannot command her destiny. Anne is able to do so only until she succeeds in getting Henry to marry her and thereby succumbs to a much less powerful, more precarious status.

Academic research on Elizabeth I continues to debate what it means that Elizabeth never married. Did she refuse to, fail to, or "in the event" just never wind up doing it? Did she deliver a "resounding No" to marriage, a typically indecisive "maybe," or a tentative but ineffectual "yes"?[22] Some scholars emphasize that Elizabeth's attitudes toward marriage varied over time according to the proposed suitor and other circumstances.[23] Some dwell on her political motives for remaining unmarried;[24] others invite us to consider Elizabeth's desires. Was her desire thwarted or facilitated by her unmarried life? Was her sexuality against, outside, or simply apart from marriage?[25] Should we define her by the marriage she refused or failed or couldn't manage, or by the alternative state she positively chose?

In popular biographies and novels, the answer is simple. Elizabeth did not marry because she had learned from her mother and stepmothers that it was better not to. Since Elizabeth was only two years old when Anne was beheaded, and we have no record that she ever referred directly to her mother, it is hard to know what her attitude toward her mother might have been.[26] But novelists and biographers alike assume that, as Alison Weir puts it, "what is certain is that the knowledge of what had happened to Anne Boleyn had a traumatic effect on Elizabeth, and may well have crippled her emotionally for life."[27] In her "feminist reinterpretation" of the saga of Henry's wives, Karen Lindsey reflects upon the lesson Elizabeth might have learned from her mother, her halfsister, and her stepmothers.

Marriage . . . was not safe. Mary had destroyed herself through marriage. Ann Boleyn had briefly gained power by marrying Henry VIII, then lost both the power and her life. And her successors? The insipid Jane Seymour had died providing Henry with a son. Kathryn Howard had been the king's pretty toy, crushed and discarded when it became soiled. Wise, motherly Katherine Parr had survived two marriages, barely escaped execution in a third, and then died in childbirth after being betrayed by the one husband she really loved. Even the ghost of Henry's first wife haunted Elizabeth. The daughter of the most powerful ruler in Europe had been abandoned when her body could no longer offer pleasure or produce a son. Only one of Henry's wives had lived happily, the wife who was not a wife, Anne of Cleves. But she lived in obscurity. Elizabeth had learned her lesson from all these women. For fifty years she reigned alone, her own consort, her own ruler.[28]

In Lindsey's vision, Elizabeth learns that marriage always entails risk and loss for women and often leads to their deaths—and so she becomes "her own consort."

Novel after novel suggests that Anne Boleyn's fate is at the root of the supposed mystery of why Elizabeth never married. Most novels about Elizabeth make some reference to her mother. Again and again, we find a queen who chooses queenship over marriage and does so in part because her history suggests that the two roles are incompatible and that marriage is a death sentence. In *The Tidal Poole*, the second in Karen Harper's series of mysteries featuring Elizabeth, the young queen visits her mother's unmarked grave, under the paving stones of St. Peter in Chains Church on the grounds of the Tower, and identifies herself as "your Bess grown and now queen in my own right with no husband to obey or please."[29] In Fiona Buckley's *Doublet Affair*, sleuth Ursula Blanchard explains:

The Queen isn't cold of heart. . . . She fears marriage. When she was two, her father had her mother beheaded. She was too young then to understand what it meant, but when she was eight he had her young stepmother Catherine Howard beheaded as well. The one illuminated the other. Anne Boleyn and Catherine Howard both saw an adoring husband turn into the monster who sighed [sic] their death warrant. Elizabeth will not forget.[30]

Harper and Buckley both depict Elizabeth as deeply suspicious of men because of her mother's (and stepmothers') fates. Elizabeth wants power over men and is unwilling to grant them any power over her.

Most novels include some acknowledgment that, as a queen regnant rather than a queen consort, Elizabeth would not be as vulnerable as Henry's wives had been, but they presume that Elizabeth has compelling reservations, rooted in her childhood, about men and marriage. In Rosalind Miles's *I, Elizabeth*, the queen explains to readers that it is through reflecting on her parents' relationship that she has come to realize "that a maiden should keep her head," by which she means that she should preserve her maidenhead or virginity and thus her own life by having the sense to "have the power without losing the power." In this novel, Elizabeth constantly articulates a fear of "what marriage was, what marriage did, even to a queen"—a fear that is based, as usual, on her observation of other royal women. As a consequence, she decides, "if I had to marry, I would much rather *be* a husband than have one! For I had seen at first hand with Dame Katherine and sister Mary what it was to be a wife, to be subject to a man and bound to obey his will. *In marriage men gain, women lose!*[31] In that last phrase, Miles's Elizabeth boldly articulates the marital economy of scarcity, in which one spouse's benefit comes at the other's expense.

In most novels, Elizabeth confides in readers her canny understanding of this zero-sum game, her assumption that it is inescapable, and her determination to wind up on the plus side. In Jean Plaidy's *Queen of This Realm*, Elizabeth reflects at the end of her life on how she has differed from other women: "I did not seek to subjugate myself to men. I demanded their submission to me." As to why she never married, she explains that, while she liked men, and even preferred them to other women,

> I wanted perpetual courtship, for when the fortress is stormed and brought to surrender, the battle is lost. The relationship between men and women is a battle of the sexes with the final submission of the woman to the man. The act itself is the symbol of the triumph of the strong over the weak. I was determined never to give any man that triumph. The victory must always be mine. . . . I wanted, during every moment of my life, to be in absolute control.

Casting her relationships to men in terms of a "battle" in which only one can achieve "triumph" or "victory," Elizabeth explains that she could only ensure that she would "remain the commander of them all" by foregoing both intercourse and marriage.[32]

In Susan Kay's novel *Legacy* (1985), Elizabeth explains in the most vivid terms her shrewd calculation about how much she has to lose and how little to gain in marriage. This novel also makes the link between Anne's history and Elizabeth's choices central to its assessment of Elizabeth's character, choosing as its title the key word in my study, signaling a relationship between the present and the past. In this novel, Elizabeth is Anne's legacy to the world; hating and distrusting men is Anne's legacy to Elizabeth. After her mother is executed, Elizabeth beheads one of her dolls and then keeps that doll as a cherished, hidden reminder of the debt she owes the past and of the future to which she must not submit. Early in the novel Anne says to the toddler Elizabeth, who has been waving at Henry and been spurned, "when he rots in hell you will be King and Queen both and the whole of England will wave to you. . . . Let no man take it from you!"[33] From the start of the novel, Elizabeth declares that she will never marry. But the novel's most remarkable passage, for my purposes here, is one in which Elizabeth explains why she cannot marry Robert Dudley, Earl of Leicester, who is consistently depicted in novels as her greatest love and most likely mate.

> Death waited in a lost corridor of her mind, waited for Robin in the glittering guise of her love. She knew now what she feared, what held her back from taking the very thing she desired. She could not trust herself with his life.

For marriage would not content him. Men like Robin were never content, and men like Robin were all she would ever love, grasping, ambitious reflections of herself. Once he knew that the crown matrimonial would never be his, that she would not make him king in his own right, he would begin to plot and scheme behind her back, building up a court faction to force her hand. Robin was too like his father, neither men to be ruled by their wives. To emerge from that final conflict as the victor, it would be necessary to kill him. And she knew she was capable of doing it—it was as simple as that. His company, his friendship, his passionate attachment were all that she dared to take from him; she loved him too much to let him pay the price of owning her, body and soul. (302)

According to Martha Tuck Rozett, who also quotes this passage at length, "there is something nearly tragic about this realization; Kay attempts to make sense of Elizabeth and Leicester's lifelong relationship by endowing her subject with an acute recognition of the impasse in which she finds herself."[34] But Rozett does not probe what that impasse is or the gothic terms in which it is expressed. While this is a wholly fabricated "recognition," it connects Elizabeth to a way of understanding marriage that does have its roots in the early modern period. In terms strikingly familiar from the many different kinds of texts I have examined in this book, Elizabeth describes a marriage between equals as murderous conflict from which one spouse can only emerge "as the victor" by killing the other. Should she marry, she assumes she will be forced to choose between the roles of her headless mother or her murderous father. In Kay's novel, as in so many others, Elizabeth decides that she can avoid becoming her mother—and being ignominiously executed—only by not marrying. But Kay's Elizabeth also wants to avoid becoming her father, the murderous spouse on top. To dodge this fate, too, she must avoid marriage.

Even as an unmarried woman she cannot escape a "winner-take-all" relationship to others. The novel suggests that she employs some kind of witchcraft to waste Cecil and Dudley. Dudley worries that "slowly the flame of her life was consuming him, eating away his manhood, almost his identity; he had sunk his life in hers, lost himself so deeply in her shadow that it seemed without her he would no longer exist."[35] While Elizabeth does not marry and therefore kill Dudley, she does overshadow him, as she fears a husband would a wife. She reduces Dudley to the cipher, the person who loses his identity and even life in the course of the relationship. Furthermore, Kay's Elizabeth does not simply conclude that marriage would require her to kill or be killed. She assumes that she owes her mother a sacrifice. Ultimately, she offers Dudley's stepson Essex, who identifies himself as the perfect choice when he boasts, "I can be the only master she has ever had!" In turn, she vows to make a "final stand and show him that there was in this land but one mistress and no master." She cannot pardon him, she feels. "Like her, he was caught up and controlled by a dreadful whirlpool from the past—the chosen sacrifice which would expiate her father's crime in murdering her mother. He had no choice but to work against her; and now she had no choice but to kill him for it."[36] Elizabeth's "legacy" from her mother is thus an inescapable obligation to destroy any man who challenges her self-possession. And yet it is this maternal inheritance itself that limits Elizabeth and compromises her autonomy. A "dreadful whirlpool," the past is destructive, irresistible, and wholly determining.

Michael Dobson and Nicola Watson point out that the novel is "described in its quaintly retrograde publicity materials as 'the story of a woman in search of a master'."[37] But the publicity materials do not address what happens in the novel after a woman finds the man who would be her master: she contemplates killing him (Dudley) and actually does so (Essex). This is a retrograde fantasy, but not quite the one those publicity materials might lead one to expect.

Febrile and extravagant, Legacy participates in some of the features of the gothic but with interesting twists. According to Michelle Massé, what she calls the "marital gothic" explores "how and why the figure who was supposed to lay horror to rest [i.e., the husband] has himself become the avatar of horror who strips voice, movement, property and identity itself from the heroine." In Legacy, Elizabeth assumes that any man worth marrying—"grasping, ambitious reflections of herself"—would eventually attempt to divest her of her crown, her identity, her life.[38] But if, as Tania Modleski argues, one function of the gothic is to "convince women that they are not their mothers," Legacy performs this function by assigning to Elizabeth—a queen after all and no average wife—the capacity to imagine herself as the husband, the tyrant, the "avatar of horror."[39] Although she has more power and mobility than most, Kay's Elizabeth cannot escape the marital gothic. Any marriage would cast her as either victim or killer, mother or father, wife or husband.

The emotions that Legacy attributes to Elizabeth and her companions are so extreme that the novel is often inadvertently funny. Everything about Elizabeth's pathology is exceptional, even supernatural. Kay's Elizabeth is damaged goods, fighting her own "womanly" impulses and becoming insane as a result. She is only able to escape the horrifying ghost of her headless mother after her death, when she can finally join Dudley as "joyfully, *triumphantly*, he took her hand and pulled her forward into infinity."[40] Apparently, with Essex's execution and Elizabeth's own death, her mother is finally appeased. But death does not seem to end the struggle for rule between Dudley and Elizabeth as much as it frees her to surrender to him at last. In the end, he is "triumphant," which sounds very much like "emerg[ing] from that final conflict as the victor." *He* pulls *her* forward. As bizarre as Legacy is, it shares assumptions about marriage that inform other accounts of Elizabeth's character and her choices.

Most novels explore the possibility that what people want from marriage is an equal. But the longed-for match of equals is feared to degenerate quickly into a rivalry or antagonism. In Margaret Irwin's *Elizabeth, Captive Princess*, the second in her trilogy of novels about Elizabeth, Robert Dudley longs for "an equal mate in courage, wits and knowledge of the world, a woman of complicated and baffling charm, . . . an impossible combination, he knew; but then . . ." Dissatisfied with his own wife, he finds in Elizabeth this possible equal. While they are both held prisoner in the Tower, they are "fellow-prisoners," a term that "pleased them both" since "it showed them equal, more free together in prison than ever they could be outside it." Yet Irwin's novel presents this fantasy of equality as unsustainable in the world outside of prison. Dudley oscillates between viewing Elizabeth as an equal or as a challenge. Pages after he cherishes their status as "fellow-prisoners," he views her as a trophy and her easy camaraderie with him as an obstacle to his attempts to win her. "To love her would be a wild adventure. He longed to essay it, as a young knight might long to prove his manhood in some desperate action. What a trophy her love would be! Yet how difficult to begin to make it when she talked thus, like one young man with another." He fears, too, her "icy self-control that would always give her the whip-hand over others." The "equal mate" for whom he longs, the fellow prisoner whose "equal" friendship he values, unsettlingly resembles another young man, and thereby seems to disrupt what he thinks courtship requires, what marriage might mean. When she refuses to play the role of "trophy," then he perceives her as demanding the whip hand. The equal mate cannot seem to hold a position in between these extremes. In the novel, Elizabeth too discovers that Robin is not quite what she longs for. She is too canny to marry "a younger son of a disgraced family of upstarts." Furthermore, "a fierce and lonely pride told her, even in this moment of passionate regret, that he was not the mate equal to, no, greater than herself, who must compel her to the ultimate surrender of herself. Had she ever met him? No, and most probably never would."[41] Just as Dudley wants an equal and a chance to "prove his manhood," so Elizabeth wants a mate equal to as well as "greater than" herself who would "compel" her to "surrender." The novel repeatedly insists that passionate people want to marry their equals and that this was not yet achievable in the sixteenth century. But in Elizabeth's and Dudley's musings on their desire for an "equal mate," we also find confusion as to what equality between a man and a woman might mean and how long it might last.

Surveying many of the novels about Elizabeth, Dobson and Watson offer a provocative account of how these novels change in the second half of the twentieth century. In the 1940s and 1950s, they argue, "Elizabeth makes her debut as a thoroughly normal would-be (and on occasion actual) wife and mother, a doubling prefiguration (albeit in more interesting clothes) of Elizabeth II." This offers a provocative way of thinking about how Irwin's Elizabeth (in a novel first published in 1948) longs for marriage, even though she never achieves it. In contrast to Dobson and Watson, I emphasize that Irwin's novel encodes a contradiction: an expectation that marriage should match equals yet a creeping sense that it will inevitably, perhaps even should, entail the wife's surrender to her superior, rather than her insistence on holding the whip hand. This is not an uncritical endorsement of marriage as female destiny; it is an undigested, contradictory set of expectations of what marriage should be.

I also find Dobson and Watson's description of the connection between social change and novels about Elizabeth I both interesting and incomplete.

By the 1970's, however, in the context of feminism, permissiveness, the now widely available Pill, and a steeply rising divorce-rate, the issue of Elizabeth's failure to marry and reproduce all but vanishes. In a cultural environment in which sexuality was now severed from marriage and reproduction, and in which women increasingly were expecting to wield equal power in the public sphere, the Virgin Queen was magically transformed into a role model for career women, eventually coming to double the career-politician-cum-dominatrix, Mrs. Thatcher, who in the 1980s reunited femininity and the realities of state power.[42]

Meanings for readers in the United States, who did not experience the marked shift in female icons of power from Queen Elizabeth II to Prime Minister Margaret Thatcher, would have been different. Furthermore, the correspondence between social and political change, on the one hand, and the popular versions of Elizabeth's story, on the other, is not so neat. Despite the rupture between sexuality and reproduction, and despite the recognition that a woman might want power *and* sex, the stories continue to present marriage as both desirable and dangerous.

Critics such as Dobson and Watson have tended to focus on how the novels ignore the particular complexities of the early modern period in order to explore female dilemmas particular to the periods in which they are written and marketed.[43] Certainly, the twists and turns in these novels are in part the products of the specific concerns of a given novelist or of the particular historical moment in which the novels were first published. Both of these factors are important. But all these novels are still in print today, suggesting that those written in the 1940s or 1980s remain appealing to readers now. They are also remarkably similar when it comes to how they depict what marriage means for women. I am interested in the ways that these novels apprehend, exaggerate, and perpetuate a way of imagining marriage that is as much early modern as it is modern. I have downplayed what is particular to their moments to emphasize what they actually borrow from the period they depict.

In these novels, women who are larger than life, who refuse to be eclipsed or subjugated, who demand to have it all—these are the ones who find marriage restrictive. They have more to lose. Focusing on queens thus enables identification and distancing. "It's true," a reader might think, "marriage would be a loss for a character such as Elizabeth I. But that wouldn't necessarily apply to me. The problem has been resolved by historical progress. Furthermore, I, after all, am not a queen." And yet, as I've argued in this book, the construction of marriage as an economy of scarcity suggests that all wives risk losing part of themselves and restricting their orbit in marriage. These novels allow their readers to probe that fear without necessarily having to own it.

Reflecting on the appeal of stories about accomplished men who fall in love with their subordinates, such as James Brooks's film *Spanglish* and Richard Curtis's film *Love Actually* (both from 2003), Maureen Dowd contrasts them to "all those great Tracy/Hepburn movies more than a half-century ago." In the earlier films, "it was the snap and crackle of a romance between equals that was so exciting. Moviemakers these days seem far more interested in the soothing aura of romances between unequals."[44] As we have seen, especially in the previous chapter, there is a long tradition of interest in the notion that hierarchy is "soothing" because it prevents the struggle for mastery assumed to accompany the "snap and crackle of romance between equals." The fantasy of the tender and solicitous subordinate, like that of the tamed shrew, is nothing new.

Historical novels about queens appeal to a rather different set of needs, offering cautionary tales, warnings against the fairytale of marrying the prince. Novels about Anne Boleyn, for instance, allow readers to contemplate what it might be like to marry a king. What if the man who promises to raise you from lady-in-waiting to queen, as Henry did for Anne Boleyn, ends up having you killed? Is it clear that kings are catches? This fearful perspective on "marrying up" is encoded in an ad from the Family Violence Prevention Council, warning that "it's not worth being his queen one day if you're his victim the next" (see Figure 1).

If Anne Boleyn's story suggests that romances between unequals might be less than soothing when viewed from below, what is the effect of stories about Elizabeth's romances with her subordinates? At the end of Dowd's column, she quotes actor Carrie Fisher as saying that she no longer dates because powerful men want to date women in the service professions and so do men in the service professions. "I found out," Fisher says, "that kings want to be treated like kings, and consorts want to be treated like kings, too."[45] Fisher, presumably, is a queen. Fisher's

It's not worth being his queen one day if you're his victim the next.

If you're trapped in a violent relationship, call:

We'll help you to change your life while the word still has meaning.

Developed by the Family Violence Prevention Fund © 1987
383 Rhode Island St., Suite 304   San Francisco, CA 94103 - 5133

Figure 1. This ad from the Family Violence Prevention Council uses the specter of Henry VIII to warn women about the perils of marriage. Reproduced by permission of the Family Violence Prevention Fund.

quip depends on a hierarchical vision in which social status should make men either kings or consorts but the entitlements of masculinity trump class, preventing the men from knowing and accepting their place and from acknowledging any woman as a queen, that is, as their equal or superior. Popular novels about Renaissance women also assume a rigidly hierarchical society. If novels about Anne Boleyn enable readers to confront the nightmarish possibilities of marrying a king, those about Elizabeth explore what it is like at the top of the hierarchy. Like Elizabeth herself, these novels insist that status should be more important than gender, and a queen should not subordinate herself to any man. They depict a queen who spurns lovers who aspire to share or usurp her power, threatens those who presume upon her favor, and banishes or executes upstarts. Perhaps, they suggest, it could be good to be queen. But the pleasures and privileges assigned to Elizabeth remain those imaginable within an economy of scarcity; they are the pleasures of killing rather than being killed, of being the king and not the consort. Novels about Elizabeth suggest that women can have power or marriage but cannot have both.

"Nothing can it add unto you": Elizabeth, Marriage, and the Zero-Sum Game

Much of the scholarly discussion regarding Elizabeth's attitudes toward marriage—and there has been a lot—has assumed that she was expected and pressured to marry. Surely marriage would offer material dividends in the form of a kingly supplement to the queen's power and, eventually, an heir to the throne. Therefore, any analysis of the fact that Elizabeth did not marry must have to probe the specifics of her own feelings or the political situation and the suitors available to her so as to understand why she would not take a course so obviously desirable to her contemporaries. But Elizabeth's subjects and advisors were more ambivalent than this, as some recent scholars have emphasized.[46] It was possible in the period to imagine that Elizabeth had little or nothing to gain and much to lose through marriage.

First, there was concern about the symbolic and practical consequences of a dynastic marriage for the country represented by the wife. If marriage was routinely used as an analogy for loving but hierarchical alliances in which one party must be the head and one the foot, one the leader and one the follower, one the husband and one the wife, then wouldn't the country headed by a queen inevitably find itself in the subordinate position and thus subject to a foreign sovereign? In A Gaping Gulf, John Stubbs argued that, while it was always dangerous for a sovereign to marry a foreigner, it was much worse when that sovereign was a woman because she, and her country, would inevitably be subordinated. As a marginal note advises the reader, "as the wife is subject to hir husband, so is hir country to hys land." As a consequence, "both she and we poor sules, are to be mastered, and which is worse, mistrised to" [mistressed too].[47]

While one might think that this concern could be resolved by the queen's marrying an English subject rather than a foreign sovereign, the second concern was that the queen would be disparaged by such a match because, as a wife, she would be unable to raise her husband and he would instead bring her down to his level. This uncertainty draws on the assumption that a wife had little to offer her husband. John Knox, for instance, advises that women cannot give anything to their husbands "because it is against the nature of her kinde, being the inferiour membre to presume to geve any thing to her head."[48] Similarly, Patrick Hannay, in his "Directions for a Maid to Chuse Her Mate," advises that men who marry a woman of lower birth are excused for choosing love and beauty and "as his place, his Wife shall be esteem'd."

> But when a Woman of a noble race
> Doth match with Man of farre inferiour place,
> Shee cannot him innoble, he is still
> In place as shee first found him, good, or ill.[49]

Not only can she not "innoble" her husband but, the implication is, she is made no better, and is perhaps slightly lessened, through marriage to her inferior. This would be a poor match for any noblewoman. A queen's disparagement might ripple outward to engulf all of her subjects.

The fear that a queen might be diminished through marriage informs some of the best-known responses to the prospect of Elizabeth's marriage to the duke of Alençon; this match was first contemplated in 1572, but then pursued and debated most vigorously between 1579 and 1583.[50] In the letter he wrote to Elizabeth advising against the marriage, Sir Philip Sidney, probably writing as a spokesman for the faction of his uncle, Robert Dudley, Earl of Leicester, describes the queen as already complete in herself.[51] "To your estate, what can be added to the being an absolute born, and accordingly respected, princess?" Later, he answers his own question. "Nothing can it [marriage] add unto you, but only the bliss of children." Sidney handles this possible boon more delicately than did John Stubbs, who, in print, tactlessly expressed his doubt that Elizabeth could still conceive at forty-six.[52] As Sidney points out, the duke of Alençon is no more capable of fathering a child than any other possible suitor. As a consequence, the only benefit marriage might offer is "no more his, than anybody's," to give the queen, "but the evils and dangers are particularly annexed to his person and condition." He cannot or will not enrich her country with treasure; and he cannot "stay" the queen's cares. Even if he could, Sidney explains, staying her cares would entail "the easing you of being a queen and sovereign." In other words, to share the burden of sovereignty is to lose power. As a consequence, Sidney concludes, this marriage would be "either full of hurt, or void of help." Describing Elizabeth as the country's "head" and Monsieur as a "second head or countenance" Sidney suggests that a queen needs a husband like she needs two heads.[53] Furthermore, the country is better off with a queen as its head than with a supernumerary head.

William Camden's report on Elizabeth's reluctance to marry in 1581 attributes to the queen a calculation regarding the profits and losses of marriage. Camden rehearses the problems with both subjects and strangers as prospective spouses. He imagines Elizabeth "as foreseeing that if she married a subject, she should disparage herself by the inequality of the match, and give occasion to domestical heart-burnings, private grudges, and commotions; if a stranger, then she should subject both herself and her people to a foreign yoke, and endanger religion." He concludes with the image of Elizabeth as a kind of sun queen: "Her glory also, which whilst she continued unmarried she retained entire to herself and uneclipsed, she feared would by marriage be transferred to her husband."[54] These passages from Sidney and Camden have been much discussed. What I want to emphasize is the assumption that Elizabeth is "entire to herself and uneclipsed," and that as a result marriage can "add nothing unto" her. Indeed, marriage threatens to diminish her, reduce her from entire to partial, from sovereign to subordinate.

The prospect of an Elizabeth rendered partial rather than complete through marriage is also expressed in two oft-recounted episodes. Neither of these key moments is recorded in Elizabeth's own speeches or letters; both are reported by male witnesses, recollecting her reign long after her death. Both have since become staples of popular biographies and novels. The first episode is one in which the Scots ambassador claims, in memoirs written long after the occasion, that, when Elizabeth confided to him in 1564 that she hoped to remain unmarried, he replied: "I know the truth of that, madam, said I; you need not tell it me. Your Majesty thinks, if you were married, you would be but Queen of England; and now you are both King and Queen. I know your spirit cannot endure a commander."[55] Melville asserts an ability to read Elizabeth's mind; he says what he "knows" she thinks but won't necessarily say; retrospectively, he remembers his own prescience in understanding why she would choose not to marry.[56]

Another defining episode supposedly occurred when Dudley threatened to have one of Elizabeth's servants discharged for denying him entrance. The servant, a gentleman usher, prostrated himself before the queen, begging to know "whether my Lord of Leicester were King, or her Majesty Queen?" Elizabeth responded by warning Dudley, "God's death, my lord, I have wished you well, but my favor is not locked up for you that others shall not partake thereof, for I have many servants unto whom I have and will at my pleasure bequeath my favors and likewise re-assume the same, and if you think to rule here, I will take a course to see you forthcoming. I will have here but one mistress and no master."[57] In this episode, Elizabeth identifies herself as a mistress but not one in search of a master. She also positions Dudley as himself a servant, de-pendent on her favor. The source of this story, Robert Naunton, offers no indication of the year in which this supposedly occurred or the au-thority on which he can recount it; he says only that he has it on "assured intelligence." Like Melville's story, this one was recorded considerably later. But popular biographers and novelists usually reproduce some ver-sion of this claim, although the contexts vary.[58] For instance, we have al-ready seen that, in Susan Kay's *Legacy*, Elizabeth vows to show Essex that "there was in this land but one mistress and no master," and that Anne Boleyn advises her daughter in her *Secret Diary* "let no man be your mas-ter."[59] This episode thus provides the term used to describe what Eliza-beth must refuse and what she must choose in her unmarried state: to be unmastered and masterful.

Whether or not either of these episodes actually happened, they have been found worth remembering or inventing and worth repeat-ing because they depict moments in which Elizabeth asserts herself as a composite—the king and queen, master and mistress who does not need marriage because she already embodies its fusion of two into one. Be-cause she is not less than a king but already more than one, she risks los-ing the masterful or kingly part of herself should she take a husband. Stripped of the complicated contexts in which they were supposedly ut-tered, unburdened of their dubious provenance, the phrases "both king and queen" and "one mistress, no master" pithily sum up Elizabeth's sta-tus as a couple unto herself. Condensed and unmoored, they linger in the imagination and circulate through fictions. According to Mary Beth Rose, Elizabeth, in her own speeches, took "rhetorical advantage of the special prestige of both female and male subject positions as these were understood in the Renaissance without consistently privileging either."[60] While my own emphasis is somewhat different, I draw on Rose's illu-minating argument about how Elizabeth occupied multiple positions, sometimes sequentially and sometimes simultaneously. However Eliza-beth imagined or located herself, some of her contemporaries justified, promoted, or commemorated her decision not to marry by casting her as simultaneously occupying the positions of husband and of wife; that is, as always already a couple.

How did Elizabeth and her contemporaries reconcile the assumption that she should marry, as all women and all sovereigns should, and the fear that her marriage would diminish rather than enhance her (and by extension England)? Fictions and fantasies made it possible to imagine her as married without having to deal with the practical difficulties of an actual spouse. These fantasies served contemporaries, then, as an "imaginary 'solution'" to a "real contradiction," as Fredric Jameson describes the operation of romance.[61] One fantasy, constantly replayed in novels about Elizabeth, is that she was married to her kingdom. Scholars have disputed whether Elizabeth actually said, "I am already bound unto an husband, which is the kingdom of England," as she displayed her coronation ring. William Camden's 1615 translation of Elizabeth's 1559 answer to the Commons' petition that she marry includes these lines and this stage direction. His version has been widely cited; it is a standard feature in popular representations of Elizabeth. But, as the editors of Elizabeth's writings point out, Camden's version "freely embroiders upon . . . the speech as we have it from the early sources."[62] Recognizing this story as a myth has not stopped anyone from repeating it.[63] Novels cherish the fantasy of an Elizabeth married to England, in part because it solves a problem; it shores up marriage as a desirable even inevitable state without actually subjecting Elizabeth to it. In Camden's account of this moment, Elizabeth clearly and reassuringly identifies the kingdom as the husband and herself as the wife. Yet other contemporaries thought of her as the husband. In 1569, Thomas Norton reminded readers that "her highnesse is the Husband of the common weale, married to the realme, and the same by ceremonie of ring as solemnely signified as any common marriage is, to our great comfort and confidence I reherse it." As a consequence, rebelling against her is as unacceptable as having one's own wife, children, or servants rebel.[64] In political terms, this makes more sense. The fiction of her marriage to her kingdom, so often retold, fudges these contradictions, casting her as wife but granting her the husband's authority and autonomy.

Another possibility was a "shadow husband." Anne McLaren convincingly argues that Robert Dudley played just such a role. According to McLaren, in his special relationship with Elizabeth, Dudley was able to represent the interests of a collective of Protestant male subjects and advisors; he was also able to promote the appearance that the queen needed, wanted, and had a male consort. In McLaren's view, Dudley provided "a king figure to compensate for the perceived deficiencies of female rule, at many points symbolically, at others (especially in relation to military affairs) actually." He was perfect for the role; "his equivocal status made his candidacy, for her hand and for a commanding political role, *almost* impossibly difficult for her councilors to accept" and therefore Elizabeth was able to use him for almost twenty years. "Dudley's promotion certainly strengthened Elizabeth's position as queen in her own right ... [and] allowed her to pursue, with remarkable tenacity and success, her primary political goal of securing unchallenged possession of the English crown."[65] McLaren suggests that the "shadow husband" was both an imaginative solution and a real one, in that he stood in the place of a husband, performing some of his real and ceremonial roles, without ever threatening the queen's autonomy. In the shadow, then, he stood in something like the position of the wife, supporting by not competing with or eclipsing the sovereign. Whether or not McLaren is correct, Dudley serves as a "shadow" husband in popular novels, which pair him with Elizabeth as the man she loves but cannot or will not marry.

A marriage between two regnant queens, Elizabeth I of England and Mary Stuart of Scotland, was another fantasy solution. At first, this would seem to promise a yoking of equals in which neither would be eclipsed. But Elizabeth and Mary were no more equal than were their countries. The fantasy of their alliance depended on one or the other queen becoming a man, and therein lay the problem. On December 31, 1560, an "unknown person" wrote to Robert Dudley: "Me thinkethe it were to be wisshed of all wyse men and her majesties good subjectes, that one of those two quenes of the ile of Bryttaine were transfermed into the shape of a man to make so happie a marriage, as therby ther might be an unitie of the holl ile [whole isle]."[66] The dream that either of the queens could be transformed is disingenuous; English political interests would require that Elizabeth become the man and act as the husband.[67] Pressured to choose a husband who would insure continued amity between the two queens and their countries, Mary asked the English ambassador, "Is the Queen of England become a man?" Who else, after all, would be a suitable mate for the queen of Scotland? In part, Mary was toying with the ambassador and trying to force Elizabeth to name a mate she would find acceptable (eventually she named her own favorite, Dudley). But the fantasy of marriage between the two queens was not as radical as Mary's vision of the two as sisters, that is, as equals. "How much better were it, that we being two Queens so near of kin, neighbours and living in one Isle, should be friends and live together like sisters, than by strange means divide ourselves to the hurt of us both."[68] Living as sisters would serve Mary's interests better than marrying the sovereign of a more powerful country. After all, if two queens were able to marry, all of the problems of marriage would reassert themselves. The disparate status of spouses would pertain even if both were of the same sex.

We can see this clearly in another oft-quoted passage from the period. Elizabeth told the Spanish ambassador, Guzman de Silva, that she would like to meet the widowed Princess Juana: "how well so young a widow and a maiden would get on together, and what a pleasant life they could lead. She (the Queen) being the elder would be the husband, and her Highness [the princess] the wife. She dwelt upon this for a time."[69] Note that even when Elizabeth imagines a marriage between two women, whatever we make of this fantasy, she imagines particular and hierarchical roles for the spouses and herself in the role of husband—because she is the elder.[70] It is from the perspective of the husband's position, defined as one of gain rather than loss, that such a marriage looks like a good idea.

Adapting these imaginary solutions, first devised during her reign, novels about Elizabeth I depict her as asserting that she is married to her kingdom and needs no other spouse from the beginning of her reign or even before her accession. Yet they avoid the complexities regarding whether she is the husband or wife in that union. They pair her up with a "shadow husband," usually Dudley, so that, effectively, she is a member of a couple, desiring Dudley, resisting him, scheming with him, seeking his advice. Interestingly, while novels love the face-off between the rival queens, Elizabeth Tudor and Mary Stuart, one blonde, one brunette, one single, one thrice-married, they never entertain the fantasy that Mary and Elizabeth could teasingly articulate—that two queens might marry one another. Nor do they pick up on Mary's truly inventive suggestion that the ideal, "win-win" relation between persons and between countries, the relation that would be equitable and amicable rather than hierarchical, would have to be imagined outside of the institution or the metaphor of marriage. After all, as these sister queens both learned, they, too, were in a life or death struggle only one would win. As we will see, Philippa Gregory's fictional accounts of the relationships between sisters Mary and Anne Boleyn or Mary and Elizabeth Tudor depict them in deadly competitions for one king or one crown.

These novels, for all of their variety, draw from a repertoire of sixteenth- and seventeenth-century fantasies to take the edge off Elizabeth's unmarried state. Her thwarted desire for Dudley and later for Essex, and her longing to wear someone's ring, give her a more conventional female story and make her a more accessible heroine. At the same time, these ways of narrating Elizabeth's story retreat from the challenge of depicting a woman who is not defined by her relations to men, who wields power, and who effectively has no private life.[71] That is, the novels retreat from finding a way to tell a new and different woman's story. Contemplating her relation to Dudley or her marriage to her kingdom, the Elizabeth of historical novels is a marital pundit rather than a political tactician. Yet these fantasy solutions of an Elizabeth married to her kingdom or bonded to a shadow husband until death they do part do not resolve contradictions as much as they expose them, suggesting that the contradiction between female power and marriage has no practicable resolution. Presenting Elizabeth as outside or above the constraints she herself attributes to marriage, these novels dwell on her as an exception and emphasize the personal loss entailed in settling for sovereignty.

My Partner in This Venture: Philippa Gregory's Happy Endings

Since novels about Anne Boleyn and Queen Elizabeth, taken together, suggest that marriage is fatal for one spouse or the other, and therefore best avoided, some novels set in the period attempt to expand the options by looking a little to the side, at the margins of the historical record, outside the court, and in the realms of invention. The chances for happiness located there for today's reader are simultaneously modern—sex and personal fulfillment—and reactionary. In these novels, the marriage capacious enough for the modern woman is one that allows her to have true love, orgasms, meaningful work, (limited) autonomy—and stay at home with her children. The heroines voice critiques of marriage as an economy of scarcity yet they don't end as Anne or Elizabeth do, defeated by marriage or abstaining from it. Instead, they turn to a marriage they claim to have remodeled, presenting this as an innovative happy ending. I want to use as my case study Philippa Gregory, whose novels about Tudor women have been enormously successful. Although Gregory has written numerous books about the period, I will focus on two in which her double message about marriage is most clear.

Gregory's breakthrough hit was *The Other Boleyn Girl*, about Anne Boleyn's sister Mary, who preceded her as Henry VIII's mistress in the second or third decade of the sixteenth century.[72] In contrast to Anne, Mary settled for being a mistress rather than a wife and queen, perhaps even having a child or two by Henry before he cast her off. Other biographers and novelists who focus on Anne Boleyn also include some reference to Mary. Gregory makes Mary the central character.[73] Her approach has proved so popular that the novel has been adapted by BBC television and Hollywood.[74] Gregory depicts Mary's experience as a cautionary tale for Anne, teaching her that she will retain Henry's interest and her own influence only as long as she defers having sex with him. Yet the lesson Mary ultimately teaches Anne, and by extension readers, is a rather different one.

Mary is not paired with Anne only as the stand-in through whom she learned how to manage and profit from Henry's desire, because Mary's story did not end when her affair did or when her first husband died. In 1534, Mary made a secret and "unsuitable" second marriage to William

Stafford, "one of the hangers-on at court, the second son of minor Midlands gentry";[75] when the marriage was discovered because of Mary's pregnancy, she was banished from court and her allowance cut off. Pleading with the king's secretary, Thomas Cromwell, to restore her allowance, Mary wrote a letter that has become central to the popular notion that she married for love. "For well I might a' had a greater man of birth and a higher, but I ensure you I could never a had one that should a loved me so well nor a more honest man. . . . But were I at my liberty and might choose . . . I had rather beg my bread with him than to be the greatest Queen christened."[76] (An interesting twist on this assertion is attributed to Elizabeth, who supposedly told her half-sister, Mary Tudor, "I would rather be a beggar and single than a Queen and married.")[77] Although it is unclear that Anne Boleyn would have seen this letter, many biographers speculate that Mary's assertion was the cause of conflict between the sisters. Alison Weir claims that Anne could not forgive this because the "taunt went too deep"; Carolly Erickson avers, "poor as she was, and disowned by her family, Mary's story had come to a happy ending. It was for this, quite possibly, that Anne could not forgive her"; Karen Lindsey suggests that Mary "must have realized that Ann herself had married not for love, but in hope of becoming 'the greatest queen christened.' . . . Ann might have resented her sister's happiness."[78] One of the most authoritative biographers of Anne Boleyn, Eric Ives, offers a rather different, and compelling, interpretation. He claims that Anne resented Mary's disregard for her authority, and the fact that Mary transacted her own marriage in secret rather than deferring to Anne. It was Mary's insubordination, not her happiness, that Anne resented.[79]

Whatever caused the friction between the sisters, novelists dwell on the idea that, unlike Anne, Mary values love over power and so achieves the happier fate. In Jean Plaidy's *Lady in the Tower*, Anne concedes that her "simple-minded sister who thought love was more important than ambition" might be wiser in the end.

She had a great capacity for happiness. For the first time in my life I was envious of Mary, with her children and her happy marriage; she was serene and secure. She declared that Will Stafford was the perfect husband; he had made up for the loss of dear Will Carey [her first husband]. It seemed to me that Mary had found the right way to live. Perhaps I could have learned from her if it had not been too late.[80]

While it is too late for Anne in this novel, it is not, of course, too late for readers. Perhaps, Anne suggests, the problem isn't marriage but marriage to kings. Had she been less ambitious, had she settled for marriage to a lesser man, perhaps she might have found happiness, or at least survival. She demanded too much and wound up with nothing.

Gregory's novel builds on this tradition of contrasting the sisters, but Gregory makes Mary, rather than Anne, her heroine. Gregory suggests that the two sisters compete for the role of the novel's heroine, as they do for Henry's affections, because they are locked in fierce rivalry. As Mary baldly states: "For a moment we glared at each other, stubborn as cats on the stable wall, full of mutual resentment and something darker, the old sense between sisters that there is only really room in the world for one girl. The sense that every fight could be to the death."[81] In this sororal contest, it seems at first that Anne wins, supplanting Mary and achieving what she did not: marriage and the throne. But, ultimately, the novel suggests that Mary is the winner, achieving both love and survival.

By focusing on Mary, with peripheral glances at Anne, Gregory is able to depict early modern marriage as particularly constraining while also investing it with the potential to create happiness. The novel is especially interested in the consequences of coverture (examined at length in Chapter 1) for married women's control over property. As Mary puts it at one point, "I don't own anything on my own account." Her husband, William Carey, doubles his income, gains a knighthood, and amasses land grants for "being England's most famous cuckold" and for conferring legitimacy on the two children Mary supposedly has by Henry. According to Gregory, the king also confers titles and prominence on her other family members as a "reward" for Mary's pregnancies. Yet the novel emphasizes that even as everyone profits from her sex work, Mary accrues little benefit in her own right. She gains children she loves, but she is often separated from them and has little control over their upbringing. As her husband points out in a moment of sympathy: "All of us are thriving very handsomely and in the middle of it all ... is you, being eaten alive by every one of us. Perhaps you should have married a man who could have loved and kept you and given you a baby that you could have suckled yourself, without interruption."[82] This is, indeed, Mary's vision of what happiness would have meant for her.

Yet William's sympathy for Mary does not prevent him from collecting what profits he can from her liaison with Henry, or from asserting his own control over her. When he reclaims her after she is no longer Henry's mistress, he states: "You are my wife. Everything that is yours is mine. Everything that is mine I keep. Including the children and the woman who carries my name."[83] As a consequence, despite some guarded affection she feels for her husband, William, Gregory's Mary still views his sudden death as a liberation and an opportunity.

Now I realized that his death had set me free. If I could escape another husband, I might buy a little manor farm on my family's lands in Kent or Essex. I might have land that I could call my own and crops that I could watch grow. I might at last become a woman in my own right instead of the mistress of one

man, the wife of another, and the sister of a Boleyn. I might bring up my children under my own roof. Of course, I had to get some money from somewhere,
I had to persuade some man, Howard [her mother's family], Boleyn, or king, to
give me a pension so that I could raise my children and feed myself, but it might
be possible for me to gain enough to be a modest widow living in the country on
my own little farm.[84]

We have seen the exuberant response to a husband's death, actual or
imagined, in numerous other texts, especially those discussed at the end
of Chapter 1. The reflections Gregory attributes to Mary Boleyn are distinctive only in their frank concern with financial independence. Mary
repeats the phrase "my own" four times in this passage. She goes on
to explain that she wants to "escape another husband" because the
"women's work" of marriage is the same whatever your status. "It's earning no money for yourself and everything for your husband and master.
It's obeying him as quickly and as well as if you were a groom of the
servery. It's having to tolerate anything he chooses to do, and smile as
he does it." When her brother, George, challenges her fantasy of rural
independence, asking how she could deny her little daughter "a great
place in the world," Mary articulates the impossible position of women
at court: "If only women could have more . . . If we could have more in
our own right. Being a woman at court is like forever watching a pas-
trycook at work in the kitchen. All those good things, and you can have
nothing."[85] Gregory's Mary articulates the most extreme understanding
of coverture. Coverture, especially as it is experienced by women who
are beggars at the feast of the Tudor court, seems to be one reason that
Gregory chooses to set novels about marriage in the Tudor period. By
Gregory's account, coverture sums up the legal meaning of sixteenth-
century marriage. References to coverture mark her novels and her protagonists' fears and frustrations as "historical"; the version of coverture
she presents also justifies robust, passionate critiques of marriage that
splatter the present even as they claim to focus on superseded legal stric-
tures and the very particular position of Boleyn girls at court.

Despite Mary's persistent critique of what marriage means, at least for
Tudor wives, the novel allows her to achieve her dream not as a widow
but as a wife, married to a man who once worked for her uncle and ends
up working for the king. This union is romanticized as one in which
Mary can take her part as an equal. "In a world where women were
bought and sold as horses I had found a man I loved; and married for
love."[86] She achieves that love—and her survival—outside of the court.
But the ideal of marrying for love sits uncomfortably with Mary's earlier
critiques of marriage. Will love solve all of these inequalities? How can it
if the problems are built into the institution of marriage? The novel simply leaves these critiques behind, in the heart of the novel and in the

past, where coverture limits women's control of marital property. Moving from a disillusioned critique of marriage and women's status to her assertion that marrying for love—that is, making her own choice—has released her from her status as property, Mary reassures readers that there is a solution and that it lies in their hands. Simply choose the right spouse and embrace "rustication" or banishment from the center of power. This was Mary's punishment but the novel depicts it as her reward. Earlier in the novel, Mary claims that all wives are beggars. Ultimately, the novel suppresses Mary's insight that marriage enslaves more than it empowers women, suggesting that some wives can achieve queenly self-possession—but only outside the court.

Gregory's novel *The Queen's Fool* similarly combines a sustained critique of marriage with the reversion to a love match as the novel's happy ending. Many historical characters weave through the novel, including Robert Dudley, his pathetic wife, Amy, a sympathetically depicted Mary Tudor, and a rather ruthless Elizabeth. But the heroine is Gregory's own invention, the plucky Hannah Green. From the start, Hannah resists marriage as "the servitude of women hoping for safety, to men who cannot even keep them safe." She describes being a wife as being "a nothing."[87] For a time, Hannah wears breeches, a choice with which both Elizabeth and Mary Tudor sympathize. Elizabeth, for instance, says that the lack of choice is "always the same for all women. . . . The only people who can choose their lives are those in breeches. You do right to wear them."[88] But in the course of the novel, Hannah will surrender her breeches and marry. As in her account of Mary Boleyn's second marriage, Gregory presents Hannah's marriage as the ultimate way of "choosing [one's] life."

For my purposes here, the most interesting feature of the novel is the lengthy negotiation between Hannah and her betrothed, later her husband, an apprentice physician from whom she is twice estranged, first because of her refusal to obey him, and later because she learns that he has had a child during their first separation. These passages in the novel constitute Hannah's quest to be "a wife without descending."[89] In the letters they exchange, her husband angrily asserts his belief that their marriage, like every marriage, is a hierarchy and that her self-assertion initiates an unseemly contest for mastery. "I cannot do as you desire and set you up as the master of our home. . . . I am ordained to be your master. I cannot hand over the mastery of our family; it is my duty and responsibility; it cannot be yours." Given that he believes this, Hannah thinks that "a women who loved him would have to learn obedience, and I was not yet ready to be an obedient wife."[90] This might lead a reader to expect that the novel will chart the process by which she becomes ready to obey him. Just a few pages later, observing Mary Tudor's happiness early in her marriage to Philip II, Hannah wonders if she, too, might be ready for wifehood:

I watched her and thought that if a woman as fiercely virginal and as intensely spiritual as the queen could find love, then so perhaps could I. It might be that marriage was not the death of a woman and the end of her true self, but the unfolding of her. It might be that a woman could be a wife without having to cut the pride and the spirit out of her self. A woman might blossom into being a wife, not be trimmed down to fit.[91]

Hannah begins to imagine that there might be something in marriage worth pursuing and she evokes the assumption that marriage is a zero-sum game precisely so she can question it. Perhaps a wife might "unfold" and "blossom" rather than die or diminish. But, as any reader of history or historical fiction knows, Mary Tudor cannot serve long as the inspiring model of the blooming wife. In the course of this novel and its sequel, *The Virgin's Lover*, as in most other accounts, Mary suffers humiliating "phantom" pregnancies, her husband's neglect and absence, and severe illness. Just four years after she marries Philip, Mary dies.[92]

The novel suggests that blossoming as a wife is not just a matter of finding love or being ready. Hannah's vision of another kind of marriage requires that her husband become a new man. The novel thus charts the process by which Hannah teaches her husband, Daniel, to think differently about marriage.

I do not want to rule over you, but I do not want you to rule over me. I need to be a woman in my own right, and not only a wife.... I am used to having my own way: this is the woman I have become. I have traveled far and lived according to my own means, and I seem to have adopted a lad's pride along with breeches. I don't want to lay aside the pride when I surrender the livery. I hope that your love for me can accommodate the woman that I will grow to be. I would not mislead you in this, Daniel, I cannot be a servant to a husband, I would have to be his friend and comrade. I write to ask you if you could have a wife like this?[93]

Daniel proves better able to imagine new arrangements than he'd thought at first. He agrees that "this is a new world that we are making . . . it must be possible that a man and a wife could be married in a new way also. I do not want you as my servant, I want you as my love."[94] It takes some time and further adventures and misadventures until the couple is ready to reconcile and attempt this new life they have imagined. But Hannah teaches more than she learns in preparation for this new marriage.

Gregory links their supposedly trailblazing invention of a new and improved or "modern" model of marriage to an openness to scientific discovery (personified by Galileo) and what looks very much like re-form Judaism. Daniel assures Hannah:

> We shall live as suits us. . . . I won't have the Christian rules that forbid my learn-ing, I won't have Jewish rules that forbid my life. I shall read books that ask if the sun goes around the earth or the earth around the sun, and I shall eat pork . . . I shall accept no prohibitions on my thoughts or my actions except those that make sense to me. . . . Your letters and everything you have ever said makes sense to me only if I see you as my partner in this venture. Yes. You shall find your own way and I hope we will agree. We shall find a new way to live and it will be one that honors our parents and their beliefs, but which gives us a chance to be ourselves, and not just their children.[95]

This passage somehow links the possibility that spouses might be full part-ners "in this venture" with the freedom to eat pork! This vision of what it would mean to follow one's own beliefs and to "find a new way to live" will be made possible, Hannah claims, "in the England that Elizabeth will make."[96] Presumably, Elizabeth will make the readers' world, the modern world, the world of pork and partnership. While Elizabeth cannot achieve love and fulfillment herself, she makes it possible for others.

In *The Queen's Fool*, as in *The Other Boleyn Girl*, what constitutes the ful-fillment worth waiting and negotiating for, the fulfillment that eludes queens, is the freedom to stay home with one's children, to stay out of the court. These novels suggest that this is what women really want. Gre-gory depicts Anne Boleyn and Elizabeth I, the women who wanted to be queens, as ruthless and considerably less sympathetic than their sisters, Mary Boleyn and Mary Tudor. Casting marriage and motherhood as bold new discoveries and daring achievements, the novels depict wives and mothers as shaking off constraints depicted as both early or pre-modern and as related to the pesky political obligations of queens and courtiers.

Gregory's novels include vivid articulations of just what is wrong with marriage as a zero-sum game, as well as the insistence that marriage and motherhood are more fulfilling than life at the court and on the throne. They spend a great deal of time critiquing marriage even as they suggest that what they critique is an outmoded idea of marriage that forward-thinking women, unafraid to challenge authority, can move beyond. Reading the novels, one can simultaneously identify with the critique of marriage, an institution that seems strikingly familiar even as it is de-picted as archaic, and enjoy the message that if Renaissance women, with all of the particular constraints under which they labored, can fig-ure out how to make marriage work for them, then modern women can too. Gregory's novels presume that all women are heterosexual and that heterosexual women want marriage. Both of these novels build on Mary Boleyn's claim that it's better to be a beloved wife than a great queen.

Yet Gregory also assumes that marriage needs to be remodeled before it can serve the purposes assigned to it. In Gregory's novels about queens' sisters and servants, which are so much more invested in rehabilitating marriage than most historical novels about Anne and Elizabeth, the critique is as memorable, if not more so, than the reassurance that marrying for love really is the solution to everything.

While I share the investment in the prospect of equal, loving partnership that Gregory assigns to Mary Boleyn and Hannah Green, I am also aware of the evasions the endings require. Gregory suppresses the critiques she has assigned to her heroines and sidesteps the dilemma many of her readers face: how to combine meaningful work, perhaps even influence on the world outside the home, with this dream of loving equality? Gregory offers us the pleasure of love, marriage, and motherhood but at the expense of power. Her novels are thus the mirror image of those novels about Anne Boleyn and Elizabeth that offer us the prospect of power achieved at the cost of love and happiness (also defined as heterosexual marriage). Even as they celebrate plenitude, then, they assume scarcity. Whether we read about Anne or Mary Boleyn, Elizabeth or Mary Tudor, historical novels set in the Tudor period advise us that women have to make tough choices; they cannot have it all.

Gregory's last word on Henry's wives, *The Boleyn Inheritance* (2006), the story of Henry's fourth and fifth wives, Anne of Cleves and Katherine Howard, depicts Henry's death as the happy ending for Anne, who manages to outlive him and all his other wives. After her divorce from Henry, living on a pension in Anne and Mary Boleyn's former home, Hever Castle, Anne begins to suspect that "it may be a better thing to be a single woman with a good income in one of the finest palaces of England than to be one of Henry's frightened queens." Gregory's Anne frankly assesses the price she must pay for this independence; she loses political influence and she will never be able to marry or have children. Despite these losses, she decides that if she can survive the "dangerous proximity" of sharing Christmas with her mercurial exhusband at Hampton Court, she might "make a life for myself as a single woman in Henry's kingdom, which I plainly could not do as a wife." The novel concludes with Anne's rapturous response to Henry's death: "I am a free woman now, free from him and finally free from fear. . . . I will own a cat and not fear being called a witch; I will dance and not fear being named a whore. . . . I shall live my own life and please myself. I shall be a free woman. It is no small thing, this, for a woman: freedom."[97]

In this rousing conclusion, Gregory returns us to the insights that Mary Boleyn and Hannah Green repress or surpass, to the robustly negative view that independence can only be achieved outside of marriage. In Anne of Cleves, we find an anomalous figure who achieves freedom by being neither a queen nor a wife and mother, who gets what she wants by surrendering the political aspirations attributed to Anne Boleyn and Elizabeth I and the domestic ones Gregory assigns to Mary Boleyn and Hannah Green. Ending on Anne's celebration of Henry's death, the novel suggests that the Tudor period and the Boleyn inheritance inspire fictional explorations of marriage precisely because they restrict the wife's options to being divorced, beheaded, executed, or widowed—or, in the case of Elizabeth, the Boleyn heir, opting out entirely.[98] Through the threatening figure of Henry VIII and the perceived constraints of coverture on what married women could call their own, the Tudor court emerges as an arena of "extreme marriage," in which one can see the institution's dangers and constraints in the most exaggerated terms. Lodged in the past yet "hot" in the present, the Tudor court allows us to rehearse this negative vision of marriage without having to imagine a way out of the stalemate.[99] Anne of Cleves, divorced *and* widowed, achieves her happy ending alone.

Afterword

"If marriage didn't exist, would you invent it?"
—*Doug Stanhope,* Deadbeat Hero

The answer to comedian Doug Stanhope's question is "no." And "yes." Depending on who you are. In the United States today, many straight people are opting out of marriage. At the same time, many same-sex couples are struggling for inclusion. Their struggle recognizes marriage as a valuable sign of legitimacy under the law, as a license. One problem, as Judith Butler has pointed out, is "the lexicon of that legitimation." We are not really free to "invent" marriage at this point. While "one may wish for another lexicon altogether," marriage conveys legitimacy precisely to the extent that it figures a new story in the terms of an old one: "marriage, given its historical weight, only becomes an 'option' by extending itself as a norm (and thus foreclosing options), one which also extends property relations and renders the social forms for sexuality more conservative."[1] This historical weight is one reason that the state remains deeply invested in marriage: as a mechanism for conferring and withholding such legitimacy, as a system for distributing (and restricting) benefits, and as a structure for controlling sexuality and reproduction.

Concerns about a supposed marriage "crisis" are most often expressed in terms of individuals who expect too much and sacrifice too little, or same-sex couples who, by demanding to participate in marriage, somehow threaten it. Little attention is paid to reforming policies and practices outside the family that determine the possibilities within it. According to Stephanie Coontz, for instance,

The big problem doesn't lie in differences between what men and women want out of life and love. The big problem is how hard it is to achieve equal relationships in a society whose work policies, school schedules, and social programs were constructed on the assumption that male breadwinner families would always be the norm. Tensions between men and women today stem less from different aspirations than from the difficulties they face translating their ideals into practice.[2]

Similarly, Mary Shanley points out the need to "suggest reforms that would create greater equality between men and women in both public and private realms of activity" and "to rethink the social and economic structures that make it so difficult for adults who are responsible for children to do remunerative work and care for those children at the same time." According to Shanley, only broad reforms will "rectify the imbalance between the demands of the market and the demands of caregiving."[3] But such reforms seem to command less attention and fewer resources all the time.

Government initiatives to "support" marriage operate on the assumption that encouraging some people to marry will enable the state to be less responsible for them. These initiatives mostly target low-income people of color. A visit to the U.S. government Healthy Marriage Initiative Web site reveals that there are special programs for African Americans, Hispanics, and Native Americans, but no "healthy marriage initiative" directed at white people. One report, *Marriage, Divorce, Childbirth, and Living Arrangements Among African American or Black Populations,* advises African Americans that they are falling behind the pack when it comes to marriage. "On the whole, Blacks or African Americans (hereafter called Blacks) have lower rates of marriage and marital stability than all other ethnic groups. They also have higher rates of single-headed families than other groups."[4] These statistics are taken as evidence of moral and social failure. The goal of the "healthy marriage initiative" is to encourage people to marry and to stay married. Little inquiry is made into why people might prefer not to marry. Instead, they are advised that they will be healthier and wealthier if they do. Some studies suggest that this is, in fact, the case. But rather than offer people incentives to marry or supports once they have married (such as improved health care or child care), government programs instead promote marriage as itself the solution to problems of social welfare. If male breadwinners take responsibility for their female partners and their children, it is assumed, then the state will not have to. Lisa Duggan outs this purportedly moral campaign as an "economic agenda," a thinly disguised "privatization" scheme. And as she emphasizes, it is a nonpartisan platform, advanced as much by President Clinton's support in 1996 for the Defense of Marriage Act and the Personal Responsibility and Work Opportunity Reconcilement Act (widely known as "welfare reform") as by George W. Bush's "healthy marriage initiative" and opposition to same-sex marriage. According to Duggan, "Republicans and Democrats are by and large in agreement that as social programs are whittled away, gender-differentiated marriage (heterosexual, with different expectations for women and men) should pick up the slack."[5] Amendments and initiatives to defend and protect marriage, then, promulgate a narrowly conceived notion of what marriage is—a notion that, as I have argued, we have inherited from early modern England—and depend on this particular version of marriage to forestall the critical reflection, reform, and innovation that might promote equality both within and outside of marriage.

If financial need presses many couples to abandon their disdain for women working outside the home and for day care, financial surfeit enables some very privileged people to roll back to an ideal of wifehood and motherhood that, as Stephanie Coontz has shown, never was a dominant model of the family. They can recapture, in her phrase, the "way we never were."[6] In recent newspaper and magazine stories about women who are graduates of Ivy League universities or partners in big law firms, and who choose to stay at home with their children, economics remains a determining factor. Only women who are so privileged that working outside the home is a choice can present themselves as traditionalists who wish to reclaim the role of the stay-at-home wife, a role they might not covet if they understood it more deeply. Their prosperity and privilege protect them from confronting the scarcity built into this particular ideal of marriage.

Even as legislators, pundits, and moralists simultaneously saturate marriage with moral significance, depend on it as a disciplinary mechanism, and strip it of meaningful supports, many people are opting out of it. According to the 2000 U.S. Census, "the most common household type in the U.S. is people living alone," and "there are currently about 11 million people living with an unmarried partner in the U.S.," including "both same-sex and different-sex couples."[7] Given such statistics, one might argue that gay people are the only demographic group demanding inclusion and therefore adding luster to marriage as the ultimate sanction of sexual and emotional attachment. As Nancy Cott says, "contestation over same-sex marriage has, ironically, clothed the formal institution with renewed honor."[8] As some same-sex couples assert their own investment in marriage as the means by which a couple is recognized, legitimized, and secured, many other couples choose to forego marriage for a host of reasons. Both trajectories—straight people opting out of marriage and gay people struggling to get in—are placing productive pressure on the institution of marriage.

All these stories—about initiatives to lure more low-income couples into marriage; privileged women who want a return to the way we never were; individuals and couples who opt out of marriage; and same-sex couples who want in and people who mobilize to keep them out—reveal the material basis of the economics of scarcity that structures our conceptual and figural understanding of marriage. These phenomena are all so new and newsy that they obscure their indebtedness to the past. But by attracting our attention to who does and doesn't or must and mustn't marry, these stories also blind us to the most basic questions about marriage: what does it mean and what does it cost to be married? As I have argued, our early modern legacy limits the possible answers to that question, at least at the level of figuration and representation. To imagine different futures and different households, and to tell new stories, we need to confront and dissect the history that binds our present to that constraining past.

It is also important to acknowledge the powerful pull marriage continues to exert, despite its flaws. Politicians are interested in marriage because it is a useful mechanism for managing scarce resources and for disciplining unruly sexual subjects. But there is much more to it than that. As George Chauncey asks, "why did getting married matter so much to so many people in a culture that seemed no longer to place much stock in the institution?" He concludes that gay people wanted to be recognized as fully equal to straight people; "The fierce resistance to same-sex marriage had impressed on people the power of marriage to symbolize that equality." For Chauncey, "the rush to marry bore testimony to the continuing power of marriage as a symbol of personal commitment and as a means of gaining recognition for that commitment from others."[9] My point here is that the institution so regarded is also indebted to and shaped by inequality, by misrecognition. Its early modern legacy, the historical weight bearing down on it, is a deep suspicion that marriage cannot really accommodate two equal partners. For marriage to fulfill its promise, then, it needs to be expanded from within by new participants with different stakes and assumptions and with different stories to tell, and supported from without by social changes that accommodate and promote equality rather than suppressing it as divisive.

Notes

Introduction

Epigraphs: Chris Rock, *Never Scared*, dir. Joel Gallen (HBO Home Video, 2004); Larry David, "Mel's Offer," *Curb Your Enthusiasm: The Complete Fourth Season* (2002), dir. Andy Ackerman (HBO Home Video, 2005), episode one.

1. George W. Bush, January 2004 State of the Union Address, *New York Times*, January 21, 2004, A13. On the Bush administration's 1.5 billion dollar drive to promote marriage, see *New York Times*, January 14, 2004, A1, A16. See also Sharon Lerner, "Marriage on the Mind: The Bush Administration's Misguided Poverty Cure," *The Nation* (July 5, 2004): 40–42.

2. On the Defense of Marriage Act (H.R. 3396: To Define and Protect the Institution of Marriage), "passed by overwhelming margins in both the House and the Senate" and "signed into law by President Clinton in September 1996 in the middle of the night," see Andrew Sullivan, ed., *Same-Sex Marriage: Pro and Con* (New York: Vintage), 200–238; and Nancy F. Cott, *Public Vows: A History of Marriage and the Nation* (Cambridge, Mass.: Harvard University Press, 2000), 218–21.

3. James Dobson, *Marriage Under Fire: Why We Must Win This War* (Sisters, Ore.: Multnomah, 2004), 9, 79, 82.

4. Michael Grossberg, *Governing the Hearth: Law and the Family in Nineteenth-Century America* (Chapel Hill: University of North Carolina Press, 1985).

5. Amy Louise Erickson, *Women and Property in Early Modern England* (London: Routledge, 1993); Natasha Korda, *Shakespeare's Domestic Economies: Gender and Property in Early Modern England* (Philadelphia: University of Pennsylvania Press, 2002); Timothy Stretton, *Women Waging Law in Elizabethan England* (Cambridge: Cambridge University Press, 1998). For a fuller discussion of coverture and women's property, see Chapter 2.

6. I first identified what I then called an "economy of marital subjectivity," in *Dangerous Familiars: Representations of Domestic Crime in England, 1550–1700* (Ithaca, N.Y.: Cornell University Press, 1994), 36–38. This book expands on that earlier idea.

7. Jessica Benjamin, *The Bonds of Love: Psychoanalysis, Feminism, and the Problem of Domination* (New York: Pantheon, 1988), 7, 8.

8. C. B. Macpherson, *The Political Theory of Possessive Individualism: Hobbes to Locke* (Oxford: Oxford University Press, 1962), 1, 3. Macpherson explores the complex attitudes of the Levellers to women's political rights, claiming that

women were assumed to be men's spiritual equals but also to have "authorized their men to exercise their political rights" (296).

9. Catherine Gallagher, "Embracing the Absolute: The Politics of the Female Subject in Seventeenth-Century England," *Genders* 1 (1988): 24–39; Maureen Quilligan, *Incest and Agency in Elizabeth's England* (Philadelphia: University of Pennsylvania Press, 2005); and Katharine Gillespie, *Domesticity and Dissent in the Seventeenth Century: English Women Writers and the Public Sphere* (Cambridge: Cambridge University Press, 2004).

10. Macpherson, *Political Theory of Possessive Individualism*, 3.

11. Wendy Brown, *States of Injury: Power and Freedom in Late Modernity* (Princeton, N.J.: Princeton University Press, 1995), 150, 162. See also Mary L. Shanley, "Unencumbered Individuals and Embedded Selves: Dichotomous Thinking in Family Law," in *Debating Democracy's Discontent: Essays on American Politics, Law, and Public Philosophy*, ed. Anita L. Allen and Milton C. Regan, Jr. (Oxford: Oxford University Press, 1998). This volume offers an extended response to Michael J. Sandel, *Democracy's Discontent* (Cambridge, Mass.: Harvard University Press, 1996).

12. Lawrence Stone, *The Family, Sex, and Marriage in England: 1500–1800* (New York: Harper and Row, 1977).

13. See Lena Cowen Orlin's invaluable review essay, "Rewriting Stone's Renaissance," *Huntington Library Quarterly* 64, 1–2 (2002): 189–230.

14. Milton C. Regan, Jr., *Alone Together: Law and the Meanings of Marriage* (New York: Oxford University Press, 1999), 2, 5, 107, 133.

15. Stephanie Coontz, *Marriage, a History: From Obedience to Intimacy or How Love Conquered Marriage* (New York: Viking, 2005); Cott, *Public Vows*; David Cressy, *Birth, Marriage, and Death: Ritual, Religion, and the Life-Cycle in Tudor and Stuart England* (Oxford: Oxford University Press, 1997); Hendrick Hartog, *Man and Wife in America: A History* (Cambridge, Mass.: Harvard University Press, 2000); and Stone, *Family, Sex, and Marriage in England*.

16. Lena Cowen Orlin, *Private Matters and Public Culture in Post-Reformation England* (Ithaca, N.Y.: Cornell University Press, 1994); and Mary Beth Rose, *The Expense of Spirit: Love and Sexuality in English Renaissance Drama* (Ithaca, N.Y.: Cornell University Press, 1988).

17. Amy Erickson, "Coverture and Capitalism," *History Workshop Journal* 59 (2005): 1–16, esp. 1. Erickson claims that, first, "the incapacities placed on marrying women necessitated complex legal maneouvres which produced complex financial instruments and a populace accustomed to using them; and second, that the legal and therefore financial freedom of unmarried English women increased the proportion of the population able to engage in financial markets by fifty per cent" (3).

18. Mary S. Hartman, *The Household and the Making of History: A Subversive View of the Western Past* (Cambridge: Cambridge University Press, 2004), 12, 32.

19. Stone's *Family, Sex, and Marriage in England* is organized around an argument for the shift from patriarchal to companionate models for marriage; the subtitle of Coontz's *Marriage, a History* is "from obedience to intimacy or how love conquered marriage"; John Witte traces the shift *From Sacrament to Contract: Marriage, Religion, and Law in the Western Tradition* (Louisville, Ky.: Westminster John Knox, 1997).

20. In a particularly detailed and interesting study, Martha Howell explores the emergence and significance of marriage contracts in fourteenth- and fifteenth-century Douai. Martha Howell, *The Marriage Exchange: Property, Social Place, and*

Gender in Cities of the Low Countries, 1300–1550 (Chicago: University of Chicago Press, 1998).

21. Victoria Kahn shows that it was certainly possible to imagine marriage as a contract but not really one between equals. See *Wayward Contracts: The Crisis of Political Obligation in England, 1640–1674* (Princeton, N.J.: Princeton University Press, 2004), 171–95. Craig Muldrew argues that while it was possible to imagine marriage as an "equal contract" in the early modern period, attitudes toward marriage lagged behind the shift toward a contractual view of economics and politics. See Muldrew, "'A Mutual Assent of Her Mind'? Women, Debt, Litigation and Contract in Early Modern England," *History Workshop Journal* 55 (2003): 47–71.

22. Grossberg, *Governing the Hearth*; Amy Dru Stanley, *From Bondage to Contract: Wage Labor, Marriage, and the Market in the Age of Slave Emancipation* (Cambridge: Cambridge University Press, 1998).

23. Many feminists challenge the assumption that viewing marriage as a contract necessarily entails viewing spouses as equals. See Brown, *States of Injury*, 135–65; Pamela Haag, *Consent: Sexual Rights and the Transformation of American Liberalism* (Ithaca, N.Y.: Cornell University Press, 1999), 25–60; and Carole Pateman, *The Sexual Contract* (Stanford, Calif.: Stanford University Press, 1988).

24. Hugh Amory and David D. Hall, *The Colonial Book in the Atlantic World* (Worcester, Mass.: American Antiquarian Society; Cambridge: Cambridge University Press, 2000); David Hall, *Cultures of Print: Essays in the History of the Book* (Amherst: University of Massachusetts Press, 1996), 36–96; Ned C. Landsman, *From Colonials to Provincials: American Thought and Culture, 1680–1760* (Ithaca, N.Y.: Cornell University Press, 1997), 32, 42; Louis B. Wright, *The Cultural Life of the American Colonies, 1607–1763* (New York: Harper and Row, 1962), 136–37.

25. Samuel Huntington, *Who Are We? The Challenges to America's National Identity* (New York: Simon and Schuster, 2004), 63, 59, 61.

26. Debra Meyers, *Common Whores, Vertuous Women, and Loveing Wives: Free Will Christian Women in Colonial Maryland* (Bloomington: Indiana University Press, 2003). See also Alexandra Walsham, *Charitable Hatred: Tolerance and Intolerance in England, 1500–1700* (Manchester: Manchester University Press, 2006). Walsham describes Maryland as a "haven" (183). See her study more generally for a discussion of the status of and attitudes toward religious minorities in England.

27. Huntington, *Who Are We?* 92.

28. Robert H. Vasoli, *What God Has Joined Together: The Annulment Crisis in American Catholicism* (New York: Oxford University Press, 1998), 211. See also Patrick W. Carey, *Catholics in America: A History* (Westport, Conn.: Praeger, 2004); and Chester Gillis, *Roman Catholicism in America* (New York: Columbia University Press, 1999).

29. William Pencak, *Jews and Gentiles in Early America, 1654–1800* (Ann Arbor: University of Michigan Press, 2005), vii. See also Eli Faber, *A Time for Planting: The First Migration, 1654–1820*, Jewish People in America 1 (Baltimore: Johns Hopkins University Press, 1992); and Jeffrey S. Gurock, ed., *American Jewish History*, 8 vols., vol. 1, *The Colonial and Early National Periods, 1654–1840* (New York: Routledge, 1998).

30. Sylvia Barack Fishman, *Double or Nothing? Jewish Families and Mixed Marriage* (Boston: Brandeis University Press, 2004), 13.

31. Influential studies of Judaism in antiquity have emphasized its difference both from Christianity and from subsequent developments within Judaism. See, for instance, Daniel Boyarin, *Carnal Israel: Reading Sex in Talmudic Culture*

(Berkeley: University of California Press, 1993); and Michael L. Satlow, *Jewish Marriage in Antiquity* (Princeton, N.J.: Princeton University Press, 2001).

32. Lawrence H. Fuchs, *Beyond Patriarchy: Jewish Fathers and Families* (Boston: Brandeis University Press, 2000), 3. See also Michael J. Broyde, *Marriage, Sex, and Family in Judaism* (Lanham, Md.: Rowman and Littlefield, 2005).

33. Michael A. Gomez, "Muslims in Early America," *Journal of Social History* 60, 4 (1994): 671–710, esp. 708.

34. Barbara C. Aswad and Barbara Bilgé, eds., *Family and Gender Among American Muslims: Issues Facing Middle Eastern Immigrants and Their Descendants* (Philadelphia: Temple University Press, 1996).

35. Marilyn Yalom, *A History of the Wife* (New York: HarperCollins, 2001), 156, xviii.

36. Walter Benjamin, "Theses on the Philosophy of History," in *Illuminations*, trans. Harry Zohn (New York: Schocken, 1969), 255.

37. Michel de Certeau, "Making History: Problems of Method and Problems of Meaning," in *The Writing of History*, trans. Tom Conley (New York: Columbia University Press, 1988), 19–55, esp. 23.

38. Hugh Grady argues that historicism has become so dominant "that more 'presentist' approaches—that is, those oriented towards the text's meaning in the present, as opposed to 'historicist' approaches oriented to meanings in the past— are in danger of eclipse." Hugh Grady, *Shakespeare's Universal Wolf: Studies in Early Modern Reification* (Oxford: Clarendon, 1996), 5. A decade later, this seems to be less the case as negotiations between present and past are proliferating.

39. Unlike many critics of presentism, Ezell concedes that "the desire to find similitude, however, in itself is not, I think, a bad move" (338). Margaret J. M. Ezell, "Looking Glass Histories," *Journal of British Studies* 43, 3 (July 2004): 317–38, esp. 338.

40. Tilottama Rajan, "Introduction" to special issue on "Imagining History," *PMLA* 118, 3 (2003): 427–35, esp. 428.

41. David Kastan, *Shakespeare After Theory* (New York: Routledge, 1999), 17. For an incisive reading of these passages, see Terence Hawkes, *Shakespeare in the Present* (New York: Routledge, 2002), 1–3. See also Robin Headlam Wells, "Historicism and 'Presentism' in Early Modern Studies," *Cambridge Quarterly* 29, 1 (2000): 37–60.

42. Ewan Fernie, "Shakespeare and the Prospect of Presentism," *Shakespeare Survey* 58 (2005): 169–84, esp. 171, 174. Fernie argues that "historicism and presentism are oddly at one."

43. Rebecca Ann Bach, *Shakespeare and Renaissance Literature before Heterosexuality* (New York: Palgrave, 2007); David Cressy, "Gender Trouble and Cross-Dressing in Early Modern England," *Journal of British Studies* 35, 4 (October 1996): 438–65; Mario DiGangi, *The Homoerotics of Early Modern Drama* (Cambridge: Cambridge University Press, 1997), especially his chapter on "Queering the Renaissance Family"; Cynthia B. Herrup, *A House in Gross Disorder: Sex, Law, and the 2nd Earl of Castlehaven* (New York: Oxford University Press, 1999); Valerie Traub, *The Renaissance of Lesbianism in Early Modern England* (Cambridge: Cambridge University Press, 2002); and Wendy Wall *Staging Domesticity: Household Work and English Identity in Early Modern Drama* (Cambridge: Cambridge University Press, 2002), 159.

44. Karma Lochrie, *Heterosyncrasies: Female Sexuality When Normal Wasn't* (Minneapolis: University of Minnesota Press, 2005), xxviii.

45. Hawkes, *Shakespeare in the Present*, 22.

46. Jonathan Goldberg and Madhavi Menon, "Queering History," *PMLA* 120, 5 (2005): 1608–17, 1609, 1616, 1610. See also Judith Halberstam's proposal for a "perverse presentism as not only a denaturalization of the present but also an application of what we do not know in the present to what we cannot know about the past," *Female Masculinity* (Durham, N.C.: Duke University Press, 1998), 53.

47. Louise Fradenburg and Carla Freccero, eds., *Premodern Sexualities* (New York: Routledge, 1996), xix.

48. David Halperin, *How to Do the History of Homosexuality* (Chicago: University of Chicago Press, 2002), 17.

49. Fradenburg and Freccero, *Premodern Sexualities*, xix, xxi.

50. Carla Freccero, *Queer/Early/Modern* (Durham, N.C.: Duke University Press, 2006), 5.

51. Michel Foucault, *Discipline and Punish: The Birth of the Prison*, trans. Alan Sheridan (New York: Vintage, 1979), 31; Halperin, *How to Do the History*, 23.

52. I hope to contribute toward the new kind of historicism that Valerie Traub calls "achieving the difficult and delicate balance between historical sameness and difference, continuism and alterity; of resisting teleology while tracking change; of recognizing both the relative incoherence and relative power of past and present conceptual categories; of integrating questions of representation with questions about lived experience; of attempting to create knowledge of the past while keeping the past productively unknown." Valerie Traub, "The Present Future of Lesbian Historiography," in *A Companion to Lesbian, Gay, Bisexual, Transgender, and Queer Studies*, ed. George Haggerty and Molly McGarry (Oxford: Blackwell, 2007).

53. Hélène Cixous, "Sorties: Out and Out: Attacks/Ways Out/Forays," and Toril Moi, "Feminist, Female, Feminine," in *The Feminist Reader: Essays in Gender and the Politics of Literary Criticism*, ed. Catherine Belsey and Jane Moore (New York: Blackwell, 1989), 101–16, 117–32, esp. Moi, 125, and Cixous, 102.

54. Valerie Traub, *The Renaissance of Lesbianism*, 20. "Material weight" is Traub's phrase. See also de Certeau, *Making History*, 37.

55. Judith Butler, "Contingent Foundations: Feminism and the Question of 'Postmodernism'," in *Feminists Theorize the Political*, ed. Butler and Joan W. Scott (New York: Routledge, 1992), 3–21, esp. 17. See also Teresa de Lauretis, "The Violence of Rhetoric: Considerations on Representation and Gender," in *The Violence of Representation: Literature and the History of Violence*, ed. Nancy Armstrong and Leonard Tennenhouse (London: Routledge, 1989), 239–58.

56. Judith Bennett, "Confronting Continuity," *Journal of Women's History* 9, 3 (1997): 73–94, esp. 88.

57. George Chauncey, *Why Marriage? The History Shaping Today's Debate over Gay Equality* (New York: Perseus, 2004), xviii, 122.

58. Chauncey, *Why Marriage?* 60, 69, 60, 148.

59. Christina Hoff Sommers, *Who Stole Feminism? How Women Have Betrayed Women* (New York: Simon and Schuster, 1994), 200; see also Donald G. Dutton, "Patriarchy and Wife Assault: The Ecological Fallacy," in *Domestic Partner Abuse*, ed. L. Kevin Hamberger and Claire Renzetti (New York: Springer, 1996), 125–51. Sommers is responding to Claire M. Renzetti, *Violent Betrayal: Partner Abuse in Lesbian Relationships* (Newbury Park, Calif.: Sage, 1992). Renzetti is continually revising her arguments about the phenomenon of same-sex partner abuse. For more recent work on the topic, see Claire M. Renzetti and Charles Harvey Miley, eds., *Violence in Gay and Lesbian Domestic Partnerships* (New York: Harrington Park, 1996); Ellyn Kaschak, *Intimate Betrayal: Domestic Violence in Lesbian Relationships*

(New York: Haworth, 2001), also issued as *Women and Therapy* 23, 3 (2001); and Jana L. Jasinski and Linda M. Williams, eds., *Partner Violence: A Comprehensive Review of Twenty Years of Research* (Thousand Oaks, Calif.: Sage, 1998). Janice L. Ristok argues against any of the existing ways of assessing and explaining violence in lesbian relationships in *No More Secrets: Violence in Lesbian Relationships* (New York: Routledge, 2002).

60. Valerie Lehr, *Queer Family Values: Rethinking Inclusion in Marriage and Private Life* (Philadelphia: Temple University Press, 1999), 26.

61. Michael Warner, *The Trouble with Normal: Sex, Politics, and the Ethics of Queer Life* (New York: Free Press, 1999), 82 and passim. Warner, like Lehr, is not confident that marriage can so easily be transformed into a more egalitarian institution (127–31). See also Judith Butler, "Is Kinship Always Already Heterosexual?" *differences: A Journal of Feminist Cultural Studies* 13, 1 (2002): 14–44, esp. 18.

62. William Eskridge, *The Case for Same-Sex Marriage: From Sexual Liberty to Civilized Commitment* (New York: Free Press, 1996), 8, 9, 118.

63. Jim Holt, "A States' Right Left?" *New York Times Magazine*, November 21, 2004, 27.

64. As Lisa Duggan and Richard Kim put this, "the 'threat' of gay marriage" allowed conservatives "to portray marital households as under assault (from homosexuals and judges) without addressing any of the economic factors that put marital households under stress and without directly attacking any of the related legal and social transformations (no-fault divorce, new reproductive technologies, women in the workplace) that most Americans would be reluctant to reject." Lisa Duggan and Richard Kim, "Beyond Gay Marriage," *The Nation* (July 18–25, 2005): 24–27.

Chapter 1. One Flesh, Two Heads: Debating the Biblical Blueprint for Marriage in the Seventeenth and Twentieth Centuries

1. William Perkins, *Oeconomie: or, Houshold-Government. A Short Survey of the Right Manner of Erecting and Ordering a Family, According to the Scriptures*, in *The Workes of That Famous and Worthy Minister of Christ in the Universitie of Cambridge, M. W. Perkins*, 3 vols. (London, 1631), 3: sig. Qqqq5v. The *Oxford Dictionary of National Biography* describes Perkins as a Church of England clergyman, fellow of Christ's College, Cambridge, and "the most significant English theologian of his age." His complete works went through eleven editions between 1602 and 1635. *Oeconomie* was also published separately as *Christian Oeconomie* in 1609.

2. Quoted in Nancy F. Cott, *Public Vows: A History of Marriage and the Nation* (Cambridge, Mass.: Harvard University Press, 2000), 199.

3. Elisabeth Elliott laments that the "blueprint has been lost" (*Let Me Be a Woman: Notes to My Daughter on the Meaning of Womanhood* [Wheaton, Ill.: Tyndale, 1976], 110); Gary Smalley describes Ephesians 5 as a "Biblical blueprint for loving leadership in a home" (Gary Smalley, *Love Is a Decision: Thirteen Proven Principles to Energize Your Marriage and Family* [New York: Pocket Books, 1989], 114). See also James Walker, *Husbands Who Won't Lead and Wives Who Won't Follow* (Minneapolis: Bethany House, 1989), 11, 13.

4. Carol Gilligan argues for "an affinity between love and democracy," with which I am in sympathy, but that affinity is not a given (*The Birth of Pleasure* [New York: Knopf, 2002], 208). Early modern writing on marriage assumes the importance of love but does not think of it as incompatible with hierarchy. On the early

modern period, see: Dympna Callaghan, "The Ideology of Romantic Love: The Case of *Romeo and Juliet*," in *The Weyward Sisters: Shakespeare and Feminist Politics*, ed. Dympna Callaghan, Lorraine Helms, and Jyotsna Singh (Oxford: Blackwell, 1994), 59–101; Judy Kronenfeld, *King Lear and the Naked Truth: Rethinking the Language of Religion and Resistance* (Durham, N.C.: Duke University Press, 1998), 122; Sara Mendelson and Patricia Crawford, *Women in Early Modern England* (Oxford: Clarendon, 1998), 133; J. A. Sharpe, "Plebeian Marriage in Stuart England: Some Evidence from Popular Literature," *Transactions of the Royal Historical Society* 5th ser. 36 (1986): 69–90; Alexandra Shepard, *Meanings of Manhood in Early Modern England* (Oxford: Oxford University Press, 2003), 70–89; Debora Shuger, *Habits of Thought in the English Renaissance: Religion, Politics, and the Dominant Culture* (Berkeley: University of California Press, 1990), 246; Eileen Spring, "Love and the Theory of the Affective Family," *Albion* 16 (1984): 1–20.

5. Lawrence Stone, *The Family, Sex, and Marriage in England: 1500–1800* (New York: Harper and Row, 1977). See also John Gillis, *For Better, for Worse: British Marriages, 1600 to the Present* (New York: Oxford University Press, 1985); and Randolph Trumbach, *The Rise of the Egalitarian Family* (New York: Academic Press, 1977).

6. On continuities in marriage advice, see Kathleen M. Davies, "Continuity and Change in Literary Advice on Marriage," in *Marriage and Society: Studies in the Social History of Marriage*, ed. R. B. Outhwaite (New York: St. Martin's, 1981); and Margot Todd, *Christian Humanism and the Puritan Social Order* (Cambridge: Cambridge University Press, 1987). On continuities in marriage law, see Eric Josef Carlson, *Marriage and the English Reformation* (Cambridge, Mass.: Blackwell, 1994). On continuities in family structures and ideologies, see Peter Laslett, *The World We Have Lost: England before the Industrial Age*, 3rd ed. (New York: Scribner's, 1984); Ralph Houlbrooke, *The English Family, 1450–1700* (London: Blackwell, 1986); and Alan Macfarlane, *Marriage and Love in England: Modes of Reproduction, 1300–1840* (Oxford: Blackwell, 1986).

7. Keith Wrightson, *English Society, 1580–1680* (New Brunswick, N.J.: Rutgers University Press, 1982).

8. David Cressy, *Birth, Marriage and Death: Ritual, Religion, and the Life-Cycle in Tudor and Stuart England* (Oxford: Oxford University Press, 1997), 9.

9. Pamela Allen Brown, *Better a Shrew Than a Sheep: Women, Drama, and the Culture of Jest in Early Modern England* (Ithaca, N.Y.: Cornell University Press, 2003); Bernard Capp, *When Gossips Meet: Women, Family, and Neighbourhood in Early Modern England* (Oxford: Oxford University Press, 2003); Heather Dubrow, *A Happier Eden: The Politics of Marriage in the Stuart Epithalamium* (Ithaca, N.Y.: Cornell University Press, 1990), 1–27, esp. 14; Anthony Fletcher, *Gender, Sex, and Subordination in England, 1500–1800* (New Haven, Conn.: Yale University Press, 1995); Laura Gowing, *Domestic Dangers: Women, Words, and Sex in Early Modern London* (Oxford: Clarendon Press, 1996); Mary Beth Rose, *The Expense of Spirit: Love and Sexuality in English Renaissance Drama* (Ithaca, N.Y.: Cornell University Press, 1988), 116–31, esp. 118–19; and Alison Wall, *Power and Protest in England, 1525–1640* (London: Arnold, 2000), 81–96.

10. Rebecca Ann Bach, *Shakespeare and Renaissance Literature Before Heterosexuality* (New York,: Palgrave Macmillan, 2007); Fletcher, *Gender, Sex, and Subordination*; Valerie Traub, *The Renaissance of Lesbianism in Early Modern England* (Cambridge: Cambridge University Press, 2002).

11. Many reviewers of Stone's *Family, Sex, and Marriage*, and many subsequent histories of marriage and the family in the period, have used an expanded range of sources in order to challenge the "trickle down" model. For instance, Mary S.

Hartman, synthesizing demographic research and exploring its implications, argues that important changes in early modern attitudes and arrangements moved "from the bottom up rather than the top down" (*The Household and the Making of History: A Subversive View of the Western Past* [Cambridge: Cambridge University Press, 2004], 61, cf. 31 and passim). Debates about the family thus resemble those about the origins of the Reformation or the causes of the civil war. Some scholars argue that change is imposed from the top down; others argue for grass roots movements; and still others argue for messy, hard-to-diagram processes of change.

12. Douglas Brouwer, *Beyond "I Do": What Christians Believe about Marriage* (Grand Rapids, Mich.: Eerdmans, 2001), 40. I have gotten many of these books through interlibrary loan from community libraries. Most copies are heavily highlighted, underlined, and commented on, suggesting that their readers approach them as textbooks for happiness.

13. William Whately, *A Care-Cloth: or a Treatise of the Cumbers and Troubles of Marriage: Intended to Advise Them That May, to Shun Them; That May Not, Well and Patiently to Beare Them* (London, 1624), sig. A3v.

14. Nancy Nason-Clark, *The Battered Wife: How Christians Confront Family Violence* (Louisville, Ky.: Westminster John Knox, 1997), 24. See also John Bartkowski, *Remaking the Godly Marriage: Gender Negotiation in Evangelical Families* (New Brunswick, N.J.: Rutgers University Press, 2001), 54; Brenda E. Brasher, *Godly Women: Fundamentalism and Female Power* (New Brunswick, N.J.: Rutgers University Press, 1998); Sally K. Gallagher, *Evangelical Identity and Gendered Family Life* (New Brunswick, N.J.: Rutgers University Press, 2003), 12, 84, 148–49, and passim.

15. See the "Puritan paperbacks" series from Grace and Truth books. Although this series does not reprint any of the conduct books I discuss here, it does reprint other titles by William Perkins, for instance, arguing that such works form the "solid gold" foundation of a Christian family library. I am grateful to David Kay for telling me about this phenomenon.

16. David S. Katz, *God's Last Words: Reading the English Bible from the Reformation to Fundamentalism* (New Haven, Conn.: Yale University Press, 2004).

17. Kristen E. Kvam, Linda S. Schearing, and Valarie H. Ziegler, eds., *Eve and Adam: Jewish, Christian, and Muslim Readings on Genesis and Gender* (Bloomington: Indiana University Press, 1999), 371.

18. Gallagher, *Evangelical Identity and Gendered Family Life,* 69.

19. On the history of conflict within the Southern Baptist Convention, and the triumph of conservatives with a particular interest in excluding women from leadership roles, see Kvam, Schearing, and Ziegler, *Eve and Adam,* 373; and R. Albert Mohler, Jr., "Against an Immoral Tide," *New York Times,* June 19, 2000, A23.

20. Kvam, Schearing, and Ziegler, *Eve and Adam,* 388.

21. For the basic history of the organization, see Judith Newton, *From Panthers to Promise Keepers: Rethinking the Men's Movement* (Lanham, Md.: Rowman and Littlefield, 2005), 214–15, and the organization's Web site, www.promisekeepers.org.

22. *Seven Promises of a Promise Keeper* (Colorado Springs, Colo.: Focus on the Family Publishing, 1994), 79–80, as quoted in Ken Abraham, *Who Are the Promise Keepers? Understanding the Christian Men's Movement* (New York: Doubleday, 1997), 106; see also 59. Newton points out that while these lines have been frequently cited as summing up the organization's attitudes toward gender, Evans's and the organization's rhetoric was considerably more complicated (3). Furthermore, it was often African American platform speakers, like Evans, who emphasized men's domestic responsibilities (*Panthers to Promise Keepers,* 28, 223–24).

23. Abraham, *Who Are the Promise Keepers?* 59.

24. William H. Lockhart, "'We Are One Life,' But Not of One Gender Ideology: Unity, Ambiguity, and the Promise Keepers," in *Promise Keepers and the New Masculinity: Private Lives and Public Morality*, ed. Rhys H. Williams (Lanham, Md.: Lexington, 2001), 73–92. See also other essays in this collection. John Bartkowski emphasizes that, within movement writings, "traditionalist and egalitarian discourses of godly manhood overlap and complement one another" (John Bartkowski, *The Promise Keepers: Servants, Soldiers, and Godly Men* [New Brunswick, N.J.: Rutgers University Press, 2004], 56). For a simpler and more negative reading of the movement, see Michael A. Messner, *Politics of Masculinities: Men in Movements* (Thousand Oaks, Calif.: Sage, 1997), 24–35.

25. On the complexities of these formulations see Bartkowski, *Remaking the Godly Marriage*, 54–68. Bartkowski points out that "servant leadership" is a term appropriated from "popular organizational consultant Robert Greenleaf" (59); Judith Stacey attributes to feminists within evangelical Christianity "the ingenious and, to my mind, somewhat forced doctrine of mutual submission" (*Brave New Families: Stories of Domestic Upheaval in Late-Twentieth-Century America* [Berkeley: University of California Press, 1998], 142).

26. Kvam, Schearing, and Ziegler, *Eve and Adam*, 28–29. Throughout this chapter, my discussion of scriptural and exegetical traditions is indebted to this invaluable sourcebook. Schwartz emphasizes the differences between the two accounts: "in one, after a vast cosmos has been delineated, humankind is created; in the other, humans are created first and the cosmos has shrunk to a garden that suits their needs. Together, these accounts tell that humankind is both the periphery and the center, that the universe is both incomprehensibly vast and intimate" (Regina M. Schwartz, *The Curse of Cain: The Violent Legacy of Monotheism* [Chicago: University of Chicago Press, 1997], 173). See also Mieke Bal, *Lethal Love: Feminist Literary Readings of Biblical Love Stories* (Bloomington: Indiana University Press, 1987), 104–30; and Pamela Norris, *Eve: A Biography* (New York: New York University Press, 1998).

27. Naomi Tadmor, "Women and Wives: the Language of Marriage in Early Modern English Biblical Translations," *History Workshop Journal* 62, 1 (Autumn, 2006): 1–27, esp. 1.

28. Kvam, Schearing, and Ziegler, *Eve and Adam*, 35. This sourcebook includes those who depict hierarchy as paradisal (Augustine, Rashi, Aquinas, Calvin) and as punishment (Chrysostom, Luther).

29. Calvin, in Kvam, Schearing, and Ziegler, *Eve and Adam*, 280. Bartkowski points out that many twentieth-century evangelical commentators "interpret the Genesis 3 account of humankind's 'fall' from grace as a confirmation of the pitfalls of feminine leadership in marriage" (*Remaking the Godly Marriage*, 65). As some commentators point out, however, other husbands in the Bible do and should listen to their wives. For instance, God says to Abraham, regarding Sarah, "in all that Sarah has said to you, hearken to her voice" (Gen. 21:12) (Kvam, Schearing, and Ziegler, *Eve and Adam*, 135).

30. Chrysostom, from homily 17 on Genesis, in Kvam, Schearing, and Ziegler, *Eve and Adam*, 146.

31. Luther, from Lectures on Genesis, vols. 1–8, in Kvam, Schearing, and Ziegler, *Eve and Adam*, 274–75.

32. John Brinsley, *A Looking Glasse for Good Women* (London, 1645), sig. F2.

33. Kvam, Schearing, and Ziegler, *Eve and Adam*, 393–94. The Danvers Statement also claims that, as a consequence of the fall, "in the home, the husband's

loving, humble headship tends to be replaced by domination or passivity; the wife's intelligent, willing submission tends to be replaced by usurpation or servility" (Kvam, Schearing, and Ziegler, *Eve and Adam*, 389).

34. Stacey, *Brave New Families*, 142.

35. Judith Newton, "The Politics of Feeling: Men, Masculinity, and Mourning on the Capital Mall," in *Boys Don't Cry? Rethinking Narratives of Masculinity and Emotion in the U.S.*, ed. Milette Shamir and Jennifer Travis (New York: Columbia University Press, 2002), 243. See also *From Panthers to Promise Keepers*, 226–29.

36. Brasher, *Godly Women*, 154, 164, 168–69.

37. Bartkowski, *Remaking the Godly Marriage*, 116, 117, 116, 121, 123, 129, 123.

38. Tim Elmore, *Soul Provider* (San Bernardino, Calif.: Here's Life Publishers, 1992), 22.

39. Gallagher, *Evangelical Identity and Gendered Family Life*, 69, 84.

40. Stacey, *Brave New Families*, 133. See also Judith Stacey and Susan Elizabeth Gerard, "'We Are Not Doormats': The Influence of Feminism on Contemporary Evangelicals in the United States," in *Uncertain Terms: Negotiating Gender in American Culture*, ed. Fay Ginsburg and Anna L. Tsing (Boston: Beacon, 1990), 98–117; Judith Newton, "The Politics of Feeling," esp. 239, and *From Panthers to Promise Keepers*, 146 and passim.

41. Like Judith Stacey, Faludi finds southern California to be "ground zero" of a crisis in masculinity that is transforming the family. Susan Faludi, *Stiffed: The Betrayal of the American Man* (New York: William Morrow, 1999), esp. chap. 5, "Where Am I in the Kingdom? A Christian Quest for Manhood," 41.

42. Harry Brod, "Pornography and the Alienation of Male Sexuality," in *Gender Violence: Interdisciplinary Perspectives*, ed. Laura L. O'Toole and Jessica R. Schiffman (New York: New York University Press, 1997), 454–66, esp. 461; Alan Soble, *Pornography: Marxism, Feminism, and the Future of Sexuality* (New Haven, Conn.: Yale University Press, 1986), 82.

43. David Savran, "The Sadomasochist in the Closet: White Masculinity and the Culture of Victimization," *differences* 8, 2 (1996): 127–52, esp. 128, 129.

44. On Promise Keepers' commitment to racial integration and white members' resistance, see Newton, *From Panthers to Promise Keepers*, 5, 10, 30, 242–45.

45. Brouwer, *Beyond "I Do,"* 101.

46. Walker, *Husbands Who Won't Lead*, 119.

47. Elliott, *Let Me Be a Woman*, 133. According to James Dobson, one of the problems with the culture of the 1990s was that "the concept that a man and woman should become one flesh, finding their identity in each other rather than as separate and competing individuals, is said to be intolerably insulting to women" (James Dobson, *Straight Talk* [Dallas: Word, 1991], 128–29). Mary Pride has been an especially influential opponent of feminism, arguing for a return to biblical models of marriage and promoting wifely submission and maternal sacrifice. Her book *The Way Home: Beyond Feminism, Back to Reality* (Westchester, Ill.: Crossway, 1985), has been called a "founding text" of the Quiverfull movement, which repudiates birth control and encourages women to home school their large families. See Kathryn Joyce, "The Quiverfull Conviction: Christian Mothers Breed 'Arrows for the War'," *The Nation* (November 27, 2006): 11–18.

48. Susan D. Rose, "Women Warriors: The Negotiation of Gender in a Charismatic Community," *Sociological Analysis* 48, 3 (1987): 245–58, esp. 250, 256.

49. Beverly LaHaye, *The Spirit-Controlled Woman* (Irvine, Calif.: Harvest House, 1976), 73, 74.

50. Gary Smalley, *Hidden Keys of a Loving Lasting Marriage: A Valuable Guide to Knowing, Understanding, and Loving Each Other* (Grand Rapids, Mich.: Zondervan, 1988), 49. This volume conjoins two of Smalley's earlier titles: *If Only He Knew* and *For Better or for Best.*

51. Walker, *Husbands Who Won't Lead*, 21, 119.

52. Dobson, *Straight Talk*, 151.

53. Hilary Hinds, *God's Englishwomen: Seventeenth-Century Radical Sectarian Writing and Feminist Criticism* (Manchester: Manchester University Press, 1996), 44–50; Constance Jordan, *Renaissance Feminism: Literary Texts and Political Models* (Ithaca, N.Y.: Cornell University Press, 1990), 214–20, 248–307; Mendelson and Crawford, *Women in Early Modern England*, 31, 132; Keith Thomas, "Women and the Civil War Sects," *Past and Present* 13 (1958): 42–62; Laurel Ulrich, "'Vertuous Women Found': New England Ministerial Literature, 1668–1735," in *A Heritage of Her Own: Toward a New Social History of American Women*, ed. Nancy F. Cott and Elizabeth H. Pleck (New York: Simon and Schuster, 1979), 58–80. Regarding colonial America, Richard Godbeer argues that the soul was considered sexless, not adopting the gender of the body it inhabited; Elizabeth Reis argues that the soul was often understood as feminine. See Richard Godbeer, "'Love Raptures': Marital, Romantic, and Erotic Images of Jesus Christ in Puritan New England, 1670–1730," *New England Quarterly* 68, 3 (1995): 355–84; and Elizabeth Reis, *Damned Women: Sinners and Witches in Puritan New England* (Ithaca, N.Y.: Cornell University Press, 1997), 93–120.

54. Phyllis Mack, *Visionary Women: Ecstatic Prophecy in Seventeenth-Century England* (Berkeley: University of California Press, 1992); Rachel Trubowitz, "Female Preachers and Male Wives: Gender and Authority in Civil War England," *Prose Studies* 14, 3 (1991): 112–33; Marie B. Rowlands, "Recusant Women, 1560–1640," in *Women in English Society, 1500–1800*, ed. Mary Prior (London: Methuen, 1985), 149–80.

55. Robert Pricke, *The Doctrine of Superioritie, and of Subjection* (London, 1609), sig. L2; Thomas Gataker, *Marriage Duties Briefely Couched Togither; Out of Colossians, 3.18, 19* (London, 1620), sigs. C3, Ev.

56. Richard Allestree, *The Ladies Calling: In Two Parts* (Oxford, 1673), 2: 41.

57. Smalley, *Hidden Keys*, 319 (emphasis mine).

58. Laura Doyle, *The Surrendered Wife: A Practical Guide to Finding Intimacy, Passion, and Peace with a Man* (New York: Simon and Schuster, 1999), 153.

59. Elisabeth Elliot, *Let Me Be a Woman*, 114 [chap. 34 title], 116.

60. Gallagher, *Evangelical Identity and Gendered Family Life*, 53. In *The Case for Marriage: Why Married People Are Happier, Healthier, and Better Off Financially* (New York: Doubleday, 2000), Linda J. Waite and Maggie Gallagher emphasize that one of the keys to marriage is "the powerful magic of specialization—the process of finding out who is good at or enjoys certain tasks" (29). Note that Maggie Gallagher is a syndicated columnist who had a $21,000 contract with the Department of Health and Human Services for writing and advisory work on marriage policy. She did not disclose this contract to her readers. "Marriage czar" Wade Horn insists that she was not paid "to utilize her role as a columnist to promote the president's healthy marriage initiative"; she concurs (*New York Times*, January 27, 2005, A18).

61. Dobson, *Straight Talk*, 33.

62. Doyle, *Surrendered Wife*, 200. This idea has a long reach. In an article in *Health* magazine about the strains created by an "equal marriage," a drop-in box on "Equal Marriage: A Bumpy Ride" explains that "sex is often secondary" in marriages between equal partners. The assumption throughout the article

and in its accompanying box is that only opposites attract. Linking desire with conflict, this article insists that equality robs couples of passion. These popular formulations suggest that the conflict between "opposites" fuels heterosexual passion but also that this conflict is contained by hierarchy, in which one spouse is acknowledged as the superior. So the passionate yet peaceful marriage requires gender contrast to heighten desire but gender hierarchy to limit conflicts of authority. *Health* (March 2000), 92. Research by Amy Weaver, based on Judith Wallerstein and Sandra Blakeslee, *The Good Marriage* (New York: Warner, 1995).

63. Tim LaHaye, *How to Be Happy Though Married* (Wheaton, Ill.: Tyndale House, 1968), 7, 21. On the "Left Behind" series, co-authored by LaHaye and Jerry B. Jenkins, see http://www.leftbehind.com/.

64. Smalley, *Hidden Keys*, 13. In a later work, *Love Is a Decision: Thirteen Proven Principles to Energize Your Marriage and Family* (New York: Pocket Books, 1989), Smalley tries to address the problem of seeming to suggest that men and women are naturally incompatible by arguing that men and women are different by design, having been fashioned by God as complements to one another.

65. Walker, *Husbands Who Won't Lead*, 15, 16.

66. Alison Wall, "Elizabethan Precept and Feminine Practice: The Thynne Family of Longleat," *History* 75, 1 (February 1990): 23–38, esp. 37, 28–29, 35; Zachary Lesser, *Renaissance Drama and the Politics of Publication: Readings in the English Book Trade* (Cambridge: Cambridge University Press, 2004), 132; Tim Meldrum, *Domestic Service and Gender, 1660–1750: Life and Work in the London Household* (Harlow: Longman/Pearson, 2000), 40. See also Bernard Capp, *When Gossips Meet*, 20–25 and passim.

67. Faludi, *Stiffed*, 42. I then invert Judith Newton's description of "a patriarchy more mythic than actual" cited above (Newton, "The Politics of Feeling," 243).

68. In his commentary on Genesis, Augustine argues that a male companion would have been more suitable for Adam: "How much more agreeably could two male friends, rather than a man and woman, enjoy companionship and conversation in a life shared together. . . . Consequently, I do not see in what sense the woman was made a helper for the man if not for the sake of bearing children" (Kvam, Schearing, and Ziegler, *Eve and Adam*, 150–51). Donne quotes this passage in a wedding sermon (*The Sermons of John Donne*, ed. George R. Potter and Evelyn M. Simpson, 10 vols. [Berkeley: University of California Press, 1955], 2: 339). James Grantham Turner discusses this passage, and Donne's response to it, in *One Flesh: Paradisal Marriage and Sexual Relations in the Age of Milton* (Oxford: Clarendon, 1987), 98–101, 114–15. See also John Salkeld, *A Treatise of Paradise* (London, 1617), sig. N3.

69. The rhetoric of friendship was most fully developed with regard to men. See Alan Bray, *The Friend* (Chicago: University of Chicago Press, 2003). Jeffrey Masten suggests that male homoeroticism may have provided a model for imagining and idealizing the relationship between equals that later became the model for marriage. See "My Two Dads: Collaboration and the Reproduction of Beaumont and Fletcher," in *Queering the Renaissance*, ed. Jonathan Goldberg (Durham, N.C.: Duke University Press, 1994), 280–309. In addition, many women also idealized their relationships with one another in terms we now associate with marriage. Seventeenth-century poet Katherine Philips, for instance, describes friendship between women as the melting or transcendence of any boundaries between the two, so that they become one soul if not one flesh. "How happy are we now, whose souls are grown, / By an incomparable mixture, One" ("L'amitie: to

Mrs. M. Awbrey"). "Our chang'd and mingled souls are grown, / To such acquaintance now, / . . . We have each other so ingrost, / That each is in the union lost" ("To Mrs. M.A. at Parting"). While Philips actually insists on union in friendship she argues for a needful separateness in marriage (especially for spouses with different politics): "My love and life I must confesse are thine, / But not my errours, they are only mine" ("To Antenor, on a paper of mine which J. Jones threatens to publish to his prejudice"). *The Collected Works of Katherine Philips, the Matchless Orinda*, 3 vols., ed. Patrick Thomas (Stump Cross, Stump Cross, 1990), 1: 142, 146, 117. On female friendship, see Traub, *Renaissance of Lesbianism*, 276–325.

70. Laurie Shannon, *Sovereign Amity: Figures of Friendship in Shakespearean Contexts* (Chicago: University of Chicago Press, 2002), 56, 64–65, 67; "Likenings: Rhetorical Husbandries and Portia's 'True Conceit' of Friendship," *Renaissance Drama* n.s. 31 (2002): 3–26, esp. 7; and "Nature's Bias: Renaissance Homonormativity and Elizabethan Comic Likeness," *Modern Philology* 98, 2 (2000): 183–210, esp. 185–86. See also Thomas H. Luxon, *Single Imperfection: Milton, Marriage and Friendship* (Pittsburgh: Duquesne University Press, 2005).

71. Traub, *Renaissance of Lesbianism*, 269.

72. George Whetstone, *A Critical Edition of George Whetstone's 1582 "An Heptameron on Civill Discourses,"* ed. Diana Shklanka (New York: Garland, 1987), 204–5. Peter Lake offers an interesting biography of Whetstone as a soldier and professional hack writer, in *The Antichrist's Lewd Hat: Protestants, Papists and Players in Post-Reformation England* (New Haven, Conn.: Yale University Press, 2002), xxviii.

73. *The Memoirs of Anne, Lady Halkett and Ann, Lady Fanshawe*, ed. John Loftis (Oxford: Clarendon, 1979), 103.

74. Daniel Rogers, *Matrimoniall Honour: or, the Mutuall Crowne and Comfort of Godly, Loyall, and Chaste Marriage* (London, 1650), sig. Hh3. There were two editions of this text, in 1642 and 1650. Rogers was a Church of England clergyman.

75. Henry Smith, "A Preparative to Marriage," *The Works of Henry Smith*, 2 vols. (Edinburgh: James Nichol, 1866), 1: 5–40, esp. 25. Smith's patron, William Cecil, Lord Burghley, protected him from the consequences of his nonconformist zeal. Known as "the silver-tongued preacher," Smith consolidated his reputation and extended his persuasion by publishing his collected sermons, which then went through numerous late sixteenth- and seventeenth-century printings; his only son, also Henry, was one of the judges at Charles I's trial and signed his death warrant. Nathaniel Hardy, *Love and Fear the Inseperable Twins of a Blest Matrimony* (London, 1653), sig. Dv (this was a wedding sermon Hardy delivered and was printed again in 1658); Matthew Meade, "A Discourse on Marriage" (1684), in *Conjugal Duty: Part II. Set Forth in a Collection of Ingenious and Delightful Wedding-Sermons* (London, 1736), sig. M3. Meade was a clergyman who faced constant legal difficulties, including losing his positions at the Restoration and inprisonment in connection with the Rye House Plot, because of his nonconformity (new DNB).

76. Natasha Korda, *Shakespeare's Domestic Economies: Gender and Property in Early Modern England* (Philadelphia: University of Pennsylvania Press, 2002), 29 and passim.

77. *A Godly Forme of Houshold Government, for the Ordering of Private Families, According to the Direction of God's Word* (London, 1630), sigs. F8v and L3. This text was printed at least eight times between 1598 and 1630. The title page presents Dod and Cleaver as the amenders and augmenters of a text first "gathered" by R.C. In *Family Reformation Promoted* (London, 1656), his redaction of this book and Gouge's *Domestical Duties*, Daniel Cawdrey claims that his father, Robert Cawdrey, first wrote and published *A Godly Forme of Houshold Government*. He claims that he

does not object to Dod and Cleaver repackaging the material, but only to the fact that they put "to their Booke their own Names, concealing (or at least obscuring) the Name of the first Father of it; onely putting the two first letters of his names, R.C. which signifies nothing to a strange Reader" (Cawdrey, *Family Reformation Promoted*, sigs. A2v–A3). The new DNB includes an entry for Cawdrey, listing him as the "probable" author of this work, but not for Cleaver. The entry on Dod describes him as a "hardliner" Puritan who experienced some persecution but was widely known and influential. Since he wrote many works with Cleaver between 1605 and 1615, and the edition of the work I am using, like Cawdrey's son, names Cleaver as Dod's collaborator, I refer to the authors as "Dod and Cleaver," as is conventional. But I want to draw attention to Cawdrey's contribution.

78. Edmund Tilney, *The Flower of Friendship* (London, 1568), ed. Valerie Wayne (Ithaca, N.Y.: Cornell University Press, 1992), 112. See Wayne's commentary on this passage (62). Tilney was Elizabeth I's distant cousin and served as her "master of the revels" from c. 1577 to 1610. This text went through seven editions, three within the first year of issue (Wayne, 5).

79. Robert Wilkinson, "The Merchant-Royal: Or, Woman a Ship" (first ed., 1607), preached at White Hall at the wedding of Lord Hay and his wife Lady Honoria, in *Conjugal Duty: Set Forth in a Collection of Ingenious and Delightful Wedding-Sermons* (London, 1732), sig. C4v.

80. Ste. B., *Counsel to the Husband, to the Wife Instruction* (London, 1608), sig. E8v.

81. Allestree, *The Ladies Calling*, 1: section 2, 39. The ESTC lists 14 editions of this work between 1673 and 1787. Allestree was a Church of England clergyman and a Royalist who seems to have worked as an agent during the 1650s and who became regius professor of divinity at Oxford as well as provost of Eton College. He also had a sideline as the anonymous author of hugely popular texts such as this and *The Whole Duty of Man*.

82. *Calvin: Commentaries*, trans. and ed. Joseph Haroutunian and Louise Pettibone Smith (Philadelphia: Westminster, 1958), 358.

83. *Luther's Works*, ed. Jaroslav Pelikan, 55 vols. (St. Louis: Concordia, 1958), 1: 133–34, 138. It could be argued that this is a gender division that Christ's resurrection healed. See, for instance, Paul's famous statement in Galatians 3:27–28: "As many of you as were baptized in Christ have clothed yourselves with Christ. There is no longer Jew or Greek, there is no longer *male and female*, for all of you are one in Christ Jesus." But before long, "egalitarian gender roles lost their significance as signs of the new order, and hierarchical roles resumed" (Kvam, Schearing, and Ziegler, *Eve and Adam*, 109). As a result, Paul's second reflection on Genesis 1–3 (1 Corinthians) notoriously reinscribes gender difference and hierarchy; it has been more influential. Household codes in New Testament texts (Ephesians 5:22–6:10, Colossians 3:18–4:1, Titus 2:4–10, and 1 Peter 2:13–3:12) also reinforced hierarchy (Kvam, Schearing, and Ziegler, *Eve and Aam*, 109–10). Catherine Belsey talks about Luther's "remembrance" passage, see Belsey, *Shakespeare and the Loss of Eden: The Construction of Family Values in Early Modern Culture* (New Brunswick, N.J.: Rutgers University Press, 1999), 88.

84. Kvam, Schearing, and Ziegler, *Eve and Adam*, 77–78, 110–12, 120–24, 165, 214–15, 225; Turner, *One Flesh*, 65–71.

85. Quoted in Kvam, Schearing, and Ziegler, *Eve and Adam*, 278.

86. Smith, "A Preparative to Marriage," 1: 12.

87. Consider a statement such as: "In order to become fully human, male and female must join," Dennis Prager, "Homosexuality, the Bible, and Us: A Jewish

Perspective," in *Same-Sex Marriage: Pro and Con; A Reader,* ed. Andrew Sullivan (New York: Vintage, 1997), 65.

88. On the history of and problems caused by such an outlook, see Stephanie Coontz, *The Way We Never Were: American Families and the Nostalgia Trap* (New York: Basic, 1992), 58–65.

89. William Heale, *An Apologie for Women* (Oxford, 1609), sig. H3v; my emphasis. A clergyman, Heale wrote this book in opposition to William Gager's argument that it was lawful for husbands to beat their wives. Constance Jordan claims that "no other critic of marriage envisaged such profound changes in the legal status of the wife as did Heale" (Jordan, *Renaissance Feminism,* 297).

90. While "Puritan" is a troublesome term, it remains a useful way of identifying a distinctive "style of subjectivity and looking at the world" (Peter Lake, "Defining Puritanism—Again?" in *Puritanism: Transatlantic Perspectives on a Seventeenth-Century Anglo-American Faith,* ed. Francis J. Bremer [Boston: Massachusetts Historical Society, 1993], 3–29, esp. 9). James Grantham Turner is an excellent guide to the complexity of early modern responses to Genesis, especially with regard to the status of women and marital sexuality (*One Flesh,* 71–79 and passim). See also Philip C. Almond, *Adam and Eve in Seventeenth-Century Thought* (Cambridge: Cambridge University Press, 1999).

91. Gataker, *Marriage Duties Briefely Couched Togither,* sig. E4v, see also F. Gataker was a Church of England clergyman, and a prolific preacher, writer, and scholar. At the time that he published this text, he had lost two wives to complications following childbirth; he would marry twice more (new DNB).

92. Gouge, *Of Domesticall Duties: Eight Treatises* (London, 1622), sigs. V7, Aa3. A renowned preacher, Gouge was the minister of St. Ann's parish in Blackfriars, London, for thirty-five years (1608–43), where he drew crowds so huge that the church had to be expanded. This enormous volume was printed in 1622 and 1634 and was extremely influential. Daniel Cawdrey claims that he redacted it with Gouge's blessing because it was "too dear for many, yea most poor housholders to buy" (Cawdrey, *Family Reformation Promoted,* sig. A3v). Three years after the first printing, in 1625, Gouge's wife, Elizabeth, died after giving birth to their thirteenth child in twenty-one years of marriage; she was about thirty-nine years old (new DNB). On the importance of sexual pleasure within marriage, or "due benevolence," in passages such as this one from Gouge, see Fletcher, *Gender, Sex, and Subordination in England,* 114; and Traub, *Renaissance of Lesbianism,* 81–83. For a similar passage on sexual mutuality, see *The Honourable State of Matrimony Made Comfortable, or an Antidote against Discord* (London, 1685), sigs. E12v–Fv, M2v–M3.

93. Angus McLaren, *Reproductive Rituals: The Perception of Fertility in England from the Sixteenth Century to the Nineteenth Century* (London: Methuen, 1984), 29.

94. Traub, *Renaissance of Lesbianism,* 265. In contrast, Rebecca Bach emphasizes that conduct manuals such as the ones I am discussing here are "saturated" with "sex-negativity" (*Shakespeare and Renaissance Literature before Heterosexuality,* 15–16).

95. Gervase Babington, *Certaine Plaine, Briefe, and Comfortable Notes, upon Every Chapter of Genesis* (London, 1596), sigs. Ev-E2. This is the enlarged second version of this text, first published in 1592. Babington was bishop of Worcester and, for a time, domestic chaplain to Henry Herbert, second earl of Pembroke, and his wife, Mary Sidney Herbert, countess of Pembroke.

96. William Whately, *A Bride-Bush. or, a Direction for Married Persons* (London, 1623), sigs. G2, E4, G2v. Whately repudiated the first edition of this text (1617)

and offered an expanded version in 1619. A popular Puritan preacher known as "the Roaring Boy of Banbury," Whately was called before the Court of High Commission for his claim in this work that willful desertion should be grounds for divorce and that remarriage should be possible after such a divorce; he recanted in 1621 and this 1623 edition includes his two-page disclaimer as well as the offending passages. There were four more editions of *A Bride-Bush* in the eighteenth century. It was also reprinted by Methodist presses in the eighteenth and early nineteenth-centuries as *Directions for Married Persons* (1753, 1768, 1790, 1794, 1804).

97. John Brinsley, *A Looking-Glasse for Good Women* (London, 1645), sig. F4v; Matthew Meade, "A Discourse on Marriage," sig. M3; Gataker, *Marriage Duties*, sig. F2v. On the importance of cohabitation, see also Heinrich Bullinger, *The Golden Boke of Christen Matrimonye* (London, 1543), chaps. 14 and 15; Gouge, *Of Domesticall Duties*, sig. Q4; Perkins, *Oeconomie*, chap. 9.

98. Dod and Cleaver, *A Godly Forme of Houshold Government*, sig. O5; Gouge, *Of Domesticall Duties*, sig. P3v; Rogers, *Matrimoniall Honour*, sig. Hh3.

99. Dod and Cleaver, *A Godly Forme of Houshold Government*, sig. O7.

100. Ibid., sigs. O7, L3; Babington, *Certaine Plaine, Briefe, and Comfortable Notes*, sig. E2.

101. Whately, *Bride-Bush*, sig. G3; Rogers, *Matrimoniall Honour*, sig. Cc3.

102. John Wing, *The Crowne Conjugall, or the Spouse Royal. A Discovery of the True Honour and Happinesse of Christian Matrimony* (London, 1632), sigs. E3, E3v, E4. The author of *The Honourable State of Matrimony Made Comfortable* warns that when it comes to slander "an open enemy is not capable of doing so much wrong to him, as she that is in his bosom, because she is easily to be believed, as being supposed to know him better than any other" (sig. E5).

103. John Milton, "Doctrine and Discipline of Divorce," in *John Milton*, ed. Stephen Orgel and Jonathan Goldberg (Oxford: Oxford University Press, 1991), 214.

104. Margaret W. Ferguson draws our attention to the word "incorps'd," used once in *Hamlet* and nowhere else in Shakespeare. The word means being "made into one body," and Claudius uses it to describe how the figure Ferguson identifies as Lamord or Death "grew into" or became one with his horse. While Claudius uses the word to praise Lamord's equestrian skill, he also, Ferguson argues, brings death into the closing movement of the tragedy, reminding us of the foundation of Hamlet's fears: to be made one flesh through the matter of marriage and mothers is also to be made mortal, made a corpse through incorporation. Margaret W. Ferguson, "*Hamlet*: Letters and Spirits," in *Shakespeare and the Question of Theory*, ed. Patricia Parker and Geoffrey Hartman (New York: Methuen, 1985), 292–309.

105. Schwartz, *Curse of Cain*, 82, 83, 117. As Schwartz acknowledges, there are some narratives in the Old Testament that "do offer glimpses of another kind of deity, a God of plenitude, of generosity, one who need not protect his turf because it is infinite" (119).

106. Ibid., 5.

107. "Christian" marriage advice published in the last decade or so explicitly counters this tradition by insisting that physical abuse is never acceptable.

108. Susan Dwyer Amussen, *An Ordered Society: Gender and Class in Early Modern England* (Oxford: Basil Blackwell, 1988), 127–29; Gowing, *Domestic Dangers*, 180–231.

109. Martin Ingram, *Church Courts, Sex and Marriage in England, 1570–1640* (Cambridge: Cambridge University Press, 1987), 183. According to Ingram, in

church courts, "it is not surprising to find that it was invariably the wife who claimed cruelty," not because husbands were the more likely to be abusive, but because a husband who "tried to sue his wife for ill-treatment would no doubt have been regarded as a laughing-stock" (183). An account of the duchess of Mazarin's divorce proceedings, published in English in 1699 and cited by Mary Astell as an inspiration to her reflections on marriage, laments that the duke's advocate "will allow nothing to be a justifiable Cause of Separation, but Cruelty; by which he means downright breaking her Bones" (Monsieur de St. Evremont, *The Arguments of Monsieur Herard, for Monsieur the Duke of Mazarin, against Madam the Dutchess of Mazarin, His Spouse* [London, 1699], sigs. A7v–A8, and passim).

110. Lawrence Stone, *The Road to Divorce: England 1530–1987* (Oxford: Oxford University Press, 1992); Randolph Trumbach, *The Rise of the Egalitarian Family: Aristocratic Kinship and Domestic Relations in Eighteenth-Century England* (New York: Academic Press, 1978), 154–60.

111. Michael MacDonald, *Mystical Bedlam: Madness, Anxiety and Healing in Seventeenth-Century England* (Cambridge: Cambridge University Press, 1981), 101; Robert B. Shoemaker, *Gender in English Society, 1650–1850: The Emergence of Separate Spheres* (London: Longman, 1998).

112. Stone, *Road to Divorce*, 2, 410.

113. Carol Berkin and Leslie Horowitz, eds., *Women's Voices, Women's Lives: Documents in Early American History* (Boston: Northeastern University Press, 1998), 50. The options for non-Anglo inhabitants of the colonies and the new republic were quite different. African American couples in which one or both were slaves might be separated by sale, against their will, at any time; Native American couples had easier access to "divorce." See ibid., 53; and Carole Shammas, *A History of Household Government in America* (Charlottesville: University of Virginia Press, 2002).

114. On the greater availability of divorce in the colonies, see Cott, "Divorce and the Changing Status of Women in Eighteenth-Century Massachusetts," *William and Mary Quarterly* 3rd ser. 33 (October 1976): 586–614; Linda K. Kerber, *Women of the Republic: Intellect and Ideology in Revolutionary America* (Chapel Hill: University of North Carolina Press, 1980), chap. 6; and Marylynn Salmon, *Women and the Law of Property in Early America* (Chapel Hill: University of North Carolina Press, 1986), chap. 4. James Hammerton charts the emergence of first physical and then mental cruelty as grounds for divorce in nineteenth-century England (*Cruelty and Companionship: Conflict in Nineteenth-Century Married Life* [London: Routledge, 1992], esp. chap. 4); Richard H. Chused documents the long, slow process by which cruelty was admitted as the grounds for complete divorce in Maryland (*Private Acts in Public Places: A Social History of Divorce in the Formative Era of American Law* [Philadelphia: University of Pennsylvania Press, 1994]). In her ground-breaking book on battered women, Del Martin shows that what constitutes "cruelty," how it can be documented, and whether it should be sufficient grounds for divorce, were still at issue in the 1960s and 1970s (Del Martin, *Battered Wives*, rev. ed. [San Francisco: Volcano, 1981], 163–73).

115. Cornelia Hughes Dayton, *Women Before the Bar: Gender, Law, and Society in Connecticut, 1639–1789* (Chapel Hill: University of North Carolina Press, 1995), 136, 62, and chap. 3, esp. 114. Shammas finds this trend reversing again in the nineteenth century (Shammas, *History of Household Government in America*, 118–22).

116. Allestree, *Ladies Calling*, 2: 80.

117. Rose, *The Expense of Spirit*, 121.

118. Whately, *Bride-Bush*, sig. G2v; Gataker uses just this image, *Marriage Duties*, sig. F4.

119. Gouge, *Of Domesticall Duties*, sig. Aa4. Shepard emphasizes that marriage placed demands on and posed dangers to men: "although marriage was deemed to prove manhood, didacts also emphasized the degree to which it could endanger it" (*Meanings of Manhood*, 77).

120. M. Marsin, *The Women's Advocate: or Fifteen Real Comforts of Matrimony* (London, 1683), 87. Responding to a series of misogynist accounts of marriage including A. Marsh's *The Ten Pleasures of Marriage* (1682), this text purports to be "written by a person of quality of the female sex" and to present the female point of view.

121. Gouge, *Of Domesticall Duties*, sig. Y.

122. Whately, *Bride-Bush*, sig. Ee3v; Cotton Mather, *Ornaments for the Daughters of Zion*, facsimile of 1741 edition with introduction by Pattie Cowell (Delmar, N.Y.: Scholars' Facsimiles, 1978), 94. Mather clearly read Whately; he refers to the fact that Whately dedicated his book on the duties of a wife (by which he means *A Bride-Bush*) to his father-in-law (86). Such attitudes are not obsolete. In a letter to the *New York Times*, Frances Kissling, president, Catholics for a Free Choice, claims that the Catholic Church beatified Elisabetta Canori Mora in 1994 "because she chose to stay in an abusive marriage rather than divorce. The fact that she valued marriage over divorce was saintly; being abused was irrelevant" (*New York Times*, February 2, 2002, A18).

123. Wilkinson, "The Merchant-Royalty," sigs. Eev, C. I am grateful to Margaret Ferguson for pointing out the importance of Wilkinson's reference to Deborah in Judges.

124. Mary Astell, *Some Reflections upon Marriage* (Source Book, 1970), 24, 88.

125. Mary Beth Rose, *Gender and Heroism in Early Modern English Literature* (Chicago: University of Chicago Press, 2002), 107–11.

126. Mendelson and Crawford, *Women in Early Modern England*, 137.

127. Anna Clark, *The Struggle for the Breeches: Gender and the Making of the British Working Class* (Berkeley: University of California Press, 1995), 104. See also Naomi Graetz, *Silence Is Deadly: Judaism Confronts Wife-Beating* (Northvale, N.J.: Jason Aronson, 1998).

128. Nancy Nason-Clark, *The Battered Wife: How Christians Confront Family Violence* (Louisville, Ky.: Westminster John Knox, 1997), 46–47. Nason-Clark bases her study on in-depth interviews she conducted with 94 "Christian" women, 10 of whom she identifies as living in abusive relationships. On evangelical attitudes toward abuse today, see also Sally Gallagher, *Evangelical Identity and Gendered Family Life*, 165–66.

129. *The Lady Eleanor Her Appeal* (1646), in *Prophetic Writings of Lady Eleanor Davies*, ed. Esther S. Cope (New York: Oxford University Press, 1995), 181–97, at 186. Citations will appear in parentheses. I am grateful to Carol Neely for reminding me of Lady Eleanor's efficacious predictions.

130. As Megan Matchinske argues, Eleanor focused particular attention on her most immediate obstacles, her husbands. Megan Matchinske, *Writing, Gender and State in Early Modern England: Identity Formation and the Female Subject* (Cambridge: Cambridge University Press, 1998), 139–55, esp. 141; see also Esther S. Cope, *Handmaid of the Holy Spirit: Dame Eleanor Davies, Never Soe Mad a Ladie* (Ann Arbor: University of Michigan Press, 1992), esp. 42–44, 50, 52, 56. On Eleanor's conflicts with Charles I, see Cynthia B. Herrup, *A House in Gross Disorder: Sex, Law, and the 2nd Earl of Castlehaven* (New York: Oxford University Press, 1999), 90–91, 127–28.

131. Matchinske points out that "in an odd narrative chronology," Eleanor describes the outcome, that Douglas was "strooken bereft of his senses" (189), before she recounts her prediction (Matchinske, *Writing, Gender and State*, 146).

132. Anne Wentworth, *A Vindication of Anne Wentworth* (London, 1677), 2, 1. Citations appear in parentheses.

133. In a text written a year earlier, Wentworth makes a similar move, recasting the meaning of obedience by substituting God for her husband: "I shall not be an unfaithful wife for obeying the voice of my heavenly Husband" (*A True Account of Anne Wentworth's Being Cruelly, Unjustly, and Unchristianly Dealt With by Some of Those People Called Anabaptists* [London, 1676], 8).

134. Katharine Gillespie, *Domesticity and Dissent in the Seventeenth Century: English Women Writers and the Public Sphere* (Cambridge: Cambridge University Press, 2003), 202–10, esp. 209. See also Hinds, *God's Englishwomen*, 102–6; Vera J. Camden, "Prophetic Discourse and the Voice of Protest: The Vindication of Anne Wentworth," *Man and Nature: Proceedings of the Canadian Society for Eighteenth-Century Studies* 8 (1989): 29–38.

135. Richard Rambuss, *Closet Devotions* (Durham, N.C.: Duke University Press, 1998), 80. For bibliographic information on Rous and Collins, see Rambuss.

136. Wentworth, *True Account*, 10, 9, 18.

137. Rambuss, *Closet Devotions*, 82.

138. *Religion and Domestic Violence in Early New England: The Memoirs of Abigail Abbot Bailey*, ed. Ann Taves (Bloomington: Indiana University Press, 1989), 72 (editor's note). All citations from the *Memoirs* will refer to this edition and will appear in the text.

139. Hendrik Hartog, *Man and Wife in America: A History* (Cambridge, Mass.: Harvard University Press, 2000), 152. On coverture, see my chapter 2.

140. Taves, "Introduction" to *Religion and Domestic Violence*, 18.

141. Wentworth, *True Account*, 7.

142. Hartog, *Man and Wife in America*, 53, 62.

143. *The Honourable State of Matrimony Made Comfortable*, sig. G4v.

144. See, for instance, Karla B. Hackstaff, *Marriage in a Culture of Divorce* (Philadelphia: Temple University Press, 1999).

145. Jeannine Gilbert, "My husband's going to die," *Aglow* 22 (Summer 1975): 9–11, as cited and discussed in R. Marie Griffith, *God's Daughters: Evangelical Women and the Power of Submission* (Berkeley: University of California Press, 1997), 169, 173.

146. Newton, *From Panthers to Promise Keepers*, 222.

147. Kate Chopin, *The Awakening and Selected Stories*, ed. Sandra Gilbert (New York: Penguin, 1986), 214–15.

148. Vorse's "The Quiet Woman," in *Women in the Trees: U.S. Women's Short Stories About Battering and Resistance, 1839–1994*, ed. Susan Koppelman (Boston: Beacon, 1996), 60.

Chapter Two: Battered Women, Petty Traitors

1. On disparities among different kinds of evidence with regard to women who kill, see Frances E. Dolan, *Dangerous Familiars: Representations of Domestic Crime in England, 1550–1700* (Ithaca, N.Y.: Cornell University Press, 1994); Christine Holmlund, "A Decade of Deadly Dolls: Hollywood and the Woman

Killer," in *Moving Targets: Women, Murder, and Representation*, ed. Helen Birch (Berkeley: University of California Press, 1994), 127–51; George Robb, "Circe in Crinoline: Domestic Poisonings in Victorian England," *Journal of Family History* 22, 2 (April 1997): 176–90; Martin J. Wiener, "Alice Arden to Bill Sikes: Changing Nightmares of Intimate Violence in England, 1558–1869," *Journal of British Studies* 40 (April 2001): 184–212; and Joy Wiltenburg, *Disorderly Women and Female Power in the Street Literature of Early Modern England and Germany* (Charlottesville: University Press of Virginia, 1992). Wiener argues that cultural interest has shifted from the wife who kills her husband to the husband who kills his wife. While this is in many ways true—even the term "battered woman" emphasizes his violence rather than hers—the murderous wife continues to claim a cultural prominence out of proportion to her statistical significance.

2. Ann Jones, *Women Who Kill* (New York: Holt, Rinehart, 1980, 1996), 319–20, 346, 426; Angela Browne, *When Battered Women Kill* (New York: Free Press, 1987), 9–10; R. Emerson Dobash and Russell Dobash, "Violence Against Women," in *Gender Violence: Interdisciplinary Perspectives*, ed. Laura L. O'Toole and Jessica R. Schiffman (New York: New York University Press, 1997), 266–78, esp. 270, and R. Emerson Dobash and Russell Dobash, *Violence Against Wives: A Case Against the Patriarchy* (New York: Free Press, 1979), 15–17; Erica Goode, "When Women Find Love Is Fatal," *New York Times*, February 15, 2000, D1, D6; David Levinson, *Family Violence in Cross-Cultural Perspective* (Newbury Park, Calif.: Sage, 1989); Lorraine Radford, "Pleading for Time: Justice for Battered Women Who Kill," in *Moving Targets: Women, Murder, and Representation*, ed. Helen Birch (Berkeley: University of California Press, 1994), 172–97, esp. 182; Randolph A. Roth, "Spousal Murder in Northern New England, 1776–1865," in *Over the Threshold: Intimate Violence in Early America*, ed. Christine Daniels and Michael V. Kennedy (New York: Routledge, 1999): 65–93; Murray A. Straus, "New Theory and Old Canards About Family Violence Research," *Social Problems* 38, 2 (1991): 180–97; Murray A. Straus, "Physical Violence in American Families: Incidence, Rates, Causes, Trends," in *Abused and Battered: Social and Legal Responses to Family Violence*, ed. Dean Knudsen and JoAnn Miller (Hawthorne, N.Y.: Aldine de Gruyter, 1991); and Neil Websdale, *Understanding Domestic Homicide* (Boston: Northeastern University Press, 1999), 11, 121, 124.

3. Websdale, *Understanding Domestic Homicide*, 6–8; John M. Dawson and Patrick A. Langan, "Murder in Families" (1994), Bureau of Justice Statistics Special Report NCJ 143498, based on a survey of murder cases disposed in 1988 in large urban areas, 3, available at www.ojp.usdoj.gov/bjs/abstract/mif.htm.

4. Elizabeth Rapaport challenges the legal assumption that an unpremeditated murder committed in "hot blood" is somehow less heinous than a premeditated murder; "The Death Penalty and the Domestic Discount," in *The Public Nature of Private Violence: The Discovery of Domestic Abuse*, ed. Martha Albertson Fineman and Roxanne Mykituk (New York: Routledge, 1994), 224–51.

5. Goode, "When Women Find Love Is Fatal," D6. Goode cites two studies, one of which found that 32 percent of women killed by a partner were killed after they "threatened separation, tried to separate or had recently separated from their partners," and another that found that 32 percent of intimate partner homicides "were committed in the context of a separation." Because this is so often the case, Martha Mahoney proposes that such attacks be defined as "separation assaults" (Martha R. Mahoney, "Legal Images of Battered Women: Redefining the Issue of Separation," *Michigan Law Review* 90, 1 [October 1991]: 1–94). See also Ann

Jones, "Why Doesn't She Leave?" in *Next Time She'll Be Dead: Battering and How to Stop It* (Boston: Beacon Press, 1994), 129–66. Working from capital sentences, Rapaport argues that "a man who kills a woman who lives with him is likely to be less severely sanctioned than one who kills a woman who has left him" ("The Death Penalty and the Domestic Discount," 235). In her view, this disparity is in part because of the continued influence of coverture (238).

6. Both Ginny NiCarthy, *The Ones Who Got Away: Women Who Left Abusive Partners* (Seattle: Seal, 1987), and Ann Goeting, *Getting Out: Life Stories of Women Who Left Abusive Men* (New York: Columbia University Press, 1999) present third-person narratives based on interviews, and including long passages of first-person narration. Anna Quindlen's novel *Black and Blue* (New York: Random House, 1998) tells the first-person story of a woman who leaves her abusive husband.

7. Win Breines and Linda Gordon, "The New Scholarship on Family Violence," *Signs* 8, 3 (1983): 490–531, esp. 519; Evan Stark, Anne Flitcraft, and William Frazier, "Medicine and Patriarchal Violence: The Social Construction of a 'Private' Event," *International Journal of Health Services* 9, 3 (1979): 461–93.

8. When women end up in the emergency room, for example, physicians describe the injuries that bring them there in "passive, disembodied phrases" that objectify the women and erase their assailants: "hit by lead pipe." Carole Warshaw, "Domestic Violence Intervention Calls for More Than Treating Injuries," *Journal of the American Medical Association* 264, 8 (1990): 940. See also Elizabeth M. Schneider, *Battered Women and Feminist Lawmaking* (New Haven, Conn.: Yale University Press, 2000), 60–62.

9. Schneider points out that the term "battered woman" can erase the political roots of this status, consigning it to individual pathology. Schneider praises the Violence Against Women Act, passed in 1994, for the fact that it "equates and connects the national with the individual, the public with the private" (*Battered Women*, 188). That the civil rights remedy provided was found unconstitutional in 2000 by the U.S. Supreme Court suggests that this promise remains unfulfilled (9, 239–40n34). Schneider observes that "for a woman to kill her male partner brings back the historic view of 'treason'"; "A comparison of her situation in killing her partner ('representative of the state' in the household) with that of a man who kills the woman he has beaten (who is viewed as having no independent legal identity), underscores the underlying views of appropriate female conduct that shape these perceptions" (229). In this chapter, I hope to contribute to the project of reconnecting this present struggle to one of its political histories, and of excavating the fuller meanings of this resonance of treason. On the political ramifications of domestic violence, see also Rhonda Copelon, "Recognizing the Egregious in the Everyday: Domestic Violence as Torture," *Columbia Human Rights Law Review* 25, 2 (1994): 291–367.

10. Lenore Walker, *The Battered Woman* (New York: HarperCollins, 1980). For an extended critique of Walker, see Donald Alexander Downs, *More Than Victims: Battered Women, the Syndrome Society, and the Law* (Chicago: University of Chicago Press, 1996), 155–62. See also Browne, *When Battered Women Kill*, chap. 9. Walker was discredited in some people's eyes by the fact that she was scheduled as an expert witness in O. J. Simpson's defense, although she never testified.

11. Julie Blackman, "Emerging Images of Severely Battered Women and the Criminal Justice System," *Behavioral Sciences and the Law* 8 (Spring 1990): 121–30, esp. 127.

12. Robin West, *Narrative, Authority, and Law* (Ann Arbor: University of Michigan Press, 1993), 198, 200. See also Valerie Nash Chang, *I Just Lost Myself: Psychological Abuse of Women in Marriage* (Westport, Conn.: Praeger, 1996).

13. As quoted in Faith McNulty, *The Burning Bed: The True Story of Francine Hughes—A Beaten Wife Who Rebelled* (New York: Harcourt, Brace, 1980), 282.

14. Judith Herman, *Trauma and Recovery: The Aftermath of Violence—from Domestic Abuse to Political Terror* (New York: Basic, 1992), 91. Herman emphasizes that whatever can be said about "battered women" and other survivors of trauma, their consequent behaviors are created by the trauma itself and their strategic responses to it; nothing about them attracted that trauma.

15. Sally Engle Merry, as quoted in Schneider, *Battered Women*, 201.

16. Christine A. Littleton, "Women's Experience and the Problems of Transition: Perspectives on Male Battering of Women," *University of Chicago Legal Forum* (1989): 23–58. Martha Mahoney, too, emphasizes the reasonableness of staying and the resourcefulness of battered women, in "Legal Images of Battered Women" and in "Victimization or Oppression? Women's Lives, Violence, and Agency," in *The Public Nature of Private Violence: The Discovery of Domestic Abuse*, ed. Martha Albertson Fineman and Roxanne Mykituk (New York: Routledge, 1994), 59–92, where she discusses "the problems of equating agency in battered women with exit from violent relationships" ("Victimization" 61, 79).

17. Downs, *More Than Victims*, chap. 7; Linda Gordon, "Killing in Self-Defense," *The Nation* (March 24, 1997): 25–28. Anna Clark argues that in eighteenth- and nineteenth-century England, "moral concerns about wifebeating became symbolically linked to political debates over the citizenship of women and working-class men" and cast wife beaters as "working-class brutes who did not deserve the right to privacy" or to the vote and their wives as "passive creatures who could not determine their own fates" and of course did not deserve the vote either. Anna Clark, "Humanity or Justice? Wifebeating and the Law in the Eighteenth and Nineteenth Centuries," in *Regulating Womanhood: Historical Essays on Marriage, Motherhood, and Sexuality*, ed. Carol Smart (London: Routledge, 1992), 187–206. See also Clark, *The Struggle for the Breeches: Gender and the Making of the British Working Class* (Berkeley: University of California Press, 1995), esp. 248–71.

18. Schneider, *Battered Women and Feminist Lawmaking*; Alan Dershowitz, *The Abuse Excuse and Other Cop-Outs, Sob Stories, and Evasions of Responsibility* (Boston: Little, Brown, 1994).

19. Naomi R. Cahn, "The Looseness of Legal Language: The Reasonable Woman Standard in Theory and in Practice," *Cornell Law Review* 77 (September 1992): 1398–446, esp. 1421.

20. Wendy Brown argues that an injury is an extremely risky claim to entitlement in *States of Injury: Power and Freedom in Late Modernity* (Princeton, N.J.: Princeton University Press, 1995).

21. Frances Power Cobbe, "Wife Torture in England," in *Femicide: The Politics of Woman Killing*, ed. Jill Radford and Diana E. H. Russell (New York: Twayne, 1992), 46–52; "The Declaration of Sentiments," from the Seneca Falls Convention (1848), in Elizabeth Cady Stanton, Susan B. Anthony, and Matilda Joslyn Gage, eds., *History of Woman Suffrage*, 6 vols. (New York: Fowler and Wells, 1881), 1: 70–72; Clark, *The Struggle for the Breeches*; Linda Gordon, *Heroes of Their Own Lives: The Politics and History of Family Violence, Boston, 1880–1960* (New York: Viking/Penguin, 1988), chap. 8; Elizabeth A. Foyster, *Marital Violence: An English Family History, 1660–1857* (Cambridge: Cambridge University Press, 2005);

A. James Hammerton, *Cruelty and Companionship: Conflict in Nineteenth-Century Married Life* (London: Routledge, 1992); Margaret Hunt, "Wife Beating, Domesticity, and Women's Independence in Eighteenth-Century London," *Gender and History* 4, 1 (Spring 1992): 10–33, esp. 25–27; Jones, *Women Who Kill*, 87, 91–93, 98; David Peterson Del Mar, *What Trouble I Have Seen: A History of Violence Against Wives* (Cambridge, Mass.: Harvard University Press, 1998); Elizabeth Pleck, *Domestic Tyranny: The Making of American Social Policy Against Family Violence from Colonial Times to the Present* (Oxford: Oxford University Press, 1987); Nancy Tomes, "A 'Torrent of Abuse': Crimes of Violence Between Working-Class Men and Women in London, 1840–1875," *Journal of Social History* 11, 3 (1978): 328–45, esp. 342; Martin J. Wiener, "The Victorian Criminalization of Men," in *Men and Violence: Masculinity, Honor Codes and Violent Rituals in Europe and America, 1600–2000*, ed. Pieter Spierenburg (Columbus: Ohio State University Press, 1997), 197–212; and Martin J. Wiener, *Men of Blood: Violence, Manliness, and Criminal Justice in Victorian England* (Cambridge: Cambridge University Press, 2004).

22. On battered husbands, see Suzanne K. Steinmetz, "The Battered Husband Syndrome," *Victimology* 2, 3–4 (1977–78): 499–509; Murray A.Straus, Richard J. Gelles, and Suzanne K. Steinmetz, *Behind Closed Doors: Violence in the American Family* (New York: Anchor, 1980); Richard J. Gelles, *The Violent Home: A Study of Physical Aggression between Husbands and Wives* (Beverly Hills, Calif.: Sage, 1974); and Murray A. Straus, "Physical Assaults by Wives: A Major Social Problem," in *Current Controversies on Family Violence*, ed. Richard J. Gelles and Donileen R. Loseke (Newbury Park, Calif.: Sage, 1993). For skeptical responses, see Elizabeth Pleck, Joseph H. Pleck, Marilyn Grossman, and Pauline B. Bart, "The Battered Data Syndrome: A Comment on Steinmetz's Article," *Victimology* 2, 3–4(1977–78): 680–84; Browne, *When Battered Women Kill*, 6–9; and Jones, *Next Time She'll Be Dead*, 154–56.

23. Catharine A. MacKinnon, "Toward Feminist Jurisprudence," *Stanford Law Review* 34, 3 (February 1982): 703–37, esp. 735.

24. Holly Maguigan, "Battered Women and Self-Defense: Myths and Misconceptions in Current Reform Proposals," *University of Pennsylvania Law Review* 140 (December 1991): 379–486, esp. 388. See also Schneider, *Battered Women*.

25. Schneider, *Battered Women*, 122.

26. Ibid., 120. On women's resistance to battering, see also Foyster, *Marital Violence*, 84–128; Gordon, *Heroes of Their Own Lives*, 251–52, 271–76, 286; Mahoney, "Victimization or Oppression?," 73–81; McNulty, *The Burning Bed*; and Del Mar, *What Trouble I Have Seen*.

27. Downs, *More Than Victims*, 24.

28. Mark Kelman, "Reasonable Evidence of Reasonableness," *Critical Inquiry* 17, 4 (Summer 1991): 798–817.

29. Browne, *When Battered Women Kill*, 135.

30. Quoted from an interview in Downs, *More Than Victims*, 158.

31. Jones, *Next Time She'll Be Dead*, 101; Gordon, "Killing in Self-Defense," 28. Jones argues that the number of women who kill their abusers has declined steadily since battered women's shelters first opened in the 1970s; for her, this suggests that women don't want to kill but rather to get away, and will take nonviolent routes of escape when available.

32. Peter Laslett, *The World We Have Lost: England before the Industrial Age— Further Explored*, 3rd ed. (New York: Scribner's, 1984), 20; Lawrence Stone, *The Family, Sex, and Marriage in England, 1500–1800* (New York: Harper and Row, 1977), 195–202.

33. *The Lawes Resolutions of Womens Rights: or, the Lawes Provision for Woemen,* compiled by I. L. and revised by T. E. (London, 1632), sigs. I7, B2v. The author of this compendium, which focuses largely on the common law, has been variously imagined as Thomas Edgar, Nicholas Brady, and Sir John Doderidge. The most thorough discussion of authorship favors Edgar (1602–92), a lawyer and "puritan patriarch," as the reviser and presenter. W. R. Prest, "Law and Women's Rights in Early Modern England," *Seventeenth Century* 6, 2 (Autumn 1991): 169–87. With the running title "The Woman's Lawyer," this text addresses itself to women and presumably those offering them legal advice; we know little about its actual readership; it had only one edition. See Timothy Stretton, *Women Waging Law in Elizabethan England* (Cambridge: Cambridge University Press, 1998), 47–48.

34. William Blackstone, *Commentaries on the Laws of England,* 4 vols. (Oxford: Clarendon, 1765–69), 1: 430. See also W. S. Holdsworth, *A History of English Law,* 9 vols. (London: Methuen, 1903–26), 3: 520–33, 5: 310–15, 6: 644–48. Blackstone's formulation was widely reproduced in compilations such as *The Laws Respecting Women* (London, 1777), 65. As Hendrik Hartog argues, "when American lawyers and activists took Blackstone's lapidary paragraphs as a complete description of the received law of husband and wife, they reified what had been an evolving and changing—and limited—body of English law. . . . Blackstone's language distilled the decisions of one important legal jurisdiction—the common law courts. It sketched one body of rules located in a society filled with multiple-rule bodies, many of which participated in the constitution of marriage. It was not, on its own, the compulsory imposition of a rigid religiously sanctioned patriarchy." This inaccurate reading of Blackstone was so widespread that it became "right." "In nineteenth-century America, nearly everyone . . . agreed that Blackstone's *Commentaries* captured the central features of the received law of husband and wife. By definition, then, it did so, even if everyone thereby read Blackstone in a way that wrested the English law of coverture from its historical and jurisdictional contexts." Hartog, *Man and Wife in America: A History* (Cambridge, Mass.: Harvard University Press, 2000), 118, 120, 121.

35. David Cressy, *Birth, Marriage, and Death: Ritual, Religion, and the Life-Cycle in Tudor and Stuart England* (Oxford: Oxford University Press, 1997), 337, 343.

36. Carole Pateman, *The Sexual Contract* (Stanford, Calif.: Stanford University Press, 1988), 122–23. Of the "marital rape exemption," that is, the presumption that a husband cannot rape his wife because she cannot refuse her consent to him after marriage, Cott argues that "of all the legal features of coverture, this right of the husband to his wife's body was the longest lasting" (Nancy F. Cott, *Public Vows: A History of Marriage and the Nation* [Cambridge, Mass.: Harvard University Press, 2000], 211).

37. Sir Frederick Pollock and Frederic William Maitland, *The History of English Law Before the Time of Edward I,* 2 vols. (Cambridge: Cambridge University Press, 1895), 2: 404. On married women's legal status, see also 1: 465–68, 2: 397–434.

38. Margaret R. Hunt, "Wives and Marital 'Rights' in the Court of Exchequer in the Early Eighteenth Century," in *Londinopolis: Essays in the Cultural and Social History of Early Modern London,* ed. Paul Griffiths and Mark S. R. Jenner (Manchester: Manchester University Press, 2000), 107–29, esp. 112.

39. Natasha Korda, *Shakespeare's Domestic Economies: Gender and Property in Early Modern England* (Philadelphia: University of Pennsylvania Press, 2002), 11–12, 39–47. On the complexities of married women's legal status especially with regard to property, see also Amy Louise Erickson, *Women and Property in Early Modern England* (London: Routledge, 1993); Margot C. Finn, "Women, Consumption, and

Coverture in England, c. 1760–1860," *Historical Journal* 39, 3 (1996): 703–22; Joan R. Gundersen and Gwen Victor Gampel, "Married Women's Legal Status in Eighteenth-Century New York and Virginia," *William and Mary Quarterly* ser. 3 39, 1 (1982): 114–34; Linda K. Kerber, *Women of the Republic: Intellect and Ideology in Revolutionary America* (Chapel Hill: University of North Carolina Press, 1980), esp. chaps. 4, 5; Craig Muldrew, "'A Mutual Assent of Her Mind'? Women, Debt, Litigation and Contract in Early Modern England," *History Workshop Journal* 55 (2003): 47–71; Mary Prior, "Wives and Wills, 1558–1700," in *English Rural Society, 1500–1800: Essays in Honour of Joan Thirsk*, ed. John Chartres and David Hey (Cambridge: Cambridge University Press, 1990), 201–25; Marylynn Salmon, *Women and the Law of Property in Early America* (Chapel Hill: University of North Carolina Press, 1986), 14–18; Alexandra Shepard, "Manhood, Credit, and Patriarchy in Early Modern England, c. 1580–1640," *Past and Present* 167 (May 2000): 75–106; Linda L. Sturtz, "'As Though I My Self Was Pr[e]sent': Virginia Women with Power of Attorney," in *The Many Legalities of Early America*, ed. Christopher L. Tomlins and Bruce H. Mann (Chapel Hill and London: Omohundro Institute/University of North Carolina Press, 2001), 250–71; Garthine Walker, "Women, Theft, and the World of Stolen Goods," in *Women, Crime, and the Courts in Early Modern England*, ed. Jenny Kermode and Walker (Chapel Hill: University of North Carolina Press, 1994): 81–105; and Marlene Stein Wortman, ed., *Women in American Law*, vol. 1, *From Colonial Times to the New Deal* (New York: Holmes and Meier, 1985).

40. Stretton, *Women Waging Law in Elizabethan England*, 151, 153.

41. Hunt, "Wives and Marital 'Rights' in the Court of Exchequer," 121.

42. Stretton, *Women Waging Law in Elizabethan England*, 145; Hartog, *Man and Wife in America*, 107. Baker reminds us that the logic of this legal fiction "did not always commend itself to laymen. It prompted Bumble the beadle [in *Oliver Twist*] to utter the immortal words, 'if the law supposes that . . . then the law is a ass.'" J. H. Baker, *An Introduction to English Legal History*, 3rd ed. (London: Butterworths, 1990), 551, quoting Dickens, *Oliver Twist*, chap. 51.

43. Laurel Thatcher Ulrich, *Good Wives: Image and Reality in the Lives of Women in Northern New England, 1650–1750* (New York: Vintage, 1991), 35–50.

44. Mary Beth Norton, *Founding Mothers and Fathers: Gendered Power and the Forming of American Society* (New York: Knopf, 1996), 140.

45. Tapping Reeve, *The Law of Baron and Femme*, 3rd ed. (1862; New York: Source Book, 1970), 220.

46. Barbara Todd, "'To Be Some Body': Married Women and *The Hardships of the English Laws*," in *Women Writers and the Early Modern British Political Tradition*, ed. Hilda Smith (Cambridge: Cambridge University Press, 1998), 343–61, esp. 344.

47. Linda A. Pollock, "Rethinking Patriarchy and the Family in Seventeenth-Century England," *Journal of Family History* 23, 1 (1998): 3–27. As an example, see Elizabeth Freke, *The Remembrances of Elizabeth Freke, 1671–1714*, ed. Raymond A. Anselment (Cambridge: Cambridge University Press, 2001), in which she records and then reworks her struggles with her husband over money and property, and the burdens placed on her by his lengthy absences.

48. Hartog, *Man and Wife in America*, 168.

49. Kathleen Brown, *Good Wives, Nasty Wenches, and Anxious Patriarchs: Gender, Race, and Power in Colonial Virginia* (Chapel Hill: University of North Carolina Press, 1996), 287–91; Cornelia Hughes Dayton, *Women Before the Bar: Gender, Law, and Society in Connecticut, 1639–1789* (Chapel Hill: University of North Carolina Press, 1995), 10–11, 19–20; John Demos, *A Little Commonwealth: Family Life*

in Plymouth Colony (New York: Oxford University Press, 1970), 84–91; Gundersen and Gampel, "Married Women's Legal Status," 115, 133–34.

50. Susan Staves, *Married Women's Separate Property in England, 1660–1833* (Cambridge, Mass.: Harvard University Press, 1990); Baker, *An Introduction to English Legal History*, 554–55; Amy Dru Stanley, *From Bondage to Contract: Wage Labor, Marriage, and the Market in the Age of Slave Emancipation* (Cambridge: Cambridge University Press, 1998), 175–217; Susan Cary Nicholas, Alice M. Price, and Rachel Rubin, *Rights and Wrongs: Women's Struggle for Legal Equality*, 2nd ed. (New York: Feminist Press, 1986), 28, 32–33. As Stanley points out, courts were more likely to grant a wife title to her person, labor, and wages when her husband was absent or irresponsible: "her right to the fruits of her labor was of little value when premised on physical or economic separation from her husband" (216). This shows that even laws about earnings could not quite think their way out of coverture.

51. Hartog, *Man and Wife in America*, 131, 85, 32, 37, 294–95, 38, 224.

52. On the analogical habit of thought in England, see Susan Dwyer Amussen, *An Ordered Society: Gender and Class in Early Modern England* (Oxford: Blackwell, 1988). On its transport to the colonies, see Demos, *A Little Commonwealth*; Norton, *Founding Mothers and Fathers*; and Carole Shammas, *A History of Household Government in America* (Charlottesville: University of Virginia Press, 2002). On its persistence in American culture, see Cott, *Public Vows*. In *The Case for Marriage*, Waite and Gallagher urge the importance of reactivating awareness that "Marriage is not merely a private taste or a private relation; it is an important public good." Linda J. Waite and Maggie Gallagher, *The Case for Marriage: Why Married People Are Happier, Healthier, and Better Off Financially* (New York: Doubleday, 2000), 186.

53. Margaret Cavendish, Duchess of Newcastle, *CCXI Sociable Letters* (London, 1664), letter 16, sig. D2. Cavendish goes on to say that women govern "by an insensible power, so that as men perceive not how they are Led, Guided, and Rul'd by the Feminine Sex" (sig. D2v).

54. See Sara Mendelson and Patricia Crawford, *Women in Early Modern England* (Oxford: Clarendon, 1998), 49–58, 370–71, 396–99.

55. Linda K. Kerber, *No Constitutional Right to Be Ladies* (New York: Hill and Wang, 1998), xxiii, 11. Although all women did not marry, Kerber's point is that constructions of married women's status affected all women. See also Norton, *Founding Mothers and Fathers*, 62 and passim.

56. Candice Lewis Bredbenner, *A Nationality of Her Own: Women, Marriage, and the Law of Citizenship* (Berkeley: University of California Press, 1998). See also Cott, *Public Vows*, chaps. 4, 5; Hartog, *Man and Wife in America*, 100; Kerber, *No Constitutional Right*, 41; Jacqueline Stevens, *Reproducing the State* (Princeton, N.J.: Princeton University Press, 1999), 135–37; Barbara Todd, "'To Be Some Body,'" 360.

57. Kerber, *No Constitutional Right*, 12.

58. John Milton, *Doctrine and Discipline of Divorce*, ed. Lowell W. Coolidge, in *Complete Prose Works of John Milton*, 8 vols. in 10, gen. ed. Don M. Wolfe (New Haven, Conn.: Yale University Press, 1959), vol. 2; On Paine, see Jay Fliegelman, *Prodigals and Pilgrims: The American Revolution Against Patriarchal Authority, 1750–1800* (Cambridge: Cambridge University Press, 1982), 123–24.

59. Mary Astell, *Some Reflections upon Marriage* (1700; New York: Source Book Press, 1970), 34. Note that Astell was a Tory and upheld absolute monarchy and husbandly authority, arguing that, once entered into, the marriage contract bound wives to obedience. See Ruth Perry, *The Celebrated Mary Astell: An Early*

English Feminist (Chicago: University of Chicago Press, 1986), 150–80. According to Rachel Weil, "The writers who made an analogy between a people's right to depose a ruler and a wife's right to 'depose' a husband were generally opponents of the Revolution who wanted to illustrate the dangerous consequences of political contractarianism." Rachel Weil, *Political Passions: Gender, the Family, and Political Argument in England, 1680–1714* (Manchester: Manchester University Press, 1999), 123. See also Julia Rudolph, "Rape and Resistance: Women and Consent in Seventeenth-Century English Legal and Political Thought," *Journal of British Studies* 39, 2 (2000): 157–84. On how the use of a language of tyranny to describe husbands changed over the course of the seventeenth century, see Garthine Walker, *Crime, Gender and Social Order in Early Modern England* (Cambridge: Cambridge University Press, 2003), 278.

60. Cott, *Public Vows*; Fliegelman, *Prodigals and Pilgrims*, chap. 4; Jan Lewis, "The Republican Wife: Virtue and Seduction in the Early Republic," *William and Mary Quarterly* 3rd ser. 44, 4 (October 1987): 689–721; Belinda Roberts Peters, *Marriage in Seventeenth-Century English Political Thought* (Houndsmills, Basingstoke: Palgrave Macmillan, 2004); and Mary Lyndon Shanley, "Marriage Contract and Social Contract in Seventeenth-Century English Political Thought," *Western Political Quarterly* 32, 1 (1979): 79–91. Carole Shammas argues that the power of Anglo heads of household was, if anything, expanded in colonial America (*A History of Household Government in America*, 24–52); Kathleen Brown argues that the confrontations between Algonquians and the English "may have strengthened the value of patriarchy for each" (*Good Wives, Nasty Wenches*, 73).

61. Carole Pateman, "Conclusion: Women's Writing, Women's Standing," in *Women Writers*, ed. Smith, 365–82, esp. 369. See also Pateman, *The Disorder of Women: Democracy, Feminism, and Political Theory* (Stanford, Calif.: Stanford University Press, 1989); Pateman, *The Sexual Contract*; and Christopher Durston, *The Family in the English Revolution* (Oxford: Blackwell, 1989).

62. Paula McDowell, *Women of Grub Street: Press, Politics, and Gender in the London Literary Marketplace, 1678–1730* (Oxford: Clarendon, 1998); Kerber, *Women of the Republic*; Norton, *Founding Mothers and Fathers*; Steve Rappaport, *Worlds Within Worlds: Structures of Life in Sixteenth-Century London* (Cambridge: Cambridge University Press, 1989), 36–42; Hilda L. Smith, "Women as Sextons and Electors: King's Bench and Precedents for Women's Citizenship," in *Women Writers*, ed. Smith, 324–42. Sara Mendelson and Patricia Crawford argue that women were "negative citizens"—that is, they were accountable for acts of disloyalty yet were not granted privileges (*Women in Early Modern England*, 415).

63. On the prominence of the feminine in national iconographies, see Linda Colley, *Britons: Forging the Nation, 1707–1837* (New Haven, Conn.: Yale University Press, 1992); Lynn Hunt, *The Family Romance of the French Revolution* (Berkeley: University of California Press, 1992); Jodi Mikalachki, *The Legacy of Boadicea: Gender and Nation in Early Modern England* (London: Routledge, 1998); Shirley Samuels, *Romances of the Republic: Women, the Family, and Violence in the Literature of the Early American Nation* (New York: Oxford University Press, 1996). On the Republican Mother, see Kerber, *Women of the Republic*, chap. 9; and Lewis, "The Republican Wife."

64. Stanton et al., *History of Woman Suffrage*, 1: 93, 89. See also 261–62 and passim for critiques of marriage and especially of coverture. Stanton, letter to Gerrit Smith, January 5, 185[1?], as quoted in Stanley, *From Bondage to Contract*, 177. On the relationship between feminists and abolition, see Stanley, *From Bondage to Contract*, 175–217. Some court records suggest that abusive husbands

sometimes threatened to make their wives into slaves; see Laura Gowing, *Domestic Dangers: Women, Words, and Sex in Early Modern London* (Oxford: Clarendon, 1996), 226.

65. Teresa Michals, "'The Sole and Despotic Dominion': Slaves, Wives, and Game in Blackstone's *Commentaries*," *Eighteenth-Century Studies* 27, 2 (Winter 1993–94): 195–216, esp. 202–3.

66. Cott, *Public Vows*, chap. 3, esp. 60–61; Kristen E. Kvam, Linda S. Schearing, and Valarie H. Ziegler, *Eve and Adam: Jewish, Christian, and Muslim Readings on Genesis and Gender* (Bloomington: Indiana University Press, 1999), chap. 7.

67. Karen Sánchez-Eppler, "Bodily Bonds: The Intersecting Rhetorics of Feminism and Abolition," *Representations* 24 (Fall 1988): 28–59, esp. 33–34; Jean Fagan Yellin, *Women and Sisters: The Antislavery Feminists in American Culture* (New Haven, Conn.: Yale University Press, 1989).

68. Pateman, "Conclusion," 368.

69. On petty treason in England, see Michael Dalton, *The Countrey Justice* (London, 1618), a handbook for rural justices of the peace, 204–6; Dolan, *Dangerous Familiars*, 20–88; William Hawkins, *A Treatise of the Pleas of the Crown*, 2nd ed., 2 vols. (1724–26; New York: Arno, 1972), 1: 3, 87–88; Pollock and Maitland, *History of the English Law*, 2: 501–7; and Paul Strohm, "Treason in the Household," in *Hochon's Arrow: The Social Imagination of Fourteenth-Century Texts* (Princeton, N.J.: Princeton University Press, 1992), 121–44.

70. Dalton, *Countrey Justice*, 204; Blackstone, *Commentaries*, 4: 203–4.

71. These punishments were standard for men by the thirteenth century and for women by the fourteenth. See Dalton, *Countrey Justice*, 206; Sir Matthew Hale, *Historia Placitorum Coronae*, 2 vols. (London, 1736), 2: 399; John Selden, *A Booke of the Punishments of the Common Laws of England* (Wapping, 1678); J. H. Baker, "Criminal Courts and Procedure in Common Law 1550–1800," in *Crime in England, 1550–1800*, ed. J. S. Cockburn (Princeton, N.J.: Princeton University Press, 1977), 42; and Baker, *Introduction to Legal History*, 600. On the 1790 revocation of burning as the punishment for women adjudged of petty or high treason, see Ruth Campbell, "Sentence of Death by Burning for Women," *Journal of Legal History* 5 (1984): 44–54.

72. Kerber, *No Constitutional Right to Be Ladies*, 13; Jones, *Women Who Kill*, 19, 36–41; Stephanie Cole, "Keeping the Peace: Domestic Assault and Private Prosecution in Antebellum Baltimore," in *Over the Threshold: Intimate Violence in Early America*, ed. Christine Daniels and Michael V. Kennedy (New York: Routledge, 1999), 148–69, esp. 151–52.

73. On changing attitudes toward domestic violence, see Susan Dwyer Amussen, "'Being Stirred to Much Unquietness': Violence and Domestic Violence in Early Modern England," *Journal of Women's History* 6, 2 (Summer 1994): 70–89; Pamela Allen Brown, *Better a Shrew Than a Sheep: Women, Drama, and the Culture of Jest in Early Modern England* (Ithaca, N.Y.: Cornell University Press, 2003), 118–49; Emily Detmer, "Civilizing Subordination: Domestic Violence and *The Taming of the Shrew*," *Shakespeare Quarterly* 48 (Fall 1997): 273–94; Anthony Fletcher, *Gender, Sex, and Subordination in England, 1500–1800* (New Haven, Conn.: Yale University Press, 1995), chaps. 10, 11; Elizabeth A. Foyster, *Manhood in Early Modern England: Honour, Sex and Marriage* (London: Longman, 1999), 181–93; Foyster, *Marital Violence*; Gowing, *Domestic Dangers*, chap. 6; and Hunt, "Wife Beating, Domesticity, and Women's Independence."

74. On the ambiguity surrounding a husband's legal "right" to beat his wife, and its limits, see *Lawes Resolutions of Womens Rights*, sigs. I8v–K, and Henry Ansgar

Kelly, "*Rule of Thumb* and the Folklaw of the Husband's Stick," *Journal of Legal Education* 44, 3 (1994): 341–65.

75. Blackstone, *Commentaries*, 1: 432.

76. On the wife's ambiguous status see, among others, Catherine Belsey, *The Subject of Tragedy: Identity and Difference in Renaissance Drama* (London: Methuen, 1985), 154; Lena Cowen Orlin, *Private Matters and Public Culture in Post-Reformation England* (Ithaca, N.Y.: Cornell University Press, 1994), 98–104; and Mary Beth Rose, *The Expense of Spirit: Love and Sexuality in English Renaissance Drama* (Ithaca, N.Y.: Cornell University Press, 1988), chap. 3. On the connection between the wife's status and wife beating, see Constance Jordan, *Renaissance Feminism: Literary Texts and Political Models* (Ithaca, N.Y.: Cornell University Press, 1990), 286–97.

77. William Gouge, *Of Domesticall Duties: Eight Treatises* (London, 1622), sig. Cc3v.

78. Hugh Amory and David D. Hall, eds., *The Colonial Book in the Atlantic World* (Worcester, Mass.: American Antiquarian Society; Cambridge: Cambridge University Press, 2000); David Hall, *Cultures of Print: Essays in the History of the Book* (Amherst: University of Massachusetts Press, 1996), 36–96; Ned C. Landsman, *From Colonials to Provincials: American Thought and Culture, 1680–1760* (Ithaca, N.Y.: Cornell University Press, 1997), 32, 42.

79. Gouge, *Of Domesticall Duties*, sig. Cc4v; Robert Snawsel, *A Looking Glasse for Married Folkes* (1610, 1619, 1631), rpt. in *Conjugal Duty: Part II: Set Forth in a Collection of Ingenious and Delightful Wedding-Sermons*, Part II (London, 1736), 214.

80. Gouge, *Of Domesticall Duties*, sig. Cc4. For other claims that the notion that husband and wife are "one flesh" renders wife beating illogical, see also John Dod and Robert Cleaver, *A Godly Forme of Houshold Government, for the Ordering of Private Families* (London, 1630), sig. O2; William Heale, *An Apologie for Women* (Oxford, 1609), sigs. B2v, D4 (this text was revised and reissued in 1682); Alexander Niccholes, *A Discourse of Marriage and Wiving* (London, 1615), sig. G2v; William Perkins, *Oeconomie: or, Houshold-Government* (first published in 1609 as *Christian Oeconomie: or, a Short Survey of the Right Manner of Erecting and Ordering a Familie*), in *The Workes of That Famous and Worthy Minister of Christ in the Universitie of Cambridge, M. W. Perkins*, 3 vols. (London, 1631), vol. 3, sig. Ssss4v; and Henry Smith, "A Preparative to Marriage" (1591), from *The Works of Henry Smith*, 2 vols. (Edinburgh: James Nichol, 1866), 1: 27. *A Caution to Married Couples* (London, 1677) recounts the story of a man who intervenes in the "unnatural Co[m]bat between two that were (or at least should be) both one flesh" (6). The husband kills him and claims that he did so "not without provocation, hindring him to correct his Wife, etc." (7).

81. William Vaughan, *The Golden-Grove, Moralized in Three Bookes* (London, 1608), 2nd ed. sig. O5).

82. William Whately, *A Bride-Bush. or, a Direction for Married Persons* (London, 1623), sig. P2. This collection of Whately's sermons went through three editions in the seventeenth century. Jacqueline Eales explores the differences among the three early editions of this text, including the fact that between the 1617 and 1619 editions, "Whately had substantially changed his mind and he then argued that a husband could use blows as a corrective if his wife had repeatedly and willfully disobeyed him and refused to comply with reasonable commands." Jacqueline Eales, "Gender Construction in Early Modern England and the Conduct Books of William Whately (1583–1639)," in *Gender and Christian Religion*, ed. R. N. Swanson (Woodbridge, Suffolk: Boydell, 1998), 163–74, at 168.

83. Heale, *An Apologie for Women*, sig. C2.

84. Smith, "A Preparative to Marriage," 1: 26.

85. Gouge, *Of Domesticall Duties*, sig. Cc3v.

86. Whately, *A Bride-Bush*, sigs. P3, R2v; see also Gouge, *Of Domesticall Duties*, sig. Cc4. Hartog suggests this attitude persisted into nineteenth-century America: "Much in the law and the political culture taught a husband to think of his wife (and, to a lesser extent, his children) as an extension of himself, and husbands mobilized the image of marital unity as a justification for abuse" (Hartog, *Man and Wife in America*, 104). The inverse of this logic appears in a jest in which a woman who assaults her husband with sharp tongue and nails is asked how she can use him this way, given that he is her head. "He is my head indeed, sayes / she, 'tis true, / Sir, I may scratch my head, / and so may you" (*A Banquet of Jests . . . The Second Part* [London, 1636], 77–78).

87. Sir Francis Willoughby to Lady Elizabeth Willoughby, December 29, 1585, transcript provided by Alice T. Friedman, "Portrait of a Marriage: The Willoughby Letters of 1585–1586," *Signs* 11, 3 (1986): 542–55, esp. 553.

88. Whately, *Bride-Bush*, sigs. R2–R2v, Y4, Z–Zv, Z2, Z3, Z2v.

89. Gouge, *Of Domesticall Duties*, sigs. Cc4v, Cc5. In *The Crowne Conjugall, or the Spouse Royal: A Discovery of the True Honour and Happinesse of Christian Matrimony* (London, 1616), John Wing insists that while the husband can deprive his wife of pleasures and freedoms as a punishment, he may not strike her (F7–8, O12v–P).

90. Perkins, *Workes*, vol. 3, sig. Ssss4v.

91. Massachusetts Colony "Body of Liberties of 1641," as reprinted in Edwin Powers, *Crime and Punishment in Early Massachusetts, 1620–1692: A Documentary History* (Boston: Beacon, 1966), 542. Elizabeth Pleck calls this "the first law against wife abuse anywhere in the Western world," in Elizabeth Pleck, "Criminal Approaches to Family Violence, 1640–1980," in *Family Violence*, ed. Lloyd Ohlin and Michael Tonry (Chicago: University of Chicago Press, 1989), 19–57, esp. 22. On domestic violence in colonial America, see Larry D. Eldridge, "Nothing New Under the Sun: Spouse Abuse in Colonial America," in *Gender Violence: Interdisciplinary Perspectives*, ed. Laura L. O'Toole and Jessica R. Schiffman (New York: New York University Press, 1997), 254–65; Lyle Koehler, *A Search for Power: The 'Weaker Sex' in Seventeenth-Century New England* (Urbana: University of Illinois Press, 1980), chap. 5; Ann M. Little, "'Shee Would Bump His Mouldy Britch': Authority, Masculinity, and the Harried Husbands of New Haven Colony, 1638–1670," in *Lethal Imagination: Violence and Brutality in American History*, ed. Michael Bellesiles (New York: New York University Press, 1999), 43–66; and Pleck, *Domestic Tyranny*.

92. On displacements of wife beating onto the lower classes, see Blackstone, *Commentaries* 1: 433; Clark, "Humanity or Justice?"; Hammerton, *Cruelty and Companionship*; Hunt, "Wife Beating," 27; Del Mar, *What Trouble I Have Seen*, chap. 3; and Wiltenburg, *Disorderly Women and Female Power*, 128. On the disciplinary effects of marriage on freed slaves, see Katherine M. Franke, "Becoming a Citizen: Reconstruction Era Regulation of African American Marriages," *Yale Journal of Law and the Humanities* 11, 2 (1999): 251–309.

93. Robert B. Shoemaker, "Reforming Male Manners: Public Insult and the Decline of Violence in London, 1660–1740," and Elizabeth A. Foyster, "Boys Will Be Boys? Manhood and Aggression, 1660–1800," in *English Masculinities, 1660–1800*, ed. Tim Hitchcock and Michele Cohen (London: Longman, 1999), 133–50, 151–66; Foyster, *Marital Violence*; and Alexandra Shepard, *Meanings of Manhood in Early Modern England* (Oxford: Oxford University Press, 2003), 70–89, 127–51. This supposed "reformation of manners" might be considered in

relation to Norbert Elias' theorization of a "civilizing process" (*The Civilizing Process*, first published in 1939, trans. Edmund Jephcott [Oxford: Blackwell, 2000]) and to the purported decline in homicide rates in England since the early modern period. On trends in England, see J. S. Cockburn, "Patterns of Violence in English Society: Homicide in Kent, 1560–1985," *Past and Present* 130 (February 1991): 70–106, esp. 95–97; J. A. Sharpe, "Domestic Homicide in Early Modern England," *Historical Journal* 24, 1 (1981): 29–48; J. A. Sharpe, "The History of Violence in England: Some Observations," *Past and Present* 108 (August 1985): 206–15; and J. A. Sharpe, "Crime in England: Long-Term Trends and the Problem of Modernization," in *The Civilization of Crime: Violence in Town and Country Since the Middle Ages*, ed. Eric A. Johnson and Eric H. Monkkonen (Urbana: University of Illinois Press, 1996), 17–34; and Lawrence Stone, "Interpersonal Violence in English Society, 1300–1980," *Past and Present* 101 (November 1983): 22–33. See also Manuel Eisner, "Modernization, Self-Control, and Lethal Violence: The Long-Term Dynamics of European Homicide Rates in Theoretical Perspective," *British Journal of Criminology* 41 (2001): 618–38. Alexandra Shepard challenges the "entrenched views of a gradual abeyance of violence in early modern Europe in response to imperatives of civility and politeness and to emergent state control" and argues that "the history of violence should be approached in terms other than 'more' or 'less'" in "Violence and Civility in Early Modern Europe," *Historical Journal* 49, 2 (2006): 593–603, esp. 593, 603.

94. Hunt, "Wife Beating,," 23. On the significance and persistence of community intervention, see Amussen, "'Being Stirred to Much Unquietness,'" 81. See also Bernard Capp, *When Gossips Meet: Women, Family, and Neighbourhood in Early Modern England* (Oxford: Oxford University Press, 2003), 105–10, 116; Foyster, *Marital Violence*, 168–204; John R. Gillis, *For Better, for Worse: British Marriages, 1600 to the Present* (New York: Oxford University Press, 1985), 76–81, 131–34; Gowing, *Domestic Dangers*, 216–18, and chaps. 3, 4; Jennine Hurl-Eamon, "Domestic Violence Prosecuted: Women Binding over Their Husbands for Assault at Westminster Quarter Sessions, 1685–1720," *Journal of Family History* 26, 4 (October 2001): 435–54; Leah Leneman, "'A Tyrant and Tormentor': Violence Against Wives in Eighteenth- and Early Nineteenth-Century Scotland," *Continuity and Change* 12, 1 (1997): 31–54, esp. 43–45; Merril D. Smith, *Breaking the Bonds: Marital Discord in Pennsylvania, 1730–1830* (New York: New York University Press, 1991), chap. 4; Tomes, "'Torrent of Abuse'"; Randolph Trumbach, *Sex and the Gender Revolution*, vol. 1, *Heterosexuality and the Third Gender in Enlightenment London* (Chicago: University of Chicago Press, 1998); and Helena M. Wall, *Fierce Communion: Family and Community in Early America* (Cambridge, Mass.: Harvard University Press, 1990), chap. 3.

95. Koehler documents that in New England "between 1630 and 1699 at least 128 men and 57 women were tried for abusing their mates" and that, of those found guilty, women received considerably harsher punishments (*A Search for Power*, 137, 155). Ann Little shows that, in New Haven Colony in roughly the same period (1638–70), husband abuse was more commonly reported than wife abuse ("'Shee Would Bump His Mouldy Britch'"). Martin J. Wiener argues that changing attitudes and legal reforms particularly worked to limit men's violence against women in Victorian England (*Men of Blood*). David Peterson Del Mar argues that, at least in Oregon, wife beating varied over time, becoming less frequent in the nineteenth century, but then resurging in the twentieth (*What Trouble I Have Seen*).

96. Henry Goodcole, *The Adultresses Funerall Day: In Flaming, Scorching, and Consuming Fire; or the Burning Downe to Ashes of Alice Clarke . . . for the Unnaturall*

Poisoning of Fortune Clarke Her Husband (London, 1635), sigs. Bv–B2v; emphasis mine.

97. Ann Little argues that the limited evidence for colonial New Haven, where she finds only two prosecutions for wife beating, "suggests a correlation between the effects of coverture—the erasing of women as legal entities—and the invisibility of abused wives in the court records" ("'Shee Would Bump His Mouldy Britch,'" 46). Several readings of the O. J. Simpson trial as the replaying of an old story also emphasize that the wife's bruised face persists as a cultural blind spot. According to Shoshana Felman, "such a face is always seen (and recognized) too late" ("Forms of Judicial Blindness, or the Evidence of What Cannot Be Seen: Traumatic Narratives and Legal Repetitions in the O. J. Simpson Case and in Tolstoy's *The Kreutzer Sonata,*" *Critical Inquiry* 23 [Summer 1997]: 738–88, esp. 756). See also Barbara Hodgdon, "Race-ing *Othello,* Re-Engendering White-Out," in *The Shakespeare Trade: Performances and Appropriations* (Philadelphia: University of Pennsylvania Press, 1998), 39–73.

98. *A Warning for Bad Wives* (London 1678), 2–3; *The Proceedings at the Assizes in Southwark, for the County of Surry, Begun on Thursday the 21th, of March, and Not Ended till Tuesday the 26 of the Same Month, 1678* (London, 1678), 4.

99. *The Last Speech and Confession of Sarah Elestone* (London, 1678), sig. A3.

100. J. M. Beattie, *Crime and the Courts in England, 1660–1800* (Oxford: Clarendon, 1986), 100; Walker, *Crime, Gender and Social Order,* 141.

101. *Warning for Bad Wives,* 3, 2, 5, 6–7.

102. Walker, *Crime, Gender and Social Order,* 142, 141, 156. In accord with Walker's argument, one of several accounts of Margaret Osgood or Osily's murder of her husband presents her as taking revenge on her sleeping husband rather than acting in self-defense: "her husband gave her some blows, the which she to outward appearance seemed not to regard, but converting her resentments to private Revenge, the which she in time found opportunity to effect" (*Great and Bloody News from Farthing-Ally* [London, 1680], 1).

103. John Chamberlain to Sir Dudley Carleton (On July 6, 1616), *The Court and Times of James I,* compiled by Thomas Birch and edited by Robert Folkstone Williams (London: Henry Colborn, 1849), 1: 418. Capp discusses the emergence of "some measure of sympathy" for women who killed in self-defense as well as several instances in which the verdict was "mischance" or "manslaughter" because of evidence of what we might call self-defense (Capp, *When Gossips Meet,* 121–23).

104. An informant to Lord Scudamore, PRO Scudamore MSS C 115/M30/8082, as quoted in Esther S. Cope, *Handmaid of the Holy Spirit: Dame Eleanor Davies, Never Soe Mad a Ladie* (Ann Arbor: University of Michigan Press, 1992), 52. This particular crime does not line up with cases that were depicted in pamphlets and ballads so it is hard to know the identity of the petty traitor. For a discussion of the relationship between different kinds of evidence of petty treason, see Frances E. Dolan, "Tracking the Petty Traitor Across Genres," in *Ballads and Broadsides in Britain, 1500–1800,* ed. Patricia Fumerton and Anita Guerrini (Burlington, Vt.: Ashgate, forthcoming).

105. For a more detailed biography of Aubrey or Hobry, see my entry on her in the *New Dictionary of National Biography.*

106. In the record of the Old Bailey trial (under the name Mary Aubry), no mention is made of a history of conflict or violence or of Denis' assault on Mary preceding the murder. The record does say that Mary had made "several resolutions to perpetate [sic] the death of her Husband" and that she set upon him

when he was "fast Asleep, through Excess of Drink" (Proceedings of the Old Bailey Ref, t16880222–24).

107. *A Warning-Piece to All Married Men and Women. Being the Full Confession of Mary Hobry, the French Midwife* (London, 1688); *A Cabinet of Grief: or, the French Midwife's Miserable Moan for the Barbarous Murther Committed upon the Body of Her Husband* (London, 1688), 2; *A Hellish Murder Committed by a French Midwife, on the Body of her Husband, Jan. 27, 1687/8* (London, 1688), sig. E3v. The accusation of sexual abuse was not unique to the Hobry case. For discussion of divorce cases in which the charge of sexual misconduct figured importantly, see Elizabeth A. Foyster, "Male Honour, Social Control, and Wife Beating in Late Stuart England," *Transactions of the Royal Historical Society* 6th ser. 6 (1996): 215–24, esp. 217–18; Foyster, *Marital Violence*, passim; Hammerton, *Cruelty and Companionship*, 108–10; Gail Savage, "The Willful Communication of a Loathsome Disease: Marital Conflict and Venereal Disease in Victorian England," *Victorian Studies* 34, 1 (Autumn 1990): 35–54; and Lawrence Stone, *Broken Lives: Separation and Divorce in England, 1660–1857* (Oxford: Oxford University Press, 1993), 33–37.

108. *Hellish Murder*, sig. E3v.

109. *Hellish Murder*, sigs. E4–E4v.

110. *Cabinet of Grief*, sigs. A3, A6v.

111. *Hellish Murder*, sigs. E3v and F. For an interesting contrast, see *Alimony Arraign'd, or the Remonstrance and Humble Appeal of Thomas Ivie, Esq; from the High Court of Chancery, to His Highnes the Lord Protector of the Commonwealth of England . . . Wherein Are Set Forth the Unheard-of Practices and Villanies of Lewd and Defamed Women, in Order to Separate Man and Wife* (London, 1654), in which Ivie claims that his wife falsely accused him of infecting her with "the Pox," sodomizing her, and attempting to murder her in order to secure a separation and alimony.

112. *Hellish Murder*, sig. Fv. Interestingly, the rest of the description of the murder is offered in French. Only here is Hobry presented as a French speaker; the rest of her examination is translated.

113. *Hellish Murder*, sig. F4.

114. For a reading of the political context of Hobry's case, see Frances E. Dolan, *Whores of Babylon: Catholicism, Gender, and Seventeenth-Century Print Culture* (Ithaca, N.Y.: Cornell University Press, 1999), 212–16.

115. *Murther, Murther. or, a Bloody Relation How Anne Hamton . . . by Poyson Murthered Her Deare Husband* (London, 1641), rpt. in *The Old Book Collectors Miscellany*, ed. Charles Hindley, 2 vols. (London: Reeves and Turner, 1871–72), 2: 4–5, esp. 4; *Adultresses Funerall Day*, sig. Bv.

116. *The True Narrative of the Confession and Execution of the Prisoners at Kingstone-upon-Thames* (London, 1681), 2; *Dreadful News from Southwark: or, a True Account of the . . . Murder Committed by Margaret Osgood, on Her Husband Walter Osgood . . . July 1680* (London, 1680), 3. Another account of this case is mentioned in n. 102.

117. Whately, *A Bride-Bush*, sig. P3. In contrast, Henry Smith argues that limited access to divorce discourages rather than encourages violent conflict: "If they might be separated for discord, some would make a commodity of strife; but now they are not best to be contentious, for this law will hold their noses together, till weariness make them leave struggling; like two spaniels which are coupled in a chain, at last they learn to go together, because they may not go asunder" (Smith, "A Preparative to Marriage," 1: 38).

118. *The Passionate Morrice* (1593), ed. Frederick J. Furnivall, New Shakespeare Society 6, 2 (London: N. Trubner, 1876), 62.

119. Dod and Cleaver, *A Godly Forme of Houshold Government*, sigs. K2v, L3.

120. Daniel Rogers, *Matrimoniall Honour* (London, 1642), sig. K2; Thomas Hilder, *Conjugall Counsell: or, Seasonable Advise, Both to Unmarried, and Married Persons* (London, 1653), 43. I am grateful to Dympna Callaghan for the Hilder reference.

121. Gowing, *Domestic Dangers*, 205: Laura Gowing points out that, in the early modern period, "husband murder is a pragmatic crime: death was the only sure way of exchanging one husband for another." In *Dido's Daughters: Literacy, Gender, and Empire in Early Modern England and France* (Chicago: University of Chicago Press, 2003), Margaret W. Ferguson points out that Salome, in Elizabeth Cary's play *The Tragedy of Mariam,* raises the question "if an unjust legal system binds a partner to a marriage against her will, how unethical is it for her to resort to illegal means to gain her freedom?" (313). Pompa Banerjee argues that European travelers to India circulated a myth that widows were burned because so many had poisoned their husbands. As she shows, this story, prominent in European accounts and absent from Southeast Asian texts, says more about European assumptions and anxieties than about Indian wives. Even the most self-sacrificing wife can be seen as a potential or actual murderer; self-sacrifice collapses into execution because all wives are imagined as potential murderers, all widows as suspect. Pompa Banerjee, *Burning Women: Widows, Witches, and Early Modern European Travelers in India* (New York: Palgrave Macmillan, 2003), 137–73. It is interesting to speculate about whether there were English and colonial wives who killed their husbands and got away with it, in part because neighbors turned a blind eye, thinking he deserved it and she had no choice.

122. Isabel Marcus, "Reframing 'Domestic Violence': Terrorism in the Home," in *Public Nature of Private Violence,* ed. Fineman and Mykituk, 11–35, esp. 23. Dobash and Dobash similarly argue that "the correct interpretation of violence between husbands and wives conceptualizes such violence as the extension of the domination and control of husbands over their wives. This control is historically and socially constructed" (*Violence Against Wives,* 15; see also 33).

123. Walker, *Battered Woman,* 11–13, 33–34, 221; Del Martin, *Battered Wives,* 194; Browne, *When Battered Women Kill,* 144–45; Rapaport, "The Domestic Discount," 230, 238, 243, 247. In contrast, Waite and Gallagher argue that marriage protects women from domestic violence, which is more often visited on girlfriends than on wives: "the research clearly shows that, outside of hying thee to a nunnery, the safest place for a woman to be is inside marriage" (Waite and Gallagher, *Case for Marriage,* chap. 11, esp. 152).

124. Amy Louise Erickson, "Coverture and Capitalism," *History Workshop Journal* 59 (Spring 2005): 1–16, esp. 4; Milton C. Regan, Jr., *Alone Together: Law and the Meanings of Marriage* (New York: Oxford University Press, 1999), 93. Blackstone explains the logic of what has come to be called "spousal privilege" (Blackstone, *Commentaries,* 1: 431). Regan contends that, while support for privileging confidential spousal communication is widespread, the traditional protection against "adverse spousal testimony" is eroding. "In federal and in most state courts, the adverse testimony privilege now protects a defendant from the incriminating testimony of his spouse only if the latter chooses not to testify" (89). In a few states, spouses are absolutely barred from testifying against one another. This privilege does not cover an "alleged wrong committed by one spouse against the other" (90). Regan defends the value of this traditional privilege, although he also concedes that "in practice the adverse testimony privilege operates largely to prevent wives from testifying against their husbands" (90; see also 131).

125. Brown, *States of Injury*, 138. Brown presents Pateman as claiming in *The Sexual Contract* that "the sexual contract is where patriarchalism *lives* in the political and legal order ordinarily understood as its supersession" (136). She herself argues that "the legacy of gender subordination Pateman identifies as historically installed in the sexual-social contract is to be found not in contemporary contract relations but in the *terms* of liberal discourse that configure and organize liberal jurisprudence, public policy, and popular consciousness" (138).

126. Shoshana Felman, "Forms of Judicial Blindness," esp. 751. See also Anna Clark, *Struggle for the Breeches*: "however much radical men may have disapproved of it, wife-beating was not an aberration, but a consequence of the domestic ideal" (263).

Chapter Three. Fighting for the Breeches, Sharing the Rod

1. Stanley Cavell, *Pursuits of Happiness: The Hollywood Comedy of Remarriage* (Cambridge, Mass.: Harvard University Press, 1981).

2. Noel Coward, *Plays: Two* (London: Methuen, 1986), 11–12. Further citations will be given in parentheses in the text.

3. Elyot and Amanda are alone in the apartment in Act 2 because they have let Louise go for the evening. They joke about the "profoundly miserable" life they imagine for her at home, where her "beastly" and "absolutely vile" family "knock her about dreadfully, . . . and make her eat the most disgusting food, and pull her fringe" (41), but they never discuss what it must be like for her to work for them.

4. Eve Kosofsky Sedgwick, *Between Men: English Literature and Male Homosocial Desire* (New York: Columbia University Press, 1985). See also the work on erotic triangles involving slaves, below. In *Adulterous Alliances: Home, State, and History in Early Modern Drama and Painting* (Chicago: University of Chicago Press, 2000), Richard Helgerson considers an erotic triangle that structures many early modern European texts: a sexual predator who is somehow identified with the state (a soldier, a courtier, an aristocrat, a king) invades the nonaristocratic home (which is often figured in the nonaristocratic woman).

5. Barbara Hodgdon, *The Shakespeare Trade: Performances and Appropriations* (Philadelphia: University of Pennsylvania Press, 1998), 1. According to Ewan Fernie, "Shakespeare . . . is primarily a contemporary dramatist and writer, because he is currently taught, read and performed on a global scale unmatched by any other author. . . . [H]e is more embedded in our modern world than he ever was in the Renaissance" ("Shakespeare and the Prospect of Presentism," *Shakespeare Survey* 58 [2005]: 169–84, esp. 175).

6. M. C. Bradbrook, "Dramatic Role as Social Image: A Study of *The Taming of the Shrew*," *Shakespeare Jahrbuch* 94 (1958): 132–50, esp. 134.

7. On shrews, see Lynda E. Boose, "Scolding Brides and Bridling Scolds: Taming the Woman's Unruly Member," *Shakespeare Quarterly* 42, 2 (1991): 179–213; Valerie Wayne, "Refashioning the Shrew," *Shakespeare Studies* 17 (1985): 159–87; and Linda Woodbridge, *Women and the English Renaissance: Literature and the Nature of Womankind, 1540–1620* (Urbana: University of Illinois Press, 1984).

8. Samuel Rowlands, *A Whole Crew of Kind Gossips, All Met to Be Merry* (London, 1609), rpt. in *The Complete Works of Samuel Rowlands, 1598–1628*, 3 vols. (Glasgow: Hunterian Club, 1880), describes a wife who binds her husband to the peace with "a Faggot-sticke", 2: 9. Anthony Fletcher opines that "Rowlands knew that

his male readers were used to living with women prepared to give as good as they got, whether with tongue or fist" (*Gender, Sex, and Subordination in England, 1500–1800* [New Haven, Conn.: Yale University Press, 1995], 21). In "The Cruel Shrew: Or, The Patient Man's Woe" (c. 1600–1650), the husband describes how his wife "takes up a cudgel's end, / and breaks my head full sore"; in "The Henpeckt Cuckold" (c. 1689–91), the husband describes how his "cross-grained wife" scratches, bites, and strikes him, and knocks him down with a frying-pan; in her "answer" the wife promises to "get a lusty Rod" to "jerk and firk this Cod." See *The Roxburghe Ballads* (Herford: Ballad Society, 1870–99), vols. 1–3 ed. William Chappell, vols. 4–9 ed. J. W. Ebsworth, 1: 94–98, 7: 182–83, 7: 432–33.

9. As Valerie Traub observes of the provision under Judaic law that a hermaphrodite could marry a woman but not a man, "two penises, apparently, were considered too many in one marriage." Traub, *Renaissance of Lesbianism in Early Modern England* (Cambridge: Cambridge University Press, 2002), 50.

10. The Sam Taylor film of *Taming of the Shrew* (1929), with Mary Pickford and Douglas Fairbanks, plays with this possibility by equipping both Katherina and Petruchio with whips.

11. Thomas Hobbes, *Leviathan* (1651), edited with an introduction by C. B. Macpherson (Harmondsworth: Penguin, 1968), Part II, chap. 20, p. 253.

12. Joy Wiltenburg, *Disorderly Women and Female Power in the Street Literature of Early Modern England and Germany* (Charlottesville: University Press of Virginia 1992), 137.

13. William Whately, *A Care-Cloth: or a Treatise of the Cumbers and Troubles of Marriage* (London, 1624), sig. A2v.

14. William Gouge, *Of Domesticall Duties: Eight Treatises* (London, 1622), sig. Y3v; S.B., *Counsel to the Husband, to the Wife Instruction* (London, 1608), sig. F2v; Daniel Cawdrey, *Family Reformation Promoted* (London, 1656), sig. F9v; Gouge, *Of Domesticall Duties*, sig. S8.

15. Richard Allestree, *The Ladies Calling: In Two Parts* (Oxford, 1673), part II, section ii, 33–34. On the influence and importance of this text, see Fletcher, *Gender, Sex, and Subordination*, 384–89.

16. Gouge, *Of Domesticall Duties*, sig. S8; William Whately, *A Bride-Bush. Or, A Direction for Married Persons* (London, 1623), sigs. Bb3–Bb3v.

17. Cotton Mather, *Ornaments for the Daughters of Zion* in the facsimile of the 1741 edition with introduction by Pattie Cowell (Delmar, N.Y.: Scholars' Facsimiles, 1978), 89. There were three editions of this work (1692, 1694, 1741); emphasis mine.

18. Woodbridge, *Women and the English Renaissance*, 217. On the prevalence of the pants as a "metaphor for authority" in European popular culture, see Keith Moxey, *Peasants, Warriors, and Wives: Popular Imagery in the Reformation* (Chicago: University of Chicago Press, 1989), 104, 115–16, and woodcuts throughout chapter 5.

19. In *The Woman's Prize, or the Tamer Tamed* (1611), John Fletcher's sequel to Shakespeare's *Taming of the Shrew*, Livia proclaims "let's all wear breeches" (1.2.145). In *The Ghost, or the Woman Wears the Breeches*, a wife seizes her husband's pants, carries them on a pole as a banner of defiance and refers to him as a "breechless Booby" (written in 1640, printed in 1653); in *The City Wit, or the Woman Wears the Breeches* (London, 1653), the bossy wife doesn't actually wear breeches, but she refuses to take her husband's name, and threatens him with a truncheon. See also *The Gossips Braule, or, the Women Weare the Breeches* (London,

1655) and a ballad called "The Mock Expedition or, the Women in Breeches (Wapping, printed for Moll Tar-Breeches, 1695), which argues that the breeches are women's "by right" when they behave "like men."

20. Timothy Stretton, *Women Waging Law in Elizabethan England* (Cambridge: Cambridge University Press, 1998), 37, 131.

21. S. B., *Counsel to the Husband*, sig. C8.

22. *The Confession of the New Married Couple, Being the Second Part of the Ten Pleasures of Marriage* (London, 1683), sig. E10v.

23. Ann Rosalind Jones and Peter Stallybrass, *Renaissance Clothing and the Materials of Memory* (Cambridge: Cambridge University Press, 2000).

24. Kathleen Brown, *Good Wives, Nasty Wenches, and Anxious Patriarchs: Gender, Race, and Power in Colonial Virginia* (Chapel Hill: University of North Carolina Press, 1996), 75–80; Mary Beth Norton, *Founding Mothers and Fathers: Gendered Power and the Forming of American Society* (New York: Knopf, 1995), 190–97. This persisted into the nineteenth century. Elizabeth Fox-Genovese discusses instances in which male slaves were forced to wear women's clothing; and one in which a woman was required to wear trousers for a year in punishment for theft (*Within the Plantation Household: Black and White Women of the Old South* [Chapel Hill: University of North Carolina Press, 1988], 293). She also points out that slave owners routinely provided pants to men and skirts to women (294).

25. *The Collected Plays of Edward Albee*, 3 vols. (Woodstock, N.Y.: Overlook, 2004–5), 1: 260.

26. Penny Junor, *Burton: The Man Behind the Myth* (London: Sidgwick and Jackson, 1985), 122. Junor makes this claim in a chapter entitled "One Ego Too Many." Burton and Taylor starred in *Who's Afraid of Virginia Woolf?* a year before they made Zeffirelli's *Taming of the Shrew* (1967). On the relevance of Taylor and Burton's public personae as stars and spouses to Zeffirelli's film, see Barbara Hodgdon, *The Shakespeare Trade*, 15–19.

27. Laura Doyle, *The Surrendered Wife: A Practical Guide to Finding Intimacy, Passion, and Peace with a Man* (New York: Simon and Schuster, 1999), 156. Hendrick Hartog argues that in nineteenth-century America, sometimes speakers and writers on marriage "used the image of 'pants' or 'breeches' as a way to capture a combined sense of unity and separateness. Each leg was separate and individual; yet both were needed to make *one* pair of pants" (Hartog, *Man and Wife in America: A History* [Cambridge, Mass.: Harvard University Press, 2000], 114). Usually, however, the pants stand for an economy of scarcity within marriage. See also Anna Clark, *The Struggle for the Breeches: Gender and the Making of the British Working Class* (Berkeley: University of California Press, 1995), chap. 5.

28. Sally K. Gallagher, *Evangelical Identity and Gendered Family Life* (New Brunswick, N.J.: Rutgers University Press, 2003), 148; see also 168.

29. Maureen Dowd, "Whipping the Pants Off the Women Who Wear Them," in *Are Men Necessary? When Sexes Collide* (New York: Putnam, 2005), 108.

30. On the different status of male and female cross-dressing, see David Cressy, "Gender Trouble and Cross-Dressing in Early Modern England," *Journal of British Studies* 35 (1996): 438–65; and Jean E. Howard, *The Stage and Social Struggle* (New York: Routledge, 1994), 93–106.

31. Gouge, *Of Domesticall Duties*, sig. Cc3v.

32. John Dod and Robert Cleaver, *A Godly Forme of Houshold Government, for the Ordering of Private Families, According to the Direction of God's Word* (London, 1630), sig. D5v.

33. Whately, *A Bride-Bush,* sig. N4; Henry Smith, "A Preparative to Marriage" (1591), from *The Works of Henry Smith,* 2 vols. (Edinburgh: James Nichol, 1866), 1: 5–40, esp. 26.

34. Gouge, *Of Domesticall Duties,* sig. Cc4.

35. A. Marsh, *The Confession of the New Married Couple* (London, 1683), sig. E13. This satirical text is deeply ambivalent, even outright hostile, toward women. Yet this formulation resonates with the mixed messages in conduct books and sermons.

36. Kathleen M. Davies, "Continuity and Change in Literary Advice on Marriage," *Marriage and Society: Studies in the Social History of Marriage* (New York: St. Martin's, 1981), 58–80, esp. 68. On mistress-servant relations, see Bernard Capp, *When Gossips Meet: Women, Family, and Neighbourhood in Early Modern England* (Oxford: Oxford University Press, 2003), 127–84; Laura Gowing, "The Haunting of Susan Lay: Servants and Mistresses in Seventeenth-Century England," *Gender and History* 14, 2 (2002): 183–201; and Tim Meldrum, *Domestic Service and Gender, 1660–1750: Life and Work in the London Household* (Harlow: Longman/Pearson, 2000), 39, 42–47, 73, 118–21.

37. Daniel Rogers, *Matrimoniall Honour* (London, 1642), 299. I would like to thank Marilyn Luecke for drawing my attention to this passage. On the complexity of the mother's position, see her "The Reproduction of Culture and the Culture of Reproduction in Elizabeth Clinton's *The Countess of Lincolnes Nurserie,*" in *Women, Writing, and the Reproduction of Culture in Tudor and Stuart Britain,* ed. Mary E. Burke, Jane Donawerth, Linda Dove, and Karen Nelson (Syracuse, N.Y.: Syracuse University Press, 2000), 238–52.

38. Whately, *Bride-Bush,* sigs. N4–N4v. Another text, *The Honourable State of Matrimony Made Comfortable* (London, 1685), advises that the mother should not "chide or correct" her child in the father's presence; she must either leave this to him or "deal with the Child when the Father is gone forth" so that she does not seem to usurp his authority (sig. L8).

39. Mather, *Ornaments for the Daughters of Zion,* 107.

40. Norton, *Founding Mothers and Fathers,* 119, 116. Slave women engaged in "extensive" rather than "intensive" mothering, "in which all adult women were assumed to have competence and authority to tend to, teach, and chastise all plantation children" (Carol Berkin and Leslie Horowitz, eds., *Women's Voices, Women's Lives: Documents in Early American History* [Boston: Northeastern University Press, 1998], 52). Women's use of violence was so much the norm that it might serve as the standard by which to judge the inadequacy of non-Europeans. According to Carole Shammas, for instance, "Much to the despair of European observers, only Christianized Indian mothers engaged in physical punishment of their young" (Carole Shammas, *A History of Household Government in America* [Charlottesville: University of Virginia Press, 2002], 42).

41. Parents and employers should always punish in response to a particular fault, rather than out of anger; they should be sure that they are punishing the right party and that the punishment suits the crime, the age, and the temper of the offender; they should consider whether the mistake was intentional or accidental; and they should not disgrace the servant or child in front of others. The offender should know why he or she is being punished. See Susan Dwyer Amussen, "Punishment, Discipline, and Power: The Social Meanings of Violence in Early Modern England," *Journal of British Studies* 34, 1 (1995): 1–34, esp. 12–18.

42. Heinrich Bullinger, *The Golden Boke of Christen Matrimonye* (London, 1543), sig. L2-v.

43. See Fletcher, *Gender, Sex, and Subordination*, 216, for a discussion of how Pepys delegated the beating of a female servant to his wife in accord with such advice. Mary Beth Norton cites a case in which unruly children were ordered whipped by the parent of the same sex (*Founding Mothers and Fathers*, 48). Gendered decorum sometimes shaped relations in slave-owning households. See Marli F. Weiner, *Mistresses and Slaves: Plantation Women in South Carolina, 1830–80* (Urbana: University of Illinois Press, 1998); and Eugene D. Genovese, "Life in the Big House," in *A Heritage of Her Own*, ed. Nancy Cott and Elizabeth Pleck (New York: Simon and Schuster, 1979).

44. Wendy Wall and Alan Stewart both show that same-sex beating could certainly be construed as erotic (Wall, *Staging Domesticity: Household Work and English Identity in Early Modern Drama* [Cambridge: Cambridge University Press, 2002], 83–84, 181; Stewart, *Close Readers: Humanism and Sodomy in Early Modern England* [Princeton, N.J.: Princeton University Press, 1997], 84–121). Stewart and Wall both discuss what Wall calls Richard Mulcaster's "famous feminization of the birch": "For the private, what soever parentes say, my ladie *birchely* will be a gest at home, or else parentes shall not have their willes" (Richard Mulcaster, *Positions Concerning the Training Up of Children* [1581], ed. William Barker [Toronto: University of Toronto Press, 1994], 270; the passage is discussed by Stewart, 99, and Wall 239n59). Barker argues that "'Lady Birch' is the common expression for a form of punishment given by males to males; presumably punishment by a (symbolic) female to the male buttocks would intensify the humiliation" (446n270.7). Female teachers could also be imagined as taking pleasure in imposing pain. In *Venus in the Cloister: or the Nun in Her Smock* (London, 1683), Angelica, a more experienced nun, explains to the novice, Agnes, that she has been known to whip one of the "Scholars and Pensionaries" committed to her care "rather for my own satisfaction, than for any fault she had committed; I took great delight in contemplating her, she is very pretty, and is already thirteen years of age." Sister Agnes replies "I long for that employment of Mistriss of the School, that I might take the like divertissement!" (B8).

45. Gouge proposes an exception to the gendered division of the labor of beating, however: "if a maid should wax stout, and mannish, and turne against her mistresse, she being weake, sickly, with child, or otherwise unable to master her maid, the master may and must beat downe her stoutnesse and rebellion" (Gouge, *Of Domesticall Duties*, sig. Vv3v; cf. Henry Smith, "A Preparative to Marriage," 34). That is, if a maid-servant acts like a man, she may appropriately be treated like one.

46. Dod and Cleaver, *Godly Forme of Houshold Government*, sig. Aa3v. For a satire on what happens when such decorum is disregarded, see *The Pleasures of Matrimony* (London, 1685), which tells a story in which a husband asks his wife why she doesn't beat her "lazy Slut" of a dairy maid. The wife asks him to do it and he proposes to "exercise my Talent upon her Buttocks, as you do by your Children" and gives the maid "another sort of Chastizement than what his Wife meant." When the maid complains to the mistress, the mistress, thinking she's discussing only correction and not fornication, licenses what her husband has done and thereafter the maid "resolved never to refuse her Master's Correction when ever he was so kind as to give it her." Clearly, the text suggests, this wife was foolish to encourage her husband to meddle with the maid (sigs. H4v–H5, H5v).

47. Meldrum, *Domestic Service and Gender*, 108.

48. Gowing, "The Haunting of Susan Lay," 193. Cotton Mather also invokes Sarah but with a different spin than other writers. Of the good mistress, he says,

"though she be a Sarah, that is, a Mistress; yet she owns that she has a *Master*. And like a *Sarah* of old, she will not so much as take in, or cast out a Servant without consulting *him*" (*Ornaments of the Daughters of Zion*, 90).

49. Byrd's mother's first husband had been Samuel Filmer, son of Sir Robert Filmer, the apologist for patriarchy (in his text *Patriarcha*). See Kenneth A. Lockridge, *On the Sources of Patriarchal Rage: The Commonplace Books of William Byrd and Thomas Jefferson and the Gendering of Power in the Eighteenth Century* (New York: New York University Press, 1992), 21.

50. The book on which Byrd bases his shorthand code (William Mason's *La Plume Volante*, 1707) was published shortly after his first marriage; he begins the first diary less than three years after he marries. Kenneth Lockridge speculates that "the shorthand code may have been intended above all to hide Byrd's further-encoded self from his wife" (Kenneth Lockridge, *The Diary, and Life, of William Byrd II of Virginia, 1674–1744* [Chapel Hill: University of North Carolina Press, 1987], 48–49). The available edition of the diary is *The Secret Diary of William Byrd of Westover, 1709–1712*, ed. Louis B. Wright and Marion Tinling (Richmond, Va.: Dietz, 1941). Further citations appear in parentheses in the text.

51. Lockridge's assessment is that Lucy was "usually ill when pregnant, was pregnant most of the time, and miscarried easily and often" (Lockridge, *The Diary, and Life*, 68).

52. Two days after refusing to be bled in June of 1711, Lucy suffered a miscarriage (365). Lucy and William had four children, two of whom died in infancy. The early diary records the birth, christening, illnesses, and death of Parke in 1710. On the day of the baby's death (June 3, 1710), Byrd writes: "My wife was much afflicted but I submitted to His judgment better, notwithstanding I was very sensible of my loss, but God's will be done" (187). The Byrds occasionally fight about how to treat their daughter Evelyn's ailments: "My wife was severe to her because she was fretful" (129); "I was out of humor with my wife for forcing Evie to eat against her will" (180–81); "In the afternoon Evie had a sweat that worked pretty well but not long enough, for which I was out of humor with my wife" (181); "My wife and I had a quarrel because she neglected to give the child the bitter drink" a doctor had prescribed for her three times a day (225 [Sept. 1, 1710, with reference to August 5, 1710]). William and Lucy both beat Susan or Suky Brayne, his niece, when she is staying with them. On January 11, 1711, Byrd records that "I quarreled with my wife for being cruel to Suky Brayne, though she deserved it" (285) but himself administers a vomit and a purge (222) and two beatings to the girl. On Byrd's beating of other people's children, see Michael Zuckerman, *Almost Chosen People: Oblique Biographies in the American Grain* (Berkeley: University of California Press, 1993), 122–23.

53. Shammas, *History of Household Government*, 148.

54. Brown, *Good Wives, Nasty Wenches*, 152, 352. Brown points out that whipping servants naked was outlawed in 1705, reserving this indignity for slaves (352). See also Warren M. Billings, "The Law of Servants and Slaves in Seventeenth-Century Virginia," *Virginia Magazine of History and Biography* 99, 1 (January 1991): 45–62.

55. Unlike slaves, servants and apprentices "could petition county courts for redress of their grievances." According to Christine Daniels, "many servants understood their legal rights, sought relief for their grievances, and succeeded in their efforts." Christine Daniels, "'Liberty to Complaine': Servant Petitions in Colonial Maryland," in *The Many Legalities of Early America*, ed. Christopher Tomlins and Bruce Mann (Chapel Hill: University of North Carolina Press, 2001),

219–49, esp. 222, 225. See also Peter Linebaugh and Marcus Rediker, *The Many-Headed Hydra: Sailors, Slaves, Commoners, and the Hidden History of the Revolutionary Atlantic* (Boston: Beacon, 2000), 127, 135–39.

56. Susan Cahn, *Industry of Devotion: The Transformation of Women's Work in England, 1500–1660* (New York: Columbia University Press, 1987), esp. 86–125.

57. Byrd mentions about fifty servants by name but usually makes no distinction between indentured or enslaved, white or black. He seems to own six or seven house slaves. Michael Zuckerman identifies the people who figure so importantly as objects of Lucy's violence as slaves: Prue, Anaka, Eugene, and Jenny. Byrd also had a few male Indian slaves but they do not figure significantly in the diary. See Michael Zuckerman, "The Family Life of William Byrd," in *Almost Chosen People*, 115n48; and Pierre Marambaud, *William Byrd of Westover, 1674–1744* (Charlottesville: University of Virginia Press, 1971). While Jennifer L. Morgan challenges the assumption that female slaves were inevitably domestic servants, especially in the seventeenth century, emphasizing instead their important role in back-breaking agricultural labor (*Laboring Women: Reproduction and Gender in New World Slavery* [Philadelphia: University of Pennsylvania Press, 2004]), the female slaves in the Byrd household I am discussing here were engaged in domestic work.

58. Wright, "Introduction," *The Secret Diary of William Byrd of Westover, 1709–1712*, xiv.

59. Stone also describes Lucy as "a neurotic and difficult woman" (Lawrence Stone, *The Family, Sex, and Marriage in England, 1500–1800* [New York: Harper and Row, 1977], 564, 563). See also Marambaud, *William Byrd*, 178, 26, 27; Lockridge, *Diary, and Life*, 66, 67. In a later text, Lockridge claims that William "left" Lucy because she and a female friend who had come to live with them in 1711 "usurped his patriarchal authority within the household, taking over total control of material resources and of the house servants [and their discipline], something Byrd could not bear." His evidence for this idiosyncratic claim comes from one letter rather than the diary (Lockridge, *On the Sources of Patriarchal Rage*, 21–22). For Lockridge's evidence, see the "Dunella" letter in *The Correspondence of the Three William Byrds of Westover, Virginia, 1684–1776*, ed. Marion Tinling, 2 vols. (Charlottesville: University Press of Virginia, 1977), 1: 275–79. Richmond Croom Beatty, who wrote his biography, *William Byrd of Westover* (1932; rpt.: Hamden, Conn.: Archon, 1970), without the benefit of the diaries, which were discovered a few years later, assures his readers that Byrd's first marriage was "entirely conventional and orthodox." "Byrd's disposition was extremely agreeable. It would be a simple matter for him to live pleasantly with any lady whose temper was not positively shrewish" (61). It is interesting to wonder what his verdict would have been had he had access to the diary.

60. Terri L. Snyder, "'As if There Was Not Master or Woman in the Land': Gender, Dependency, and Household Violence in Virginia, 1646–1720," in *Over the Threshold: Intimate Violence in Early America*, ed. Christine Daniels and Michael V. Kennedy (New York: Routledge, 1999), 219–36; Zuckerman, *Almost Chosen People*, 122.

61. Snyder, "'As if There Was Not Master or Woman in the Land'," 223.

62. Capp, *When Gossips Meet*, 143, see also 137, 144. It was certainly possible for women to abuse their power over children and servants. According to J. A. Sharpe, women constituted 7 percent of those accused of nondomestic killing in assize courts, but 42 percent of those accused of killing a relative, and 41 percent of those accused of killing servants or apprentices in Essex assizes,

1560–1709; women also figured importantly in prosecutions for the murder of children, especially newborns. But women's acquittal rate was also high, suggesting a reluctance to criminalize household chastisement, even when it was inflicted by women. Of 44 persons accused of killing servants or apprentices at these assizes, only 5 were found guilty (3 men, 2 women). J. A. Sharpe, "Domestic Homicide in Early Modern England," *Historical Journal* 24, 1 (1981): 29–48, esp. 36–39; J. S. Cockburn, "Patterns of Violence in English Society: Homicide in Kent, 1560–1985," *Past and Present* 130 (February 1991): 70–106, esp. 95–97. For somewhat sympathetic accounts of male servants who murdered their mistresses, claiming that they were driven to do so by their employers' cruelty and "ill-usage," see *The Apprentices Warning-piece. Being a Confession of Peter Moore* (London, 1641); and *The Vain Prodigal Life and Tragical Penitent Death of Thomas Hellier* (London, 1680). On Hellier, see T. H. Breen, James H. Lewis, and Keith Schlesinger, "Motive for Murder: A Servant's Life in Virginia, 1678," *William and Mary Quarterly* 40, 1 (1983): 106–20.

63. Terri L. Snyder, *Brabbling Women: Disorderly Speech and the Law in Early Virginia* (Ithaca, N.Y.: Cornell University Press, 2003), 120, 133–34. Christine Daniels argues that female servants were more likely to complain about excessive physical punishment in part because it would usually have been administered to them by their mistresses ("'Liberty to Complaine,'" 238).

64. Elizabeth Fox-Genovese argues that, in the later antebellum period, mistresses' authority, and in particular their right to whip their servants, was routinely questioned and challenged. "Because the mistress lacked the full authority of the master, her relations with her servants could easily lapse into a personal struggle." While it was almost always the mistress who instigated violence, a servant, and even sometimes a slave, could understand the conflict as a negotiation in which s/he might gain or assert a right. Fox-Genovese, *Within the Plantation Household*, 24, 97, 313–14, quotation on 308.

65. Anne Kugler, *Errant Plagiary: The Life and Writing of Lady Sarah Cowper, 1644–1720* (Stanford, Calif.: Stanford University Press, 2002), 47, 48, 50, 55, 56, 224n19. The Cowpers had houses in London and in Hertford. Lady Sarah bore four sons in the first five years of her marriage. She then seems to have refrained from sexual relations with her husband to avoid having more children, whether with or without his consent is unclear. In the period 1670–1700, Cowper compiled and indexed eleven commonplace books (3,500 pages) (31). In 1700, she began keeping a detailed diary instead, perhaps because of a serious family crisis (her youngest son's trial for murder). She seems to have imagined the diary as a posthumous reproach to her husband, "the last word in a long-running argument," but was thwarted when he predeceased her (7, 9). While his death frustrated her design at one level, it also granted her the upper hand more effectively than her reading or her writing could. As Kugler concludes, "becoming a widow was more important to her control of household management than proving her case for wifely jurisdiction" (17).

66. *The Diary of Ralph Josselin (1616–1683)*, ed. Alan Macfarlane (London: Oxford University Press, 1976), entry for April 26, 1646 (59).

67. *The Autobiography of Mrs. Alice Thornton, of East Newton Co. York* (Durham: Surtees Society, 1875), 128.

68. Ralph Baxter, *A Breviate of the Life of Margaret . . . Wife of Richard Baxter* (London, 1681), 80, 74. One of the conflicts between Maria Thynne and her husband, which is registered in letters she wrote him, is her right to choose and manage her servants. See Alison Wall, "Elizabethan Precept and Feminine

Practice: The Thynne Family of Longleat," *History* 75, 1 (February 1990): 23–38, esp. 29, 34.

69. Joanne Bailey, *Unquiet Lives: Marriage and Marriage Breakdown in England, 1660–1800* (Cambridge: Cambridge University Press, 2003), 26, 76–77.

70. John Smolenski argues for the value of reading texts such as Byrd's as dialogical, even when they do not take pains to record slave voices, or as fieldnotes describing encounters that were, of course, not one-sided. "Hearing Voices: Dialogicality, Microhistory, and the Recovery of Popular Culture on an Eighteenth-Century Virginia Plantation," *Slavery and Abolition* 24, 1 (2003): 1–23.

71. See Brown, *Good Wives, Nasty Wenches*, 306. For the interplay of what Brown calls "enforced intimacy" and violence in a later period, see Fox-Genovese: "Mistresses whipped slave women with whom they might have shared beds, whose children they might have delivered or who might have delivered theirs, whose children they might have suckled and who frequently had suckled theirs. Young masters fought with young slave women with whom they had played as children and whom they might already be attempting to seduce. And masters, who embodied the ultimate authority, might have sexual relations with the women they disciplined and who indeed might be their daughters. Not surprisingly, house slaves felt that they had grounds to resist abuses of authority and even to claim a role in determining its legitimate bounds. Whether the tensions were openly acknowledged or not, slave women's lives in the big house constituted a dense pattern of day-to-day resistance that could at any moment explode into violence" (Fox-Genovese, *Within the Plantation Household*, 315).

72. These two modes of managing servants conjoin in the later Virginia diary when, on December 26, 1740, William reports giving a vomit to three slaves "for going off the plantation and staying all night, which did more good than a whipping." This later diary records fewer instances of beatings. *Another Secret Diary of William Byrd of Westover, 1739–1741, with Letters and Literary Exercises, 1696–1726*, ed. Maude H. Woodfin, translated and collated by Marion Tinling (Richmond, Va.: Dietz, 1942). By the 1730s, Byrd was arguing against slavery, on the grounds that it dehumanized whites and might drive slaves to desperate rebellions (Marambaud, *William Byrd*, 171–77). Since Lucy, whom William Byrd had married in 1706, died in 1716, she does not appear in subsequent parts of the surviving diary.

73. According to Kathleen Brown, "Byrd correctly perceived that physical contests between Lucy Byrd and the female slaves in his household did nothing to enhance white authority and much to diminish it, threatening to turn the exercise of discipline into a brawl" and to undermine Byrd's attempt "to protect his own use of 'discipline' from being confused with mere violence" (Brown, *Good Wives, Nasty Wenches*, 361). Of the infamous tongs incident, Lockridge writes, "in rescuing his authority Byrd was often literally concerned with rescuing the servants:" "Lucy's violent determination to work her will on the house servants shocked Byrd repeatedly into defending them. His objection was always to the violation of his authority as master and to the irrational passion and severity with which Lucy inflicted punishments rather than to the idea of corporal punishment itself" (*Diary, and Life*, 67, 68).

74. Relying on church court records, Elizabeth Foyster documents similar uses of children as surrogates for or supplements to violence in early modern marital conflicts. She cites cases of fathers who beat a beloved child to outrage its mother, who turn on mothers who intervene to stop the beating of children, or who urge children to beat their mothers. Elizabeth A. Foyster, "Silent Witnesses? Children and the Breakdown of Domestic and Social Order in Early

Modern England," in *Childhood in Question: Children, Parents and the State*, ed. Anthony Fletcher and Stephen Hussey (Manchester: Manchester University Press, 1999), 57–73; Foyster, *Marital Violence: An English Family History, 1660–1857* (Cambridge: Cambridge University Press, 2005), 129–67.

75. Marambaud, *William Byrd*, 166.

76. Lauren Berlant, for instance, argues that, especially in their relationships to light-skinned female slaves, slave-owning men "could mask their corporeal domination of all slaves in fantasies of masculine sexual entrapment by the slave women's availability and allure" (460). In "parodic and perverse fantasies of masking domination as love and conjugal decorum" (461), masters dressed up a favored slave in ladies' clothes, and gave her a little house and consumer goods; such materialized fantasies, Berlant argues, may have enabled men to mask both the domination inherent to slavery and that inherent to domesticity and marriage. Lauren Berlant, "The Queen of America Goes to Washington City: Harriet Jacobs, Frances Harper, Anita Hill," in *Subjects and Citizens: Nation, Race, and Gender from Oroonoko to Anita Hill*, ed. Michael Moon and Cathy N. Davidson (Durham, N.C.: Duke University Press, 1995), 460, 461.

77. As Brown argues, "dismemberments, hangings, and burnings of slaves provided planters with a foundation for authority rooted in the infliction of pain. As long as planters could exercise power over slave bodies, other domestic and political relationships need not be regularly disrupted by violence"—or one might add *maintained through* violence (Brown, *Good Wives, Nasty Wenches*, 321, see also 306).

78. Stone, *Family, Sex, and Marriage*, 564–65.

79. Zuckerman, *Almost Chosen People*, 111n33, 111, 109.

80. Meldrum, *Domestic Service and Gender*, 109–10. Meldrum argues that the Willet episode was unusual in the extent of sexual contact Pepys allowed himself and the level of disruption it caused (109).

81. Meldrum, *Domestic Service and Gender*, 92–94, 109–10. Meldrum points out that Pepys and his wife both routinely beat their servants, especially young male ones: "Pepys and his wife certainly had no compunction in beating many of their servants, particularly the footboys, one of whom was beaten at least eight times in two years" (92). See, for instance, *The Diary of Samuel Pepys*, ed. Robert Latham and William Mathhews (Berkeley: University of California Press, 1974), vol. 2 : 207; 3: 37–38, 66, 116; 4: 7–8, 13, 109, 193. Many of these beatings were inflicted on a boy the editors describe as "incorrigible" (4: 8n1). On several occasions, Pepys emphasizes that the beatings make his own arm sore. According to Meldrum, "the chastisement meted out by Samuel and Elizabeth Pepys to their female servants occurred less frequently than it did for their male servants" but it did happen. For occasions when Samuel chastised female servants, see 1: 307 and 8: 164 (when he was embarrassed to be seen by a neighbor's footboy). For occasions when Elizabeth beat female servants, see 5: 13 and 6: 39 (both times Samuel ordered her to beat their "little girl") and 8: 212.

82. Capp, *When Gossips Meet*, 152.

83. Pepys *Diary*, 4 (1663): 262. On Elizabeth's jealousy, see 4: 165. This companion, Mary Ashwell, was hired in response to Elizabeth's account of her loneliness, which Pepys destroyed (4: 9).

84. Pepys, *Diary*, 9: 119, 143, 337–39, 344, 346, 349, 362–71. These pages recount incidents from March 16, 1667, to late November 1668. Further citations will be in parentheses in the text.

85. Kate Loveman suggests that Pepys's relationship to Deb did not end when his account of it did in "Samuel Pepys and Deb Willet After the Diary," *Historical Journal* 49, 3 (2006): 893–901.

86. Perhaps because of such outbursts, Stone's assessment of Elizabeth Pepys is almost as negative as his assessment of Lucy Byrd: she is idle, "frivolous, extravagant and easily aroused to anger or the sulks" as well as "sexually inadequate for long periods of time" (Stone, *Family, Sex, and Marriage*, 552). By "inadequate," he appears to mean "incapable of intercourse."

87. Within a few weeks, Elizabeth was jealous of Samuel's interest in yet another servant. Here again, the couple's conflict served as a prelude to heightened sexual pleasure and experimentation (9: 439).

88. For a fuller discussion of "presentism," see the Introduction.

89. E. P. Thompson, "Happy Families," *New Society* (September 8, 1977): 499–501, esp. 499. I share Carolyn Strange's project, although she focuses on torture rather than marriage and domestic violence: "If the critically engaged historian's burden is to keep present the pasts we prefer to forget, we might do more to shift the West's 'shock' into the nagging pain of self knowledge" ("The 'Shock' of Torture: a Historiographical Challenge," *History Workshop Journal* 61.1 [Spring, 2006]: 135–52, esp. 149). See also Alexandra Shepard's skepticism about progress in "Violence and Civility in Early Modern Europe," *Historical Journal* 49, 2 (2006): 593–603,

90. Pepys, *Diary*, 4: 9.

91. William Shakespeare, *The Taming of the Shrew*, ed. Ann Thompson (Cambridge: Cambridge University Press, 2003). Subsequent citations refer to this edition.

92. Lynda Boose emphasizes the anachronism of the "vision of male dominance" Katherina presents in her final performance ("Scolding Brides and Bridling Scolds: Taming the Woman's Unruly Member," *Shakespeare Quarterly* 42, 2 [1991]: 179–213, esp. 184); Natasha Korda emphasizes the ways in which the model of marriage at the end of the play is "entirely new" in *Shakespeare's Domestic Economies: Gender and Property in Early Modern England* (Philadelphia: University of Pennsylvania Press, 2002), 52–75.

93. David Underdown, "The Taming of the Scold: The Enforcement of Patriarchal Authority in Early Modern England," in *Order and Disorder in Early Modern England* (Cambridge: Cambridge University Press, 1985), 116–36, esp. 117.

94. Hartog, *Man and Wife in America*, 155–56.

95. Nancy F. Cott, *Public Vows: A History of Marriage and the Nation* (Cambridge, Mass.: Harvard University Press, 2000), 12–13.

96. Korda, *Shakespeare's Domestic Economies*, 75. Korda argues that this speech articulates a "new division of labor" that erases the status of housework as work and "renders the housewife perpetually indebted to her husband, as her 'love, fair looks, and true obedience' are insufficient 'payment' for the material comforts in which she is passively 'kept'" (71–75, esp. 72).

97. Wendy Wall, *Staging Domesticity*, 158, 8.

98. Barbara Hodgdon, "Who Is Performing 'In' These Text(s)? Or, *Shrew*-ing Around," in *In Arden: Editing Shakespeare: Essays in Honour of Richard Proudfoot*, ed. Ann Thompson and Gordon McMullan (London: Thomson, 2003), 95–108. In my discussion of the play, I cite only those stage directions that do appear in the Folio text.

99. Wayne, "Refashioning the Shrew," 171.

100. See "Couragious Betty of Chick-Lane" and "The Coy Cook-Maid," *Roxburghe Ballads* 3: 641–44; 3: 627–30.

101. *The Life of Long Meg of Westminster* (London, 1635), rpt. in *The Old Book Collector's Miscellany; or, A Collection of Readable Reprints of Literary Rarities*, ed. Charles Hindley, 3 vols. (London: Reeves and Turner, 1871–73), 2: 36.

102. Pamela Allen Brown, *Better a Shrew Than a Sheep: Women, Drama, and the Culture of Jest in Early Modern England* (Ithaca, N.Y.: Cornell University Press, 2003). See also her essay "'Fie, What a Foolish Duty Call You This?' *The Taming of the Shrew*, Women's Jest, and the Divided Audience," in *A Companion to Shakespeare's Works: The Comedies*, ed. Richard Dutton and Jean E. Howard (London: Blackwell, 2003). Anthony Fletcher also discusses this proverb (*Gender, Sex, and Subordination*, 4).

103. Fletcher, *Gender, Sex and Subordination*, 198; Capp, *When Gossips Meet*, 2, 25.

104. Carol Rutter, *Clamorous Voices: Shakespeare's Women Today* (London: Women's Press, 1988), 18.

105. *A Pleasant Conceited Historie, Called The Taming of a Shrew*, ed. Graham Holderness and Bryan Loughrey (Lanham, Md.: Barnes and Noble, 1992), sig. D3. Compared to *The Shrew*, *A Shrew* also makes it more clear that, in the "wager scene," Katherina "brings her sisters forth by force . . . thrusting [them] before her." *The Taming of a Shrew* was published in 1594; *The Taming of the Shrew* was not published until 1623, in Shakespeare's First Folio. Critics have long debated the relationship between the two versions. See Graham Holderness, introduction to his facsimile edition, 34; Brian Morris, "Introduction," to William Shakespeare, *The Taming of the Shrew*, ed. Brian Morris (London: Methuen, 1981), 12–50.

106. Coppélia Kahn, *Man's Estate: Masculine Identity in Shakespeare* (Berkeley: University of California Press, 1981), 104–18, esp. 108.

107. Lynda Boose, "*The Taming of the Shrew*, Good Husbandry, and Enclosure," in *Shakespeare Reread: The Texts in New Contexts*, ed. Russ McDonald (Ithaca, N.Y.: Cornell University Press, 1994), 193–225; Richard A. Burt, "Charisma, Coercion, and Comic Form in *The Taming of the Shrew*," *Criticism* 26, 4 (1984): 295–311, esp. 299, 302.

108. Northrop Frye, *A Natural Perspective: The Development of Shakespearean Comedy and Romance* (New York: Harcourt, Brace, 1965), 80.

109. Kim F. Hall, "'I Rather Would Wish to Be a Black-Moor': Beauty, Race, and Rank in Lady Mary Wroth's *Urania*," in *Women, "Race," and Writing in the Early Modern Period*, ed. Margo Hendricks and Patricia Parker (London: Routledge, 1994), 178–94, esp. 180; Douglas Bruster, "Female-Female Eroticism and the Early Modern Stage," *Renaissance Drama* n.s. 24 (1993): 1–32, esp. 14.

110. On the problems with an idea of spouses as equal combatants, see Linda Gordon, *Heroes of Their Own Lives: The Politics and History of Family Violence: Boston 1880–1960* (New York: Viking/Penguin, 1988), 261; Demie Kurz, "Violence Against Women or Family Violence? Current Debates and Future Directions," in *Gender Violence: Interdisciplinary Perspectives*, ed. Laura L. O'Toole and Jessica R. Schiffman (New York: New York University Press, 1997), 443–53; and Richard J. Gelles and Donileen R. Loseke, eds., *Current Controversies on Family Violence* (Newbury Park, Calif.: Sage, 1993).

111. On the movement of married women into the paid labor force in the decades following World War II, see Susan Thistle, *From Marriage to the Market: The Transformation of Women's Lives and Work* (Berkeley: University of California Press, 2006); and Jessica Weiss, *To Have and to Hold: Marriage, the Baby Boom, and Social Change* (Chicago: University of Chicago Press, 2000), esp. 49–81. Amy Dru

Stanley charts the process of change instigated by wives' paid work. First, wifely dependency defined male freedom and self-possession; the free man had his meals cooked, clothes washed, and children minded by a dependent wife. When the wife needed to work for wages, and achieved equality in the form of control of those wages and of her own vote, then this formerly unpaid labor became the wage labor of someone else, often another woman. If coverture described an exchange of service for support then that exchange is finessed through hiring another woman's services, as a surrogate or supplement. See Amy Dru Stanley, *From Bondage to Contract: Wage Labor, Marriage, and the Market in the Age of Slave Emancipation* (Cambridge: Cambridge University Press, 1998).

112. Barbara Ehrenreich, *Nickel and Dimed: On (Not) Getting By in America* (New York: Metropolitan, 2001), 91n11.

113. Arlie Hochschild, *The Second Shift: Working Parents and the Revolution at Home* (New York: Viking, 1989), 121, 189. What Hochschild calls a second shift, Christine Delphy calls a "double workload" (Christine Delphy, *Close to Home: A Materialist Analysis of Women's Oppression* [London: Hutchinson, 1984], 68). See also Christine Delphy and Diana Leonard, *Familiar Exploitation: A New Analysis of Marriage in Contemporary Western Societies* (Cambridge: Polity, 1992), 234–37; and Annette Kuhn and AnnMarie Wolpe, eds., *Feminism and Materialism: Women and Modes of Production* (London: Routledge, 1978). Whereas some working women resent partners who don't do their share, some working men resent spouses who quit their jobs to stay home with the kids, viewing them as retreating from "equal-partnership marriages." Judith Warner, "Guess Who's Left Holding the Briefcase? (It's Not Mom)," *New York Times*, June 20, 2004, 4: 12.

114. Most housecleaners are women (Hochschild, The Second Shift, 25; Ehrenreich, *Nickel and Dimed*, 71n4).

115. This is the argument in Phyllis Palmer, *Domesticity and Dirt: Housewives and Domestic Servants in the United States, 1920–1945* (Philadelphia: Temple University Press, 1989).

116. Delphy, *Close to Home*, 69; Delphy and Leonard, *Familiar Exploitation*, 97.

117. Delphy and Leonard, *Familiar Exploitation*, 236.

118. Cheryl Mendelson, *Home Comforts: The Art and Science of Keeping House* (New York: Scribner, 1999), 806.

119. Ehrenreich, *Nickel and Dimed*, 91.

120. This is a controversial moment in the book and when the book was staged it was made into a dialogue with the audience so as to deal with their feelings. The playwright, Joan Holden, was concerned that "women in the audience—they would feel suddenly guilt-tripped." In the interaction with the audience that she wrote, as represented on National Public Radio, six women from the audience enter in to a discussion of appropriate pay, but only one man. Transcript of *All Things Considered* (September 27, 2002), about the production at the Mark Taper Forum in Los Angeles.

Chapter Four: How a Maiden Keeps Her Head

1. On authorship, see Martha Tuck Rozett, "Fictional Queen Elizabeths and Woman-Centered Historical Fiction," in *Constructing a World: Shakespeare's England and the New Historical Fiction* (Buffalo: State University of New York Press, 2003), 107. Book clubs appear to have mostly female members; see any Google search for "book club" and Elizabeth Long, *Book Clubs: Women and the Uses of*

Reading in Everyday Life (Chicago: University of Chicago Press, 2003). See also Janice A. Radway, *Reading the Romance: Women, Patriarchy, and Popular Literature* (Chapel Hill: University of North Carolina Press, 1991). The majority of the readers who review Gregory's fiction on Amazon.com or participate in the readers' group on her website identify themselves as women.

2. Alison Weir, *The Six Wives of Henry VIII* (New York: Grove, 1991), 8, 9, 12.

3. Antonia Fraser, *The Wives of Henry VIII* (New York: Knopf, 1992), 2–3.

4. On Catherine of Aragon, see Philippa Gregory, *The Constant Princess* (New York: Simon and Schuster, 2005); and Jean Plaidy, *Katharine of Aragon: Three Novels in One Volume* (New York: Three Rivers, 2005), which were first published separately in 1961 and 1962. The prolific Plaidy also wrote novels about Henry's other wives. Like Catherine of Aragon, Mary Stuart seems a likely candidate for novels about marriage. Her marital history included a first dynastic marriage to Francis II of France at sixteen, becoming a widow at eighteen, implication in the murder of her second husband, Lord Darnley, abduction and possibly rape by her third husband, the earl of Bothwell (widely regarded as her second husband's murderer), and her repeated attempts to have this last marriage annulled. Yet she does not dominate fiction as Anne and Elizabeth do. For an exception, see Margaret George's mammoth *Mary, Queen of Scotland and the Isles: A Novel* (New York: St. Martin's Griffin, 1992).

5. On the charges against Anne and the evidence brought in to support them, see Eric Ives, *Life and Death of Anne Boleyn* (Oxford: Blackwell, 2004), 343–52.

6. Susan Frye, *Elizabeth I: The Competition for Representation* (New York: Oxford University Press, 1993). Rozett, too, points out that Elizabeth proves a wonderful subject for fiction because she was always a fabrication ("Fictional Queen Elizabeths," 130).

7. This is a phrase I borrow from Susan Faludi, *Stiffed: The Betrayal of the American Man* (New York: William Morrow, 1999), 42. See Chapter 1.

8. As Richard Burt asks, "what might mass culture versions of Elizabeth tell us . . . that academic versions do not?" See his "Doing the Queen: Gender, Sexuality and the Censorship of Elizabeth I's Royal Image from Renaissance Portraiture to Twentieth–Century Mass Media," *Literature and Censorship in Renaissance England*, ed. Andrew Hadfield (New York: Palgrave, 2001), 201–28, esp. 208.

9. Barbara Hodgdon, *The Shakespeare Trade: Performances and Appropriations* (Philadelphia: University of Pennsylvania Press, 1998), 206. Rosemary Kegl discusses a "double-edged" turn to history—"scrupulous attention to historical detail on the one hand, a careless disregard for that detail on the other"—in "'(W)rapping Togas over Elizabethan Garb': Tabloid Shakespeare at the 1934 Chicago World's Fair," *Renaissance Drama* n.s. 28 (1997): 73–97, esp. 83.

10. Hodgdon, *Shakespeare Trade*, 112. Only rarely is Elizabeth imagined to experience homoerotic desire. See, for instance, Patricia Finney, *Unicorn's Blood* (New York: Picador, 1998).

11. On Anne Boleyn's erudition and promotion of reform, see Maria Dowling, "Anne Boleyn and Reform," *Journal of Ecclesiastical History* 35, 1 (1984): 30–46.

12. On the reliability of Sander's description of Anne, see Ives, *Life and Death*, 39–44; and Retha M. Warnicke, *The Rise and Fall of Anne Boleyn* (Cambridge: Cambridge University Press, 1989), 58–59, 243–47. According to Warnicke, Sander's "details were so compelling and so fascinating that, even though they were entirely fictitious, they have survived through the ages and still form the basis for references to her in modern textbooks" (247). These details, and the ways in which they cast Anne as a monster or witch, thus constitute what Warnicke calls

"the legacy of Nicholas Sander." This legacy lives on in novels as well as textbooks. See Robin Maxwell, *The Secret Diary of Anne Boleyn: A Novel* (New York: Scribner/Simon and Schuster, 1997), 48; and Jean Plaidy, *The Lady in the Tower* (New York: Three Rivers, 1986), 205.

13. David Starkey, *Six Wives: The Queens of Henry VIII* (New York: HarperCollins, 2003), 577.

14. Plaidy, *Lady in the Tower*, 233.

15. Suzannah Dunn, *The Queen of Subtleties* (New York: HarperCollins, 2004), 199.

16. Norah Lofts, *Anne Boleyn* (New York: Coward, McCann and Geoghegan, 1979), 36. Many novelists cite Lofts's biography.

17. In Jean Plaidy, *The Rose Without a Thorn* (New York: Three Rivers, 1993), Katherine Howard says of Jane Seymour: "So died the perfect wife. Not only had she produced the longed-for son, but she had had the good grace to die before the King had tired of her" (62). Useful chronologies can be found in Ives, *Life and Death*; Starkey, *Six Wives*; and Weir, *Six Wives*.

18. Plaidy, *Lady in the Tower*, 188–89. See also 214, 217, 242, 252, 266–67, 296, 299.

19. Carolyn Meyer, *Doomed Queen Anne* (Harcourt Books, 2002), 101–2, 121. This is a book in the Young Royals series.

20. Maxwell, *Secret Diary*, 260–61. On the chase whose only end can be capture and death, see 278–9.

21. Maxwell, *Secret Diary*, 269.

22. Valerie Traub, *The Renaissance of Lesbianism in Early Modern England* (Cambridge: Cambridge University Press, 2002), esp. 151; Jasper Ridley, *Elizabeth I: The Shrewdness of Virtue* (London: Constable, 1987), 214; Susan Doran, *Monarchy and Matrimony: The Courtships of Elizabeth I* (London: Routledge, 1996).

23. John N. King was one of the first scholars to chart how representations of Elizabeth's virginity changed over time. See "Queen Elizabeth I: Representations of the Virgin Queen," *Renaissance Quarterly* 43, 1 (Spring 1990): 30–74. Marshaling evidence from Elizabeth's speeches across her reign, Mary Beth Rose shows that Elizabeth did not consistently reject the possibility of marriage. See Mary Beth Rose, *Gender and Heroism in Early Modern English Literature* (Chicago: University of Chicago Press, 2002), 26–54.

24. For Susan Doran, the fact that Elizabeth did not marry was neither a personal failure (the traditional explanation) nor a personal triumph of self-assertion or queer desire (the more recent explanation). It was a sign of political failure; Elizabeth was unable to convince her council to support her choice. For Doran, Elizabeth didn't choose to remain single but rather "in the event" wound up that way (*Monarchy and Matrimony*). Anne McLaren challenges this as presenting "the unconvincing image of a queen ready to marry" but unable to secure an "all clear" from her fractious council. "The Quest for a King: Gender, Marriage, and Succession in Elizabethan England," *Journal of British Studies* 41 (July 2002): 259–90.

25. Queer readings of Elizabeth's virginity tend to run counter to the arguments that Elizabeth's attitude toward marriage changed over time and to depict her as committing herself early to an unmarried, but not necessarily asexual, life. Jonathan Goldberg argues that "to treat her as 'anomalous' is to assume that biological sex and gender are unproblematically sutured in 'ordinary' cases and that heterosexuality assigns men and women to stabilized and opposing positions. That is the work that marriage as an institution is supposed to do, and Elizabeth, from her accession speech on, made clear that however her femininity was to be

defined it would not be through that straitening and deforming institution" (*Sodometries: Renaissance Texts, Modern Sexualities* [Stanford, Calif.: Stanford University Press, 1992], 41). Valerie Traub also argues for a positive view of Elizabeth's sexuality, which she describes as a "countereroticism" that does not overlap with marriage. For Traub, Elizabeth's decision not to marry was not a failure (as some of her counselors would have had it) nor a resistance to marriage but rather a positive choice of an alternative state. Focusing on Elizabeth's eroticism, Traub questions other critics (such as Doran) who see both Elizabeth's courtships and her rejections of various suitors as wholly politically motivated (Traub, *Renaissance of Lesbianism*, 125–57).

26. See Michael Dobson and Nicola J. Watson, *England's Elizabeth: An Afterlife in Fame and Fantasy* (Oxford: Oxford University Press, 2002), 6; Starkey, *Six Wives*, 23; and Philippa Berry, *Of Chastity and Power: Elizabethan Literature and the Unmarried Queen* (Routledge, 1989), 72–73.

27. Weir, *Six Wives*, 354. Weir also claims that marriage, for Elizabeth, "had too close an association with death to ever seem safe" (485).

28. Karen Lindsey, *Divorced, Beheaded, Survived: A Feminist Reinterpretation of the Wives of Henry VIII* (Cambridge, Mass: Perseus, 1995), 214.

29. Karen Harper, *The Tidal Poole* (New York: Random House/Dell, 2000), 5.

30. Fiona Buckley, *The Doublet Affair* (New York: Pocket Books, 1998), 253.

31. Rosalind Miles, *I, Elizabeth: A Novel* (New York: Three Rivers, 1994), 124, 319, 291.

32. Jean Plaidy, *Queen of This Realm: A Novel (New York: Three Rivers, 1984)*, 447–48.

33. Susan Kay, *Legacy* (New York: Avon, 1985), 22.

34. Rozett, "Fictional Queen Elizabeths," 121.

35. Kay, *Legacy*, 396. Dudley "wondered briefly if Burghley felt the same"; Burghley does and considers Elizabeth a witch (536).

36. Kay, *Legacy*, 572, 610, 620, 630.

37. Dobson and Watson, *England's Elizabeth*, 28.

38. Michelle A. Massé, "Things That Go Bump in the Night: Husbands, Horrors, and Repetition," in *In the Name of Love: Women, Masochism, and the Gothic* (Ithaca, N.Y.: Cornell University Press, 1992), 12, 26. See also Joanna Russ, "Somebody's Trying to Kill Me and I Think It's My Husband: The Modern Gothic," *Journal of Popular Culture* 6, 4 (1973): 666–91; and Maria Tatar, *Secrets Beyond the Door: The Story of Bluebeard and His Wives* (Princeton, N.J.: Princeton University Press, 2006).

39. Tania Modleski, *Loving with a Vengeance: Mass-Produced Fantasies for Women* (New York: Routledge, 1982), 71. I want to thank Rhonda Minnick for drawing my attention to the relevance of Modleski's insight to popular representations of Elizabeth.

40. Kay, *Legacy*, 646; emphasis mine. On the end of the novel, see Dobson and Watson, *England's Elizabeth*, 28–29.

41. Margaret Irwin, *Elizabeth, Captive Princess* (1948; London: Allison and Busby, 1999), 258, 259, 266, 271, 291, 307. In the last novel in Irwin's trilogy, *Elizabeth and the Prince of Spain*, Elizabeth considers and rejects Philip II as a possible "partner" and "equal" (1953; London: Allison and Busby, 1999), 134.

42. Dobson and Watson, *England's Elizabeth*, 217–18.

43. In addition to Dobson and Watson, *England's Elizabeth*, see Hodgdon, *Shakespeare Trade*; Rozett, "Fictional Queen Elizabeths"; and Julia M. Walker, *The Elizabeth Icon, 1603–2003* (New York: Palgrave, 2004). See also Deanne Williams, "No Man's Elizabeth: Frances A. Yates and the History of History," in *The Impact*

of Feminism in English Renaissance Studies, ed. Dympna Callaghan (New York: Palgrave Macmillan, 2007), 238–58.

44. Maureen Dowd, "Men Just Want Mommy," *New York Times*, January 13, 2005, A31.

45. Dowd, "Men Just Want Mommy," A31.

46. See, for instance, McLaren, "Quest for a King"; and Rose, *Gender and Heroism*, 43.

47. John Stubbs, *The Discoverie of a Gaping Gulf Whereinto England is Like To Be Swallowed by an Other French Marriage* (London, 1579), sig. D3v. See also Ilona Bell, "'Sovereaigne Lord of Lordly Lady of This Land': Elizabeth, Stubbs and the Gaping Gulf," in *Dissing Elizabeth: Negative Representations of Gloriana*, ed. Julia M. Walker (Durham, N.C.: Duke University Press, 1998), 99–117, esp. 102; McLaren, "Quest for a King," esp. 276; and Anne Somerset, *Elizabeth I* (New York: St. Martin's Griffin, 1991), 35, 91, 179. The marriage of Elizabeth's predecessor and half-sister, Mary Tudor, to Philip II of Spain led many to distrust the prospect that Elizabeth would marry a foreign monarch. According to Judith M. Richards, "one fundamental problem in this royal match was the difficulty of conceiving a marriage between equals" (907). In addition, "the contemporary understandings of husband/wife relationships were such that few believed that, once married, Mary could continue to function as a fully autonomous monarch" (908). No matter what provisions were made to protect the queen's powers, "the ghosts of Adam and Eve overhung all the constitutional niceties" (924). Judith M. Richards, "Mary Tudor as 'Sole Quene'?: Gendering Tudor Monarchy," *Historical Journal* 40, 4 (1997): 895–924.

48. John Knox, "The First Blast of the Trumpet Against the Monstrous Regiment of Women" (1558), from *British Pamphleteers*, ed. George Orwell and Reginald Reynolds, 2 vols. (London: Allan Wingate, 1948–51), 1: 19–33, esp. 23.

49. Patrick Hannay, *A Happy Husband: or Directions for a Maid to Chuse Her Mate. Together with a Wives Behaviour after Marriage* (1622), rpt. in Hannay, *The Poetical Works of Patrick Hannay: A.M. MDCXXII with a memoir of the author* (Glasgow: [R. Anderson], 1875), 176.

50. Alençon later became duke of Anjou, but Elizabeth consistently called him "Monsieur." As the negotiations revealed, prospective kings consort make demands for power and influence of a sort that queens consort never do. Among other requests, Alençon wished to be crowned king and to have what amounted to "veto power." See Elizabeth's letter (c. May 1579) to Sir Amyas Paulet, her ambassador in France, in *Elizabeth I: Collected Works*, ed. Leah S. Marcus, Janel Mueller, and Mary Beth Rose (Chicago: University of Chicago Press, 2000), 233–37. On the Alençon courtship, see Somerset, *Elizabeth I*, 308–21.

51. Sidney's "letter" circulated only in manuscript until it was printed in 1663. Still, dozens of manuscript copies survive. According to Katherine Duncan-Jones and Jan Van Dorsten, editors of a collection of Sidney's prose, parallels in argument and phrasing suggest that Sidney had read Stubbs's *Gaping Gulf*—published in 1579—carefully; *Miscellaneous Prose of Sir Philip Sidney* (Oxford: Clarendon, 1973). For Sidney's role as "spokesman for the faction of his temporarily disgraced uncle [Leicester]," and the manuscript transmission of his text, see Peter Beal, *In Praise of Scribes: Manuscripts and Their Makers in Seventeenth-Century England* (Oxford: Clarendon, 1998), 110 and passim; and H. R. Woudhuysen, *Sir Philip Sidney and the Circulation of Manuscripts, 1558–1640* (Oxford: Clarendon, 1996), 100, 151.

52. Stubbs and his printer lost their right hands for writing and printing this text. Copies of the text were collected and destroyed. Because Stubbs's tract was suppressed it also survives in four manuscript copies, probably copied from the print versions (see Woudhuysen, *Sir Philip Sidney*, 147). For details of Stubbs's punishment, see *John Stubbs's "Gaping Gulf" with Letters and Other Relevant Documents*, ed. Lloyd E. Berry (Charlottesville: University Press of Virginia, 1968).

53. *Miscellaneous Prose of Sir Philip Sidney*, ed. Duncan-Jones and Van Dorsten, 46, 51, 47, 49, 50.

54. William Camden, *The History of the Most Renowned and Victorious Princess Elizabeth, Late Queen of England*, ed. Wallace T. MacCaffrey (Chicago: University of Chicago Press, 1970), 136–37. Camden's *The Annals or the History of the Most Renowned and Victorious Princess Elizabeth, Late Queen of England*, was first printed in Latin in two volumes (in 1615 and 1627) and then issued in English editions in 1635, 1675, and 1688. Thus, like many of the other sources for the most cherished episodes in Elizabeth's life, it was first recorded many years after her death.

55. Sir James Melville, *Memoirs of Sir James Melville of Halhill, 1535–1617*, ed. A. Francis Steuart (London: Routledge, 1929), 94. Carole Levin points out that Melville wrote long after the fact. *Heart and Stomach of a King: Elizabeth I and the Politics of Sex and Power* (Philadelphia: University of Pennsylvania Press, 1994), 5.

56. For versions of this statement, see Levin, *Heart and Stomach*, 132; Sir Arthur Salusbury MacNalty, *Elizabeth Tudor: The Lonely Queen* (London: Christopher Johnson, 1954), 101; J. E. Neale, *Queen Elizabeth I* (New York: Harcourt, 1934), 125; Somerset, *Elizabeth I*, 94. For its appearance in a novel, see Plaidy, *Queen of this Realm*, in which Elizabeth advises the reader "Remember it, for Melville is right" (201, 210, 448); Miles, *I, Elizabeth* (360); and Kay, *Legacy* (22), which, as we have seen, attributes the hope that Elizabeth will rule "as King and Queen both" to Anne Boleyn.

57. Robert Naunton, *Fragmenta Regalia: or Observations on Queen Elizabeth, Her Times and Favorites*, ed. John S. Cerovski (Washington, D.C.: Folger, 1985), 17. Naunton was born in 1563 and entered the service of his uncle, the English ambassador to Scotland, in 1589, a year after Robert Dudley, Earl of Leicester, died. So he could not have witnessed this exchange. Furthermore, Naunton probably composed his text in the early 1630s, when he was a reasonably old man (around seventy). The text circulated widely in manuscript and was first printed in 1641; it then went through five editions within twelve years. For biographical and bibliographical info, see Cerovski's edition. See also Levin, *Heart and Stomach*, 47; and Somerset, *Elizabeth I*, 139. The usher in the story was supposedly Simon Bowyer, who played a minor role in a complicated case involving his brother, Henry, as reconstructed by David Cressy, *Agnes Bowker's Cat: Travesties and Transgressions in Tudor and Stuart England* (Oxford: Oxford University Press, 2000), esp. 64.

58. See, for instance, Karen Harper, *The Twylight Tower* (New York: Dell, 2001), 317; Irwin, *Elizabeth and the Prince of Spain*, 266; Plaidy, *Queen of this Realm*, 210; and Kay, *Legacy*, 284.

59. Kay, *Legacy*, 620; Maxwell, *Secret Diary*, 269.

60. Rose, *Gender and Heroism*, 27.

61. Fredric Jameson, *The Political Unconscious: Narrative as a Socially Symbolic Act* (Ithaca, N.Y.: Cornell University Press), 118.

62. *Elizabeth I: Collected Works*, 59, 58n1. Richards discusses several instances early in Mary Tudor's reign in which she remarked that she was already married to her kingdom ("Mary Tudor as 'Sole Quene'," 912).

63. For "the origins of a myth," see King, "Queen Elizabeth I," 33–36. See also Doran, *Monarchy and Matrimony*, 1; Dobson and Watson, *England's Elizabeth*, 5–6; Levin, *Heart and Stomach*, 41. Despite these demythologizing efforts, the episode appears without framing in biographies such as Alison Plowden, *Marriage with My Kingdom: The Courtships of Elizabeth I* (London: Macmillan, 1977); and Somerset, *Elizabeth I*, 99–100. Novelists also love this theatrical moment. See, for instance, Miles, *I, Elizabeth* (261, 277–78); and Finney, *Unicorn's Blood* (13).

64. Thomas Norton, *To the Queenes Majesties Poore Deceived Subjectes of the Northe Contreye* (London, 1569), sig. B4v, discussed in Frye, *Elizabeth I*, 55.

65. McLaren, "The Quest for a King," 289, 284.

66. "An unknown person from Orleans" to Robert Dudley, December 31, 1560, in *Selections from Unpublished Manuscripts in the College of Arms and the British Museum*, ed. Joseph Stevenson (Glasgow: [Mallard Club], 1837), 84–85. This letter is sometimes attributed to Henry Killigrew (McLaren, "Quest for a King," 259) and sometimes to Nicholas Throckmorton; see Leah S. Marcus, "Elizabeth," in Marcus, *Puzzling Shakespeare: Local Reading and Its Discontents* (Berkeley: University of California Press, 1988), 51–105, 97; and Levin, *Heart and Stomach*, 133.

67. As Carole Levin points out, "one can hardly imagine Elizabeth not taking the position of 'husband' rather than 'wife.'" Levin goes on to explain that it was Elizabeth who could not imagine this. "The only way she could conceive of herself in marriage . . . was by being still in control and in the powerful position, and that meant playing the husband" (Levin, *Heart and Stomach*, 133).

68. John Guy, *My Heart Is My Own: The Life of Mary Queen of Scots* (London: Fourth Estate, 2004), 186, 189, 203. All of these statements are from Thomas Randolph's reports to William Cecil and Guy quotes them from the state papers. On the demand that Mary should choose a spouse "that shuld contynew the amity betwixt them two and ther contrees," see Nicholas Throckmorton's report to Elizabeth, May 21, 1565, in *Selections from Unpublished Manuscripts*, 139.

69. *Calendar of Letters and State Papers Relating to English Affairs, Preserved Principally in the Archives of Simancas*, ed. Martin A. S. Hume, 4 vols. (London: Her Majesty's Stationery Office, 1892–99), 1: 364. See also Levin, *Heart and Stomach*, 133; Leah Marcus, "Elizabeth"; and Traub, *Renaissance of Lesbianism*, 151.

70. Goldberg, *Sodometries*, 46.

71. The HBO Web page for the two-part mini series "event" *Elizabeth I* (2006), starring Helen Mirren, sums up the queen and her story in these terms: "She held absolute power over everything . . . except her heart." In this series, as in so many representations of Elizabeth, including the novels discussed here, the first part of this statement is not assumed to be a sufficient draw in itself. What makes her story "epic" is its focus on love; it is "an epic story of a legendary queen's appetite to love, and to be loved, against all odds." Barbara Hodgdon's analysis of television and film depictions of Elizabeth pertains to this newest offering, as it did to the film *Elizabeth* (dir. Shekhar Kapur, 1998).

72. Eric Ives points out that the chronology is unclear. See *Life and Death*, 15–17.

73. Karen Harper had the idea first in a novel published as *Passion's Reign* (New York: Kensington, 1983). In the wake of Gregory's much greater success, Harper's novel has been reissued as *The Last Boleyn* (New York: Three Rivers Press, 2006).

74. The BBC show was directed by Philippa Lowthorpe and broadcast by BBC 2 in 2004; the Hollywood production, released in 2007, was directed by Justin Chadwick. According to Gregory's official Web site (http://www.philippagre-

gory.com/), as of April 7, 2007, "there are approx 1.75 million copies of Philippa's work in print to date in the UK and approx 2 million copies in print to date in the US, totalling approximately 3.75 million copies in the English language in print worldwide." Her books, especially *The Other Boleyn Girl*, are favorites with online and in-person book clubs. I am grateful to Ryan Fong for directing me to Gregory's website.

75. Ives, *Life and Death*, 210.

76. Mary Stafford to Thomas Cromwell (1534), *Letters and Papers, Foreign and Domestic, of the Reign of Henry VIII*, ed. J. S. Brewer, R. H. Brodie, and James Gairdner, 21 vols. (London: Her Majesty's Stationery Office, 1862–1910), 7: 1655. On Mary's secret marriage, see also Chapuys to Charles V (7: 1554). Harper reproduces a version of this letter in *The Last Boleyn*, 521.

77. Levin, *Heart and Stomach*, 45. See its appearance in Irwin, *Captive Princess*, 291.

78. Weir, *Six Wives*, 273; Carolly Erickson, *Mistress Anne* (New York: St. Martin's Griffin, 1984), 225; Lindsey, *Divorced, Beheaded, Survived*, 105. Eric Ives mentions an apocryphal story by which Katherine Howard said at her execution "I die a queen, but would rather die the wife of Culpeper [her lover]." All of these formulations, documented and apocryphal, sharply oppose being a wife and being a queen. See Eric Ives, "Marrying for Love: The Experience of Edward IV and Henry VIII," *History Today* 50, 12 (2000): 48–53, esp. 50. In this essay, Ives argues that when kings such as Henry married for love, their wives were more rather than less vulnerable.

79. Ives, *Life and Death*, 210.

80. Ibid., 156, 171; Plaidy, *Lady in the Tower*, 325, 351.

81. Philippa Gregory, *The Other Boleyn Girl* (New York: Simon and Schuster/ Scribner, 2001), 232. The relationship between Anne and Queen Katherine of Aragon is also presented as an economy of scarcity. Anne explains to Mary: "I'll not be safe until she is dead. . . . Just as she will not be safe until I am dead. It is not just a matter now of a man or a throne, it is as if I am her shadow and she is mine. We are locked together till death. One of us has to win outright and neither of us can be sure what we have won or lost until the other is dead and in the ground" (376).

82. Gregory, *Other Boleyn Girl*, 184–85; see also 163, 183.

83. Ibid., 68, 280. See also Maxwell, *Secret Diary*, 42.

84. Gregory, *Other Boleyn Girl*, 303.

85. Ibid., 304.

86. Ibid., 518.

87. Philippa Gregory, *The Queen's Fool* (New York: Touchstone, 2004), 36. John Dee advises Hannah to avoid marriage in order to preserve her ability to foresee the future (47, 161).

88. Gregory, *Queen's Fool*, 196. Mary Tudor also understands why Hannah chooses to wear breeches to postpone womanhood and marriage (134–35).

89. Gregory, *Queen's Fool*, 441.

90. Ibid., 235–36.

91. Ibid., 247.

92. Mary Tudor married Philip II in 1554 and died in 1558.

93. Gregory, *Queen's Fool*, 249.

94. Ibid., 260.

95. Ibid., 349.

96. Ibid., 500.

97. Philippa Gregory, *The Boleyn Inheritance* (New York: Simon and Schuster, 2006), 304, 349, 514.

98. Katherine Parr may have survived Henry, just barely, but she died in 1548, a year after he did, bearing a child to Thomas Seymour, who would later be beheaded for treasonous sexual intrigue with her stepdaughter Elizabeth. Carolly Erickson's *The Last Wife of Henry VIII: A Novel* (New York: St. Martin's, 2006) emphasizes Katherine's fear of Henry ("I knew in my heart, that as long as Henry lived, I would never again know peace") and her relief when he dies ("Yes, I mourned him—though I certainly did not want him back. . . . I no longer had anything to fear from him") (248, 281).

99. The Showtime ten-part series *The Tudors* has been widely described as "hot" both in its sexual explicitness and in its popularity.

Afterword

Epigraph: Doug Stanhope, *Deadbeat Hero* (Shout Factory, 2004).

1. Judith Butler, "Is Kinship Always Already Heterosexual?" *differences: A Journal of Feminist Cultural Studies* 13, 1 (2002): 14–44, esp. 17, 18, 21.

2. Stephanie Coontz, *Marriage, a History: From Obedience to Intimacy; or, How Love Conquered Marriage* (New York: Viking, 2005), 299–300.

3. Mary L. Shanley, "Unencumbered Individuals and Embedded Selves: Dichotomous Thinking in Family Law," in *Debating Democracy's Discontent: Essays on American Politics, Law, and Public Philosophy*, ed. Anita L. Allen and Milton C. Regan, Jr. (Oxford: Oxford University Press, 1998), 236.

4. U.S. Department of Health and Social Services, Healthy Marriage Initiative Web site, http://www.acf.hhs.gov/healthymarriage/about/aami_marriage_statistics.htm.

5. Lisa Duggan, "Holy Matrimony!" *The Nation* (March 15, 2005): 14–19, esp. 16. On Welfare reform, see also Scott C. Shershow, *The Work and the Gift* (Chicago: University of Chicago Press, 2005), 115–35; and Scott Michaelsen and Scott Cutler Shershow, "Practical Politics at the Limits of Community: The Cases of Affirmative Action and Welfare," *Postmodern Culture* 12, 2 (January 2002).

6. Stephanie Coontz, *The Way We Never Were: American Families and the Nostalgia Trap* (New York: Basic, 1992).

7. U.S. Census Bureau statistics as assessed and presented at the Alternatives to Marriage Project Web site, http://www.unmarried.org/statistics.html. numbers.

8. Nancy F. Cott, *Public Vows: A History of Marriage and the Nation* (Cambridge, Mass.: Harvard University Press, 2000), 225.

9. George Chauncey, *Why Marriage? The History Shaping Today's Debate over Gay Equality* (New York: Perseus, 2004), 139, 141, 142, 165.

Index

Acknowledgments

I began this book with the help of a National Endowment for the Humanities Fellowship at the Newberry Library. I am grateful to Jim Grossman for his kindness. I learned a great deal from questions and comments from my fellow fellows at the Newberry, especially Anne Cruz, Martha Few, Amy Froide, Janine Lanza, Peggy McCracken, Jean O'Brien, Joseph Valente, Lisa Vollendorf, and Michael Willrich. My time at the Newberry was at the end of my father's life. Drawing from his research on the Chicago courts, Michael Willrich gave my father an astounding gift, information about my father's own long-dead father, Judge Harry P. Dolan. Identifying my grandfather as a hero of Chicago progressive politics in the early twentieth century, Michael became a hero for me and my father. For that stunning and timely act of generosity, I want to thank him here.

Early in the project, I also received a Summer Research Appointment from Miami University. At Miami, I benefited from conversations with and generous draft readings by Stefanie Dunning, Katie Johnson, Sally Lloyd, Timothy Melley, and Susan Morgan. Katharine Gillespie lent me her copy of *The Other Boleyn Girl*; our exchanges of and discussions about historical fiction helped me decide to write about it. Many years ago, Emily Detmer-Goebel gave me the advertisement that became my one illustration. I am grateful to her for that and for years of conversation about domestic violence.

Over the years, I have given many talks drawn from this project and I have always learned from audience's questions and suggestions. I delivered papers at the Midwest Conference on British Studies, the Modern Language Association, the Pacific Coast Conference on British Studies, and the Shakespeare Association of America. I have also spoken at the University of Akron; Arizona State University; the University of California at Davis; the University of California at Santa Barbara; University College, Dublin; Columbia University; the Columbia University Shakespeare

Seminar; the University of Connecticut at Storrs; the University of
Florida; the University of Illinois at Chicago; the University of Illinois
at Urbana-Champaign; the University of Michigan at Ann Arbor; Michi-
gan State University; Ohio State University; the University of Pittsburgh;
Stanford University; and St. John's University. Of the many interlocutors
I have encountered in these various places, I would like especially to
thank Rachel Adams, Laura Ambrose, Susan Amussen, Jonathan Arac,
A. L. Beier, Pamela A. Brown, Daphne Clark, Janet Clare, Julie Crawford,
David Cressy, Jenny Davidson, Anne Fogarty, Cora Fox, Ari Friedlander,
Patricia Fumerton, Roland Greene, Cynthia Herrup, Barbara Hodgdon,
Ruth Kaplan, Jenna Lay, Zachary Lesser, David Lieberman, Desirée
Martín, Michael McDonald, Randall McGowen, Melissa Mowry, Carol
Neely, Lori Newcomb, Curtis Perry, Catherine Robbon, Amy Rodgers,
Marjorie Rubright, Gregory Colon Semenza, David Simpson, Siobhan B.
Somerville, and David Underdown. For their help in securing fellowship
support for the project, and for professional guidance and camaraderie,
I wish to thank Dympna Callaghan, Margie Ferguson, Richard Helger-
son, Jean Howard, Arthur Marotti, Susan Morgan, Karen Newman, Mary
Beth Rose, and Valerie Traub.

An early version of part of Chapter 3 first appeared as "Household
Chastisements: Gender, Authority, and 'Domestic Violence,'" in *Renaissance Culture and the Everyday*, ed. Patricia Fumerton and Simon Hunt
(Philadelphia: University of Pennsylvania Press, 1999), 204–25. I am
grateful to Paddy and Simon for their comments on that essay and to the
press for permission to reprint it here. An earlier version of Chapter 2
was originally published in *Feminist Studies* 29, 2 (Summer 2003): 249–77.
I reprint it here by permission of the publisher, Feminist Studies, Inc.
My editor, Judith Kegan Gardiner, and the anonymous readers for the
journal helped me make the essay a better one and offered advice that
then shaped and sharpened the book. I am grateful to Sara Fewer of
the Family Violence Prevention Fund for providing a copy of the ad that
appears in Chapter 4 and for securing me permission to reproduce the
ad here.

At the University of Pennsylvania Press, I wish to thank Jerome Singer-
man for his belief in the project and for his willingness to resist it in productive ways nonetheless. The Editorial Board raised questions that
helped me clarify my arguments. At the press, I am also grateful for the
careful attention of Andrew Frisardi, Alison Anderson, and Mariana
Martinez.

In the middle of working on the book, I moved to the University of
California, Davis. I have learned so much from the participants in my
graduate seminars, especially those in the seminar on Queen Elizabeth
I. I received patient, careful, and creative research help from Natalie

Giannini, Katie Kalpin, Genna Pearson, Tara Pedersen, and Vanessa Rapatz. It would have been hard to have finished the book without them.

Margie Ferguson has been the best colleague imaginable. As icing on an already rich cake, she read the entire manuscript in the midst of numerous other obligations and offered invaluable suggestions when I most needed them. Valerie Traub gave the completed manuscript a vigorous, engaged reading that inspired me to revise it in crucial ways. She is my dream reader. Neither Margie nor Valerie should be held accountable for the final product. But I am enormously grateful to them both for the ways they've pressed me to write a better book. Throughout a long process, Robyn Muncy offered the encouragement, loyalty, perspective, counsel, and humor on which I have come to depend.

Scott Shershow made it possible for me to conceive and complete this project. He read drafts, saved me clippings, and engaged in endless conversations about my inchoate ideas. But his greatest contribution has been at the level of imagination. Scott's buoyant willingness to learn new things and try new approaches has been a revelation. His willingness to see things differently and his openness to arranging daily life in new ways have expanded my sense of possibility. His companionship has enabled me to launch a critique of marriage that is an act of optimism, a confident assertion that relationships between two people really can be imagined differently.

LaVergne, TN USA
31 August 2009
156370LV00002B/11/P